Selections from
William Cobbett's
Illustrated
Rural Rides
1821-1832

Selections from
William Cobbett's
Illustrated
Rural Rides
1821~1832

Introduction and notes by
Christopher Morris

This edition published 1992 exclusively for Fraser Stewart Book Wholesale Ltd., Abbey Chambers, 4 Highbridge Street, Waltham Abbey, Essex EN9 1DQ.

Produced by the Promotional Reprint Company Limited

ISBN 1 85648 031 3

Printed & Bound in Hong Kong
Produced by Mandarin Offset

Frontispiece: A view of Godington, Kent, by Michael 'Angelo' Rooker

CONTENTS

INTRODUCTION

Christopher Morris

That irrepressible force of nature known as William Cobbett came into being on 9 March 1763. Throughout a long and extraordinary life he was surviving, resisting or defying something; and he still defies political or social classification. One American professor has thrice used the phrase 'men like Cobbett'.[1] There were no men like Cobbett, any more than there were men like Shakespeare. One eminent French historian has called Cobbett 'middle-class',[2] and one eminent Marxist has even called him 'upper class' (in a bracket with Shelley and Peacock).[3] Cobbett always refused to accept letters addressed to 'W. Cobbett Esquire' and often called himself a 'ploughboy', 'born among husbandmen, bred to husbandry'. His grandfather was a day-labourer, his father a yeoman farmer and innkeeper of a small inn, The Jolly Farmer, on the outskirts of Farnham, who 'when a little boy drove the plough for two-pence a day' and spent his early savings on books of land-surveying.

Young William learnt the three Rs at his father's knee—though only in the winter evenings—and earned his first pennies by scaring birds, lifting turnips, hoeing peas, weeding the Bishop's paths at Farnham Castle or leading the horse that pulled the harrow. At the age of six he had his own garden, four feet square on top of a sandstone rock, carrying the soil up 'in the bosom of my little blue smock-frock'; and at fourteen he walked to Kew to see the famous garden, spending his last three pence not on supper but on Swift's *Tale of a Tub* which he read lying in a haystack. At nineteen he ran away to London, got work in a lawyer's office but felt an urge to go to sea and enlisted in the 54th infantry, mistakenly thinking them marines.

He was eight years in the army, mostly in bleak New Brunswick, rising to be regimental sergeant major but courting unpopularity by very early rising to read improving books, especially grammar books. One day he was to write a best-selling *English Grammar* (1818) illustrated with solecisms culled from the speeches of his political opponents. He discharged himself in 1791 but was soon in trouble, for exposing corruption on the part of army officers, and discreetly fled to France, having married Ann Reid (a sergeant's daughter) who was to bear him thirteen children, seven of whom grew up, and who seemed to Cobbett faultless except that she wore 'flannel next the skin'.

---

[1] John Clive, *Scotch Reviewers* (1957) p. 122 and *Macaulay. The Shaping of the Historian* (Vintage Books 1975) pp. 61 and 147.

[2] E. Halévy, *History of the English People in the 19th Century* (tr E. I. Watkin 1961) III p.44.

[3] E. P. Thompson, *The Making of the English Working Class* (1963) p.206.

From France, where he acquired a hatred of revolution, he moved in 1792 to Philadelphia where he set up a bookshop, flaunting a picture of George III in the window, and published pro-British pamphlets abusing Tom Paine, the Americans' adopted hero. Finally he lost a libel action brought by Dr Benjamin Rush whom Cobbett accused, probably correctly, of bleeding George Washington to death. In 1800 he returned to England bankrupt yet popular for his anti-French and anti-American views; and soon he was offered government patronage which subsidised his bookshop in Pall Mall and enabled him to start his famous periodical *The Weekly Register*, which was soon to sell in unprecedented numbers and to make Cobbett the greatest English journalist since Defoe. He was still a government supporter in 1802 when he had his windows broken for not lighting up to celebrate the Peace of Amiens. But by 1804 his views were changing—in a radical direction.

Cobbett's years abroad had fostered a highly idealised picture of the England he had left almost as a boy. The England he now found proved sadly disillusioning. His chief complaints were that paper money had replaced gold and that there was a crippling national debt. These together, he held, had caused inflation and had let loose a horde of parasites—speculators, stock-jobbers, tax farmers, placemen, borough-mongers; and, above all, had forced landowners to cease being paternal (as supposedly they had been) and to become oppressors of their tenants and labourers. Even the countryside as he remembered it seemed now to be swallowed up by enclosures, or by 'Wens' (Cobbett's name for cities).

All this had begun long before, though Cobbett did not know it. What was newer was the open sale of army commissions by the Duke of York's mistress, and Prime Minister Addington's bestowal of a sinecure worth £3000 a year on his twelve-year-old son. This nexus of corruption Cobbett called 'the Thing' (we now call it the Establishment) and about it he developed something verging on paranoia. His journalism took on an increasingly radical, not to say hysterical, tone. For long his pet aversion was Wilberforce, who seemed to Cobbett to reserve all his pity for black slaves abroad and to have none for white labourers at home. But later (1819) when Malthus appeared to be suggesting that the poor should cease to procreate, Cobbett wrote him an open letter saying, 'Parson, I have during my life, detested many men, but never anyone so much as you!'.

In 1809 five soldiers at Ely, finding the cost of their knapsacks deducted from their pay, protested in a 'threatening' manner and were sentenced to 500 lashes. This was too much for Cobbett, especially as the sentence was partly administered by German mercenaries. His cries of rage got him sentenced to two years in Newgate for sedition and fined £1000. He and his friends paid off the fine and paid also for moderately comfortable quarters in the gaol, from which he continued editing and writing. He emerged after serving only eight months of his sentence, but once more a bankrupt. This involved selling the parliamentary reporting carried by his *Register* to his printer Hansard, whose successors have it still. When the government put a heavy stamp duty on the *Register* Cobbett circumvented them by publishing his leading articles as separate pamphlets which he called his 'Twopenny Trash'. Eventually (1817) a series of draconian 'gag acts', suspending Habeas Corpus and making 'agitators' liable to imprisonment without trial, made Cobbett flee once more to America—partly also to escape his creditors.

Since 1805 Cobbett had owned Fairthorn farmhouse at Botley, Hampshire, and had combined his journalism with quite successful farming. In America, which he now found much more to his liking, he set up as a farmer on Long Island, though still editing the *Register* by remote control. He returned to England late in 1819, this time reverently bringing with him the bones of Tom Paine, and also the seeds of some transatlantic vegetation, chiefly maize (which he called 'Cobbett's corn'), swedes and acacias, not to mention the technique of making straw 'plaits'. To propagate all these he established a seed farm in Kensington. He had relished the freedom and relative prosperity found in America, and he had been impressed by the English village girl he met there who exclaimed, 'O what a blessed thing it is to live within the sound of the Gospel and to go to Meeting in real leather shoes!' But he had been home-sick through living in a country where 'the birds were without song and the flowers without smell'; and he admitted to feeling 'bound to England for life'.

Feeling also a need for more countrified pursuits, Cobbett started a farm at Barn Elms, in Surrey; and later he leased Normandy Farm near his native Farnham, where on 18 June 1835 he was to die. He longed to put down roots. Years later (in 1826) he was to be almost envious of the 'neat, smart and pretty woman', a mother of two, he met at Tangley, Wiltshire, who had never been more than two and a half miles from her home. She was 'a very acute woman, and as well-behaved as need be . . . It is a great error to suppose that people are rendered stupid by remaining always in the same place'.

Soon after Cobbett's return to England a government commission on agriculture was appointed, and Cobbett, distrusting their findings, set out on horseback to see things for himself, covering the whole of southern England. His periodic reports on his tours of inspection appeared for a decade in the *Register* and, in 1830, in book form as his *Rural Rides*, undoubtedly his masterpiece.[4]

In the same decade appeared several more of Cobbett's best books. *Cottage Economy* (1822) was a splendid poor man's 'do-it-yourself' instruction book. *A History of the Protestant Reformation* (1824–7) started a potent historical myth, which was to influence thinkers as diverse as Disraeli, Marx, William Morris, Hilaire Belloc and G. K. Chesterton. Cobbett boasted that it sold more copies than any English book except the Bible. The Reformation was depicted simply as an epoch of spoliation, dismantling an alleged mediaeval welfare state (in which all peasants were merry peasants), drying up the milk of charity, and taking into private hands the tithes which supposedly had all been spent on poor relief.

---

[4] An enlarged edition was published in 1853 by his son James Paul Cobbett, including several journeys made by coach much farther afield.

Advice to Young Men (1829) anticipated much that we associate with Samuel Smiles's *Self Help* and advocated education in the home in preference to school.

Cobbett, though a shade more cautious than before, was by no means politically inactive. He sided openly with Queen Caroline when George IV was refusing to have her prayed for in church services. Cobbett stood unsuccessfully for parliament at Coventry in 1820, where he was turned out of his hotel and subjected to considerable mob violence. At Preston in 1826 he failed again, more through chicanery than violence—the mayor disqualified radical voters if they described themselves as 'gentlemen'.

In 1830 there was agricultural unrest; some ricks and barns were burnt, some threshing machines wrecked, one overseer was ducked and chased out of a village, and the son of a great banker suffered a slight bruise and a badly damaged hat (for which one labourer was hanged). This was deemed a new peasants' revolt, and in July 1831 Cobbett was tried for having, allegedly, fomented it. He defended himself for fifteen hours, having slept for seven hours, risen at four a.m. and breakfasted on half a pound of mutton without bread or any liquid. His best witness was Lord Chancellor Brougham who produced evidence that Cobbett had done much to allay the violence. But Cobbett had also sub-poenaed half the cabinet, including four past, current or future Prime Ministers. In the event the jury sat up all night and failed to reach any verdict.[5] Not surprisingly Cobbett was elected, for Oldham, to the reformed parliament of 1832 and took his seat on the front opposition bench next to Sir Robert Peel.

This juxtaposition was not wholly outrageous. The Tories and Cobbett had several things in common. Both were rooted in the country and fought shy of towns. Both, on the whole, disliked 'big business'. Both preferred an older England to the new, and both feared revolution. Both hated 'doctrinaires', 'a race', said Cobbett, 'whom I hate (Oh God, how I hate them!).' Besides, as he wrote on another occasion, 'We want *great alteration* but we want *nothing new*. Alteration, modification to suit the times and circumstances; but the great principles ought to be and must be the same.' He claimed also to have no objection to hereditary aristocracy or to the institution of property. He and the Tories could both argue that the reforms they wanted were all practical and urgent, aimed at relieving physical suffering rather than conforming to high-falutin theory. 'I will allow nothing to be good with regard to the labouring classes unless it makes an addition to their victuals, drink or clothing. As to their minds, that is much too sublime a matter for me to think about.' Cobbett shared, too, the Tory landowner's aversion from 'dark satanic mills' and was happy to support the bill proposed by the Tories Michael Sadler and Lord Ashley[6] for the reduction of factory hours from twelve to ten, for those under eighteen and in textile mills alone. It was interesting, said Cobbett in his one great parliamentary speech, to learn that all of Britain's 'wealth,

---

[5] See Charles Greville, *Diary*, 10 July 1831.
[6] Better known by his later title Earl of Shaftesbury.

power and security' lay not in her virility nor in her agriculture, banking or merchandise, but in 'the labour of 300,000 little girls in Lancashire' and that if two hours of their daily work were deducted, 'away goes the wealth, away goes the capital, away go the resources, the power and the glory of England!' The bill was heavily defeated.

Cobbett had some sympathy for the Luddite machine-breakers, though he thought their policy short-sighted; and he confessed, 'I never like to see machines, lest I should be tempted to endeavour to understand them.' The knowledge he valued was that which countrymen possessed. 'The nature and qualities of all living things are known to country boys better than to philosophers.' It was nearly always to the agricultural labourers that Cobbett's pity and charity were drawn, though he made an exception in favour of weavers, for theirs was still almost a purely cottage industry.

Cobbett's reactions were invariably governed by a certain immediacy, by what he saw with his own eyes; and his eyes told him that the countryside was being depopulated. He refused to believe census returns which told him that the general population was increasing—an increase which might prove the hated Malthus right. Disregarding both history and logic, Cobbett argued that, whenever one saw a small village with a large church, the village must once have been very much more populous. He was certainly unwilling to believe that any countryman would consider migrating to a town. Admittedly the Durham miners seemed better off than agricultural labourers, but he also noticed that in Leicester the 'working people'[7] were 'in the most miserable state', living in virtually unfurnished hovels.

In general Cobbett deplored the growth of city life and everything that went with it. 'Wens devoured market towns and villages; and shops devoured markets and fairs. . . . Scarcely anyone thought of providing for his own wants. . . . To buy the thing ready-made was the taste of the day. Housekeepers bought their dinner ready cooked: nothing was so common as to rent breasts for children to suck: a man actually advertised to provide childless husbands with heirs! In this case, the articles were of course to be ready-made.'

If Cobbett's politics must have a label he might be called an Agrarian, holding an ideal society to be one of free small-holders, such as Thomas Jefferson wanted in America.[8] But, despite his early Tory sympathies and despite the common ground with some Tories which he never quite abandoned, he was of course a Radical; and he steadily became more Radical. His disillusionment with Peel's economic measures and above all with the Whigs' New Poor Law forced him to crusade for manhood suffrage and for something very like the Chartist programme. He came close to holding a 'labour theory of value', that is, that labourers alone produced wealth and were therefore entitled to rewards infinitely fairer than they in fact received. Moreover, he had hard words for 'moderate' reformers, whom he

---

[7] A phrase probably of Cobbett's own coining, now worn very thin through over-use.
[8] It may be significant that one of Cobbett's last books was a *Life of Andrew Jackson* (1834).

compared with scare-crows ('shoy-hoys') which are meant to repel birds but which the birds soon find to be harmless and indeed convenient perches.

Again, although Cobbett claimed to be an Anglican and was abusive about 'canting Methodists' (who promised the poor nothing but treasure in heaven), not to mention Jews and Quakers, he was no less abusive about Anglican clergy who encouraged 'lazy lolling in pews' or who did anything 'to teach people to starve without making a noise'. As for the philanthropic Hannah More, she was no better than 'a prime old prelate in petticoats', because she taught the poor to be thankful for their appointed lot. Nor was Cobbett any kinder about Robert Owen's commune at New Lanark, for it took away men's independence and institutionalised them; it was 'a melancholy thing to behold ... the reverse of domestic life ... it reversed the order of nature ... and, which was among the greatest of its evils, it fashioned the rising generation to habits of implicit submission.' Cobbett was no Proto-Socialist.[9]

Some of his aversions were based on sheer prejudice; and he scarcely makes a reasoned case against fir trees, canals, gas-lighting, railways, turnpike trusts, or Martello towers; nor against tea-drinking which he saw as a mere pick-me-up necessitated solely by long working hours on a meagre diet. His hatred of potatoes rested on his fear lest they might reduce English labourers to an Irish level and preclude their eating anything much else. 'Think', he wrote, 'of breakfasting on a mess of cold potatoes as the forlorn wretches do at Great Bedwin and Cricklade.' And the Chilworth paper factory is reviled because it might be making paper money. 'Scotch feelosophers' are anathema partly for being Scots and still more for being philosophers, particularly if they are disciples of Adam Smith or write for the *Edinburgh Review*.

Hazlitt, whose analysis of Cobbett[10] still has no equal, put his finger unerringly on Cobbett's counter-suggestibility. 'His principle is repulsion, his nature contradiction: he is made up of mere antipathies; an Ishmaelite indeed. ... And if any principle were likely to become popular would turn round against it to show his power in shouldering it on one side.' Nevertheless we may often be thankful that this cross-grained, crotchety, ill-tempered man never heeded the advice of an American Quaker, 'Friend William, keep thyself cool.' It was perhaps undesirable to keep cool when he saw a notice near Canterbury saying, 'Paradise Place. Spring guns and steel traps are set here'. 'A pretty idea of Paradise,' wrote Cobbett, 'to know that spring guns and steel traps are set in it! This was doubtless some stock-jobber's place ... whenever any one of them went to the country, they looked upon it that they were to begin a sort of warfare against everything around them'.

We cannot blame Cobbett for his ill-temper when hungry men are transported for life for poaching rabbits or hanged for wounding a gamekeeper at Broadlands while resisting arrest, or again when he finds half the population of Tutbury in hot

---

[9] Perhaps he had a modern counterpart in George Orwell.
[10] In *The Spirit of the Age* (1825).

pursuit of a poor man who has stolen a cabbage. Surely, too, he is justifiably sickened when skilled workers are reduced to stone-breaking to avoid starvation, or when men are found dead 'and when opened by the surgeons nothing but sour sorrel was found in their stomachs', or even when he sees pretty girls 'ragged as colts and as pale as ashes' with 'blue arms and lips'. Not surprisingly he is bitter about the uncaring spongers, 'debauchees' and 'tax-eaters' to be seen at Brighton, Bath, or Cheltenham where Cobbett felt 'disposed to squeeze my nose with my fingers'. At moments we are grateful for what Coleridge, who hated Cobbett, called 'the flaying rasp of his tongue'.[11]

Cobbett was not always truculent and had loves as well as hates. He warmed to singing birds, particularly goldfinches, to orchards and trees (except fir trees), to packs of hounds, to fields full of hares, to 'puffing' clouds, to the Wiltshire and Sussex Downs, to good crops and fertile valleys, to cottages with well-kept gardens, to farmhouses that were not 'too neat for a dirty-shoed labourer to be allowed to come into', above all, to pig-styes (Cobbett's acid test of a labourer's prosperity). Normally he liked landscapes to be tame, cultivated and utilitarian; and he displayed no romantic, Wordsworthian taste for the wild, barren, rugged or 'sublime', taking infinite trouble to avoid Hindhead.

This was not due to any fear of 'roughing it'. When he got soaked to the skin on the South Downs he dried his shirt on his back before the inn fire and hoped this would cure his whooping cough. He often rode for a whole day on an extremely frugal diet, sometimes one slice each of meat and bread, sometimes merely nuts, milk and apples. And what he might have spent on a full meal he gave readily to any on the road who seemed in need of it. Yet this diet sustained the robust, burly frame of a full-blooded man over six feet tall, rubicund in complexion, the very image of John Bull.

Nor was it only his physique which was imposing. When, at a farmers' gathering in Lewes in Cobbett's sixtieth year, it was proposed that he should be evicted from the room, 'I rose', he says, 'that they might see the man they had to put out. Fortunately for themselves, not one of them attempted to approach me. They were like mice that resolved that a bell should be put round the cat's neck.' No one harassed or persecuted Cobbett with impunity—least of all those agents of 'the Thing' whom he dubbed the 'malignant and tyrannical jolterheads at Whitehall'. The government, he wrote, had been at war with him for over half his lifetime and had 'silenced every formidable assailant except myself . . . It regarded surviving as impossible; it was deceived for once; it had never had to do with a plough-boy before.'

---

[11] Cited in R. J. White (ed.), *The Political Thought of Samuel Taylor Coleridge* (1938) p.238.

PUBLISHER'S NOTE

The text of William Cobbett's *Rural Rides* on which this edition is based is that of the Revd Pitt Cobbett, Vicar of Crofton, Hampshire, in 1885 (reissued by Reeves and Turner in 1908). It, in turn, was essentially the edition of 1853 made by Cobbett's son James Paul, which included several journeys taken by coach and not to be found in the first edition of 1830.

It is hoped that the selection appearing here will give the general reader a clear impression of Cobbett's liveliest and most characteristic passages. Some passages, mostly of more ephemeral interest, have been omitted.

The footnotes are the work of Christopher Morris, with the exception of some few signed 'P.C.' which are taken from Pitt Cobbett's edition.

RURAL RIDES

———

JOURNAL: FROM LONDON, THROUGH NEWBURY, TO BERGHCLERE,
HURSTBOURN TARRANT, MARLBOROUGH, AND CIRENCESTER, TO
GLOUCESTER.

Berghclere, near Newbury, Hants,
October 30, 1821, Tuesday (Evening).

FOG that you might cut with a knife all the way from London to Newbury. This fog does not *wet* things. It is rather a *smoke* than a fog. There are no two things in *this world;* and, were it not for fear of *Six-Acts*[1] (the "wholesome restraint" of which I continually feel) I might be tempted to carry my comparison further; but, certainly, there are no two things in *this world* so dissimilar as an English and a Long Island autumn. — These fogs are certainly the *white clouds* that we sometimes see aloft. I was once upon the Hampshire Hills, going from Soberton Down to Petersfield, where the hills are high and steep, not very wide at their base, very irregular in their form and direction, and have, of course, deep and narrow valleys winding about between them. In one place that I had to pass, two of these valleys were cut asunder by a piece of hill that went across them and formed a sort of bridge from one long hill to another. A little before I came to this sort of bridge I saw a smoke flying across it; and, not knowing the way by experience, I said to the person who was with me, "there is the turnpike road (which we were expecting to come to;) for, don't you see the dust?" The day was very fine, the sun clear, and the weather dry. When we came to the pass, however, we found ourselves, not in dust, but in a fog. After getting over the pass, we looked down into the valleys, and there we saw the fog going along the valleys to the North, in detached parcels, that is to say, in clouds, and, as they came to the pass, they rose, went over it, then descended again, keeping constantly along just above the ground. And, to-day, the fog came by *spells*. It was sometimes thinner than at other times; and these changes were very sudden too. So that I am convinced that these fogs are *dry clouds*, such as those that I saw on the Hampshire-Downs. Those did not *wet* me at all; nor do these fogs wet anything; and I do not think that they are by any means injurious to health. — It is the fogs that rise out of swamps, and other places, full of putrid vegetable matter, that kill people. These are the fogs that sweep off the new settlers in the American Woods. I remember a valley in Pennsylvania, in a part called *Wysihicken*. In looking from a hill, over this valley, early in the morning, in

---

[1] The Six Acts or "gagging acts" of 1819, restricting "seditious" meetings or publications and suspending Habeas Corpus.

November, it presented one of the most beautiful sights that my eyes ever beheld. It was a sea bordered with beautifully formed trees of endless variety of colours. As the hills formed the outsides of the sea, some of the trees showed only their tops; and, every now-and-then, a lofty tree growing in the sea itself, raised its head above the apparent waters. Except the setting-sun sending his horizontal beams through all the variety of reds and yellows of the branches of the trees in Long Island, and giving, at the same time, a sort of silver cast to the verdure beneath them, I have never seen anything so beautiful as the foggy valley of the Wysihicken. But, I was told, that it was very fatal to the people; and that whole families were frequently swept off by the "*fall-fever.*" — Thus the *smell* has a great deal to do with health. There can be no doubt that Butchers and their wives fatten upon the smell of meat. And this accounts for the precept of my grandmother, who used to tell me to *bite my bread and smell to my cheese;* talk, much more wise than that of certain *old grannies*, who go about England crying up "the *blessings*" of paper-money, taxes, and national debts.

The fog prevented me from seeing much of the fields as I came along yesterday; but, the fields of Swedish Turnips that I did see were good; pretty good; though not clean and neat like those in Norfolk. The farmers here, as everywhere else, complain most bitterly; but they hang on, like sailors to the masts or hull of a wreck. They read, you will observe, nothing but the country newspapers; they, of course, know nothing of the *cause* of their "bad times." They hope "the times will mend." If they quit business, they must sell their stock; and, having thought this worth so much money, they cannot endure the thought of selling for a third of the sum. Thus they hang on; thus the landlords will first turn the farmers' pockets inside out; and then their turn comes. To finish the present farmers will not take long. There has been stout fight going on all this morning (it is now 9 o'clock) between the *sun* and the *fog*. I have backed the former, and he appears to have gained the day; for he is now shining most delightfully.

October 31. Wednesday.

A fine day. Too many hares here; but, our hunting was not bad; or, at least, it was a great treat to me, who used, when a boy, to have my legs and thighs so often filled with thorns in running after the hounds, anticipating with pretty great certainty, a "*waling*" of the back at night. We had grey-hounds a part of the day; but the ground on the hills is so *flinty*, that I do not like the country for coursing. The dogs' legs are presently cut to pieces.

Hurstbourn Tarrant, Hants,
Nov. 2. Friday.

This place is commonly called *Uphusband*,[2] which is, I think, as decent a

---

[2] Now called Hurstbourne-Tarrant, from "bourn," a *stream* (the river Test running through the village); and "hurst," a *wood*, through which the river trends. It is about six miles from Andover. P.C.

Hurstbourne Park in Hampshire, 'commonly called Uphusband, which is, I think, as decent a corruption of names as one would wish to meet with.'

corruption of names as one would wish to meet with. However, Uphusband the people will have it, and Uphusband it shall be for me. I came from Berghclere this morning, and through the park of LORD CARNARVON, at Highclere. It is a fine season to look at woods. The oaks are still covered, the beeches in their best dress, the elms yet pretty green, and the beautiful ashes only beginning to turn off. This is, according to my fancy, the prettiest park that I have ever seen. A great variety of hill and dell. I like this place better than *Fonthill*, *Blenheim*, *Stowe*, or any other gentleman's grounds that I have seen. The *house* I did not care about, though it appears to be large enough to hold half a village. The great beauty of the place is the *lofty downs*, as steep, in some places, as the roof of a house, which form a sort of boundary, in the form of a part of a crescent, to about a third part of the park, and then slope off and get more distant, for about half another third part. A part of these downs is covered with trees, chiefly beech, the colour of which, at this season, forms a most beautiful contrast with that of the down itself, which is so green and so smooth! From the vale in the park, along which we rode, we looked apparently almost perpendicularly up at the downs. Our horses beat up a score or two of hares as we crossed the park; and, though we met with no *gothic arches* made of Scotch fir, we saw something a great deal better; namely, about forty cows, the most beautiful that I ever saw, as to colour at least. They appear to be of the Galway breed. They are called, in this country, *Lord Carnarvon's breed*. They have no horns, and their colour is a ground of white, with black or red spots, these

16

spots being from the size of a plate to that of a crown piece; and some of them have no small spots. These cattle were lying down together in the space of about an acre of ground: they were in excellent condition, and so fine a sight of the kind I never saw. LORD CARNARVON told a man, in 1820, that *he did not like my politics*. But, what did he mean by my *politics*? I have no politics but such as he *ought* to like. I want to do away with that infernal *system* which, after having beggared and pauperised the Labouring Classes, has now, according to the Report (made by the Ministers themselves to the House of Commons,[3]) plunged the owners of the land themselves into a state of distress, for which those Ministers themselves can hold out no remedy! To be sure I labour most assiduously to destroy a system of distress and misery; but, is that any reason why a *Lord* should dislike my politics? If the Landlords be well; if things be going right with them; if they have fair prospects of happy days; then what need they care about me and *my politics;* but, if they find themselves in *"distress,"* and do not know how to get out of it; and, if they have been plunged into this distress by those who "dislike my politics," is there not *some reason* for men of sense to hesitate a little before they *condemn* those politics? If no great change be wanted; if things could remain even; then, men may, with some show of reason, say that I am disturbing that which ought to be let alone. But, if things cannot remain as they are; if there must be a *great change;* is it not folly, and, indeed is it not a species of idiotic perverseness, for men to set their faces, without rhyme or reason, against what is said as to this change by *me*, who have, for nearly twenty years, been warning the country of its danger, and foretelling that which has now come to pass, and is coming to pass? However, I make no complaint on this score. People disliking my politics "neither picks my pocket, nor breaks my leg," as JEFFERSON said by the writings of the Atheists. If they be pleased in disliking my politics, I am pleased in liking them; and so we are both enjoying ourselves. If the country want no assistance from me, I am quite sure that I want none from it.

Nov. 3. Saturday.

Fat hogs have lately sold, in this village, at 7s. 6d. a score (but would hardly bring that now), that is to say, at $4\frac{1}{2}$d. a pound. The hog is weighed whole, when killed and dressed. The head and feet are included; but so is the lard. Hogs fatted on peas or barley-meal may be called the very best meat that England contains. At Salisbury (only about 20 miles off) fat hogs sell for 5s. to 4s. 6d. a score. But, then, observe, these are *dairy hogs*, which are not nearly so good in quality as the corn-fed hogs. But, I shall probably hear more about these prices as I get further towards

---

[3] The report to which reference is here made was upon agricultural distress. War expenses had vastly increased the taxes; the hoarding of money by the people (in their dread of an invasion) led to a suspension of cash payments. Bank notes were made a legal tender, except to the army and navy. The monetary pressure was especially felt by the owners and occupiers of land and by their dependents, and there was good reason to contrast, the then existing depression, with the prosperity which prevailed prior to the French Revolution. Cobbett's strictures, however, on paper money (which occur here and elsewhere in this work) must be received with considerable qualification. P.C.

the West. Some wheat has been sold at Newbury-market for £6 a load (40 bushels); that is, at 3s. a bushel. A considerable part of the crop is wholly unfit for bread flour, and is not equal in value to good barley. In not a few instances the wheat has been carried into the gate, or yard, and thrown down to be made dung of. So that, if we were to take the average, it would not exceed, I am convinced, 5s. a bushel in this part of the country; and the average of all England would not, perhaps, exceed 4s. or 3s. 6d. a bushel. A farmer told me the other day, that he got *so little* offered for some of his wheat, that he was resolved not to take any more of it to market; but to give it to hogs. Therefore, in speaking of the price of wheat, you are to take in the unsold as well as the sold; that which fetches nothing as well as that which is sold at high price.

Nov. 4. Sunday.

This, to my fancy, is a very nice country. It is continual hill and dell. Now and then a *chain* of hills higher than the rest, and these are downs, or woods. To stand upon any of the hills and look around you, you almost think you see the ups and downs of sea in a *heavy swell* (as the sailors call it) after what they call, a gale of wind. The undulations are endless, and the great variety in the height, breadth, length, and form of the little hills, has a very delightful effect. — The soil, which, to look *on* it, appears to be more than half flint stones, is very good in quality, and, in general, better on the tops of the lesser hills than in the valleys. It has great tenacity; does not *wash away* like sand, or light loam. It is a stiff, tenacious loam, mixed with flint stones. Bears Saint-foin well, and all sorts of grass, which make the field on the hills as green as meadows, even at this season; and the grass does not burn up in summer. — In a country so full of hills one would expect endless runs of water and springs. There are none: absolutely none. No water-furrow is ever made in the land. No ditches round the fields. And, even in the *deep valleys*, such as that, in which this village is situated, though it winds round for ten or fifteen miles, there is no run of water even now. It rained all Friday night; pretty nearly all day yesterday; and to-day the ground is as dry as a bone, except just along the street of the village, which has been kept in a sort of stabble by the flocks of sheep passing along to and from Appleshaw fair. The land here is excellent in quality generally, unless you get upon the highest chains of hills. They have frequently 40 bushels of wheat to the acre. Their barley is very fine; and their Saint-foin abundant. The turnips are, in general, very good at this time; and the land appears as capable of carrying fine crops of them as any land that I have seen. A fine country for sheep: always dry: they never injure the land when feeding off turnips in wet weather; and they can lie down on the dry; for the ground is, in fact, never wet except while the rain is actually falling. The flocks of sheep, some in fold and some at large, feeding on the sides of the hills, give great additional beauty to the scenery. — The woods, which consist chiefly of oak thinly intermixed with ash, and well set with underwood of ash and hazle, but mostly the latter, are very beautiful. They sometimes stretch along the top and sides of hills for miles together; and, as their edges, or outsides, joining the fields and the downs, go winding and twisting about, and as the fields and downs are naked of trees, the sight altogether is very pretty.

Nov. 5. Monday.

A *white frost* this morning. The hills round about beautiful at sun-rise, the rooks making that noise which they always make in winter mornings. The Starlings are come in large flocks; and, which is deemed a sign of a hard winter, the Fieldfares are come at an early season. The haws are very abundant; which, they say, is another sign of a hard winter. The wheat is high enough here, in some fields, "to hide a hare," which is, indeed, not saying much for it, as a hare knows how to hide herself upon the bare ground. But it is, in some fields, four inches high, and is green and gay, the colour being finer than that of any grass.—The fuel here is wood. Little coal is brought from Andover. A load of faggots does not cost above 10s. So that, in this respect, the labourers are pretty well off. The wages here and in Berkshire, about 8s. a week; but, the farmers talk of lowering them.—The poor-rates heavy, and heavy they must be, till taxes and rents come down greatly.— Saturday and to-day Appleshaw sheep-fair. The sheep, which had taken a rise at Weyhill-fair, have fallen again even below the Norfolk and Sussex mark. Some South-Down Lambs were sold at Appleshaw so low as 8s. and some even lower. Some Dorsetshire Ewes brought no more than a pound; and, perhaps, the average did not exceed 28s. I have seen a farmer here who can get (or could a few days ago) 28s. round for a lot of fat Southdown Wethers, which cost him just that money, when they were lambs, *two years ago!* It is impossible that they can have cost him less than 24s. each during the two years, having to be fed on turnips or hay in winter, and to be fatted on good grass. Here (upon one hundred sheep) is a loss of £120 and £14 in addition at five per cent. interest on the sum expended in the purchase; even suppose not a sheep has been lost by death or otherwise. The *Hampshire Journal* says, that, on 1st November (Thursday) at Newbury Market, wheat sold from 88s. to 24s. the Quarter. This would make an average of 56s. But, very little indeed was sold at 88s., only the prime of the old wheat. The best of the new for about 48s., and, then, if we take into view the great proportion that cannot go to market at all, we shall not find the average, even in this rather dear part of England, to exceed 32s., or 4s. a bushel. And, if we take all England through, it does not come up to that, nor anything like it. A farmer very sensibly observed to me yesterday, that, "if we had had such a crop and such a harvest a few years ago, good wheat would have been £50 a load;" that is to say, 25s. a bushel! Nothing can be truer than this. And nothing can be clearer than that the present race of farmers, generally speaking, must be swept away by bankruptcy, if they do not, in time, make their bow, and retire. There are two descriptions of farmers, very distinct, as to the effects which this change must naturally have on them. The word *farmer* comes from the French, *fermier*, and signifies *renter*. Those only who rent, therefore, are, properly speaking, *farmers*. Those who till their own land are *yeomen;* and, when I was a boy, it was the common practice to call the former *farmers* and the latter *yeomen-farmers.* These yeomen have, for the greater part, been swallowed up by the paper-system, which has drawn such masses of money together. They have, by degrees, been *bought out.* Still there are some few left; and these, if not in debt, will stand their ground. But all the present race of mere renters must give away, in one manner or another. They must break, or drop their style greatly; even in the latter case, their rent must, very shortly, be diminished, more than two-thirds. Then comes the *Landlord's turn;* and, the sooner the better.

Marlborough,
Tuesday noon, Nov. 6.

I left Uphusband this morning at nine, and came across to this place (20 miles) in a post-chaise. Came up the valley of Uphusband, which ends at about 6 miles from the village, and puts one out, upon the Wiltshire downs, which stretch away towards the West and South-west, towards Devizes and towards Salisbury. After about half-a-mile of down, we came down into a level country; the flints cease, and the chalk comes nearer the top of the ground. The labourers along here, seem very poor indeed. Farm houses, with twenty ricks round each, besides those standing in the fields; pieces of wheat 50, 60, or 100 acres in a piece; but, a group of women labourers, who were attending the measurers, to measure their reaping work, presented such an assemblage of rags as I never before saw, even amongst the hoppers at Farnham, many of whom are common beggars. I never before saw *country* people, and reapers too, observe, so miserable in appearance as these. There were some very pretty girls, but ragged as colts, and as pale as ashes. The day was cold too, and frost hardly off the ground; and their blue arms and lips, would have made any heart ache, but that of a seat-seller or a loan-jobber.

MARLBOROUGH, which is an ill-looking place enough, is succeeded, on my road to SWINDON, by an extensive and very beautiful down about four miles over. Here nature has flung the earth about in a great variety of shapes. The fine short smooth grass, has about nine inches of mould under it, and then comes the chalk. The water that runs down the narrow side-hill valleys is caught, in different parts of the down, in basins made on purpose, and lined with clay apparently. This is for watering the sheep in summer; sure sign of a really dry soil; and yet the grass never *parches* upon these downs. The chalk holds the moisture, and the grass is fed by the dews in hot and dry weather.—At the end of this down, the high-country ends. The hill is high and steep, and from it, you look immediately down into a level farming country; a little further on, into the dairy-country, whence the North-Wilts cheese comes; and, beyond that, into the vale of Berkshire, and even to Oxford, which lies away to the north-east from this hill.—The land continues good, flat, and rather wet, to Swindon, which is a plain country town, built of the stone which is found at about six feet under ground about here.—I come on now towards Cirencester, through the dairy-country of North Wilts.

Cirencester,
Wednesday (Noon), 7 Nov.

I slept at a dairy-farm house at Hannington, about eight miles from Swindon, and five on one side of my road. I passed through that villanous hole, Cricklade, about two hours ago; and, certainly, a more rascally looking place I never set my eyes on. I wished to avoid it, but could get along no other way. All along here the land is a whitish stiff loam upon a bed of soft stone, which is found at various distances from the surface, sometimes two feet and sometimes ten. Here and there a field is fenced with this stone, laid together in walls without mortar, or earth. All the houses and out-houses are made of it, and even covered with the thinnest of it formed into tiles. The stiles in the fields are made of large flags of this stone, and the gaps in the hedges, are stopped with them. — There is very little wood all along here. The labourers seem miserably poor. Their dwellings are little better than pig-beds, and their looks indicate, that their food is not nearly equal that of a pig. Their wretched hovels are stuck upon little bits of ground *on the road side*, where the space has been wider than the road demanded. In many places they have not two rods to a hovel. It seems as if they had been swept off the fields by a hurricane, and had dropped and found shelter under the banks on the road side! Yesterday morning was a sharp frost; and this had set the poor creatures to digging up their little plats of potatoes. In my whole life I never saw human wretchedness equal to this: no, not even amongst the free negroes in America, who, on an average, do not work one day out of four. And, this is *"prosperity,"* is it? These, Oh, Pitt! are the fruits of thy hellish system! However, this *Wiltshire* is a horrible county. This is the county that the *Gallon-loaf* man[4] belongs to. The land all along here is good. Fine fields and pastures all around; and yet the cultivators of those fields so miserable! —I met a farmer going with porkers to Highworth Market. They would weigh, he said, four score and a half, and he expected to get 7s. 6d. a score. I expect he will not. He said they had been fed on barley-meal; but I did not believe him. I put it to his honour, whether whey and beans had not been their food. He looked surly, and pushed on. — On this stiff ground, they grow a good many beans, and give them to the pigs with whey; which makes excellent pork for the *Londoners;* but which must meet with a pretty hungry stomach to swallow it in Hampshire. Between Cricklade and this place (Cirencester) I met, in separate droves, about two thousand Welsh Cattle, on their way from Pembrokeshire to the fairs in Sussex. The greater part of them were heifers in calf. They were purchased in Wales at from £3 to £4, 10s. each! None of them, the drovers told me, reached £5. These heifers used to fetch, at home, from £6 to £8, and sometimes more. Many of the things that I saw in these droves did not fetch, in Wales, 25s. And, they go to no

---

[4] Referring to Mr. John Bennett, at that time M.P. for South Wilts, who had stated that the "gallon-loaf" was a sufficiency for the maintenance of farm labourers, the poor-law allowance generally being 7d. per day for the labourer, and a gallon-loaf per week for each of the rest of the family. P.C.

The Market Place at Cirencester, *c.* 1810.

rising market! Now, is there a man in his senses who believes that this THING[5] can go on in the present way?

Gloucester,
Thursday (morning) Nov. 8.

In leaving Cirencester, which is a pretty, large town, a pretty, nice town, and which the people call *Cititer*, I came up hill into a country, apparently, formerly a down or common, but now divided into large fields by stone walls. Any thing so ugly I have never seen before. The stone, which, on the other side of Cirencester, lay a good way under ground, here lies very near to the surface. The plough is

---

[5] Cobbett's term for what is now called "the Establishment".

continually bringing it up, and thus, in general, come the means of making the walls that serve as fences. I see thirty acres here, that have less *food* upon them than I saw the other day, upon half an acre at Mr. Budd's[6] at Berghclere. With the exception of a little dell about eight miles from Cititer, this miserable country continued, to the distance of ten miles, when, all of a sudden, I looked down from the top of a high hill into *the vale of Gloucester!* Never was there, surely, such a contrast in this world! This hill is called *Burlip Hill;* it is much about a mile down it, and the descent so steep as to require the wheel of the chaise to be locked; and, even with that precaution, I did not think it over and above safe, to sit in the chaise; so, upon Sir Robert Wilson's[7] principle of taking care of *Number One*, I got out and walked down. From this hill you see the Morvan Hills in Wales. You look down into a sort of *dish* with a flat bottom, the Hills are the sides of the dish, and the City of Gloucester, which you plainly see, at seven miles distance from Burlip Hill, appears to be not far from the centre of the dish. All here is fine; fine farms; fine pastures; all inclosed fields; all divided by hedges; orchards a plenty; and I had scarcely seen one apple since I left Berkshire.—GLOUCESTER is a fine, clean, beautiful place; and, which is of a vast deal more importance, the labourers' dwellings, as I came along, looked good, and the labourers themselves pretty well as to dress and healthiness. The girls at work in the fields (always my standard) are not in rags, with bits of shoes tied on their feet and rags tied round their ankles, as they had in Wiltshire.

JOURNAL: FROM GLOUCESTER, TO BOLLITREE IN HEREFORDSHIRE, ROSS, HEREFORD, ABINGDON, OXFORD, CHELTENHAM, BERGHCLERE, WHITCHURCH, UPHURSTBOURN, AND THENCE TO KENSINGTON.

Bollitree Castle, Herefordshire,
Friday, 9 Nov. 1821.

I got to this beautiful place (Mr. WILLIAM PALMER'S)[1] yesterday, from Gloucester. This is in the parish of *Weston*, two miles on the Gloucester side of Ross, and, if not the first, nearly the first, parish in Herefordshire upon leaving Gloucester to go on, through Ross to Hereford.—On quitting Gloucester I crossed the Severne, which had overflowed its banks and covered the meadows with water.—The soil good but stiff. The coppices and woods very much like those upon the clays in the South of Hampshire and in Sussex; but the land better for corn and grass. The goodness of the land is shown by the apple-trees, and by the sort of sheep and cattle fed here. The sheep are a cross between the Ryland and Leicester, and the cattle of the

---

[6] William Budd, Clerk of the Peace for Berkshire, to whom Cobbett dedicated his treatise on *The Woodlands* (1825).

[7] General Sir Robert Wilson, cashiered for his actions against the mob at Queen Caroline's funeral, 1821.

[1] William Palmer, a close friend of Cobbett's and future father-in-law of Cobbett's son Richard.

Herefordshire kind. These would starve in the pastures of any part of Hampshire or Sussex that I have ever seen. — At about seven miles from Gloucester I came to hills, and the land changed from the whitish soil, which I had hitherto seen, to a red brown, with layers of flat stone of a reddish cast under it. Thus it continued to Bollitree. The land very rich, the pastures the finest, I ever saw, the trees of all kinds, surpassing upon an average, any that I have before seen in England. Sheltered by a lofty wood; the grass fine beneath the fruit trees; the soil dry under foot, though the rain had scarcely ceased to fall; no moss on the trees: the leaves of many of them yet green. No wonder that this is a country of *cider* and *perry;* but, what a shame it is, that here, at any rate, the owners and cultivators of the soil, not content with these, should, for mere fashion's sake, waste their substance on *wine* and *spirits!* They really deserve the contempt of mankind and the curses of their children. — I have been to-day to look at Mr. PALMER's fine crops of *Swedish Turnips*, which are, in general, called "*Swedes.*" These crops having been raised according to *my plan*, I feel, of course, great interest in the matter. The Swedes occupy two fields: one of thirteen, and one of seventeen acres. The drilled Swedes in the seventeen-acre field, contain full 23 tons to the acre; the transplanted ones in *that* field, 15 tons, and the broad-cast not exceeding 10 tons. Those in the thirteen-acre field which were transplanted before the 21st July, contain 27 if not 30 tons; and the rest of *that* field about 17 tons to the acre.

Old Hall,
Saturday night, Nov. 10.

Went to Hereford this morning. It was market-day. My arrival became known, and, I am sure, I cannot tell how. A sort of *buz* got about. I could perceive here, as I always have elsewhere, very ardent friends and very bitter enemies; but all full of curiosity. One thing could not fail to please me exceedingly: my friends were *gay* and my enemies *gloomy.* I went into the market-place, amongst the farmers, with whom, in general, I was very much pleased. If I were to live in the county two months, I should be acquainted with every man of them. The country is very fine, all the way from Ross to Hereford. The soil is always a red loam upon a bed of stone. The trees are very fine, and certainly winter comes later here than in Middlesex. Some of the oak trees are still perfectly green, and many of the ashes as green as in September. In coming from Hereford to this place, which is the residence of Mrs. PALMER and that of her two younger sons, Messrs. PHILIP and WALTER PALMER, who, with their brother, had accompanied me to Hereford; in coming to this place, which lies at about two miles distance from the great road, and at about an equal distance from HEREFORD and from Ross, we met with something, the sight of which pleased me exceedingly: it was of a very pretty pleasant-looking lady (and *young* too) with two beautiful children, riding in a little sort of chaise-cart, drawn by *an ass*, which she was driving in reins. She appeared to be well known to my friends, who drew up and spoke to her, calling her Mrs. *Lock*, or *Locky* (I hope it was not *Lockhart*) or some such name. Her husband, who

24

Right:
The ruins of Cowdray House in Sussex.
Built in the mid-sixteenth century, it
was burnt down in 1793. Watercolour
by Charles Wild.

Below:
Pages from *The Life of William Cobbett*
written by himself, in 1809, under the
pseudonym of Peter Porcupine.

Left:
Although travel was extremely hazardous in the first half of the nineteenth century, the coaching inns were havens of comfort and good cheer. (From an engraving by James Pollard.)

Below:
'Landscape with woman driving sheep' by Samuel Palmer.

Right:
A drover at Smithfield Market in 1808.
From mediaeval days this great market
had attracted produce from all over the
country.

Below:
A watercolour by Henry Edridge of a
farmhouse in 1811.

A shooting party on the moors by J. M. W. Turner.

is, I suppose, some young farmer of the neighbourhood, may well call himself Mr. *Lucky*; for, to have such a wife, and for such a wife to have the good sense to put up with an ass-cart, in order to avoid, as much as possible, feeding those cormorants who gorge on the taxes, is a blessing that falls, I am afraid, to the lot of very few rich farmers. Mrs. *Lock* (if that be her name) is a real *practical radical*. Others of us, resort to radical coffee and radical tea; and she has a radical carriage. This is a very effectual way of assailing the THING, and peculiarly well suited for the practice of the female sex. But, the self-denial ought not to be imposed on the wife only: the husband ought to set the example: and, let me hope, that *Mr. Lock* does not indulge in the use of wine and spirits, while Mrs. Lock and her children ride in a jack-ass gig; for, if he do, he wastes, in this way, the means of keeping her a chariot and pair. If there be to be any expense not absolutely necessary; if there be to be anything bordering on extravagance, surely it ought to be for the pleasure of that part of the family, who have the least number of objects of enjoyment; and, for a husband to indulge himself in the guzzling of expensive, unnecessary, and really injurious drink, to the tune, perhaps, of 50 or 100 pounds a year, while he preaches economy to his wife, and, with a face as long as my arm, talks of the low price of corn, and wheedles her out of a curricle, into a jack-ass cart, is not only unjust but *unmanly*.

Bollitree,
Monday, 12 Nov.

Returned this morning and rode about the farm, and also about that of Mr. WINNAL, where I saw, for the first time, a plough going *without being held*. The man drove the three horses that drew the plough, and carried the plough round at the ends; but left it to itself the rest of the time. There was a skim coulter that turned the sward in under the furrow; and the work was done very neatly. This gentleman has six acres of *cabbages*, on ridges four feet apart, with a distance of thirty inches between the plants on the ridge. He has weighed one of what he deemed an average weight, and found it to weigh fifteen pounds without the stump. Now, as there are 4320 upon an acre, the weight of the acre is *thirty tons* all but 400 pounds! This is a prodigious crop, and it is peculiarly well suited for food for sheep at this season of the year. Common turnips have not half the substance in them, weight for weight. Then, they are in the ground; they are *dirty*, and, in wet weather the sheep must starve, or eat a great deal of dirt. This very day, for instance, what a sorry sight is a flock of fatting sheep upon turnips; what a mess of dirt and stubble! The cabbage stands boldly up above the ground, and the sheep eats it all up without treading a morsel in the dirt. Mr. WINNAL has a large flock of sheep feeding on his cabbages, which they will have finished, perhaps, by January. This gentleman also has some "*radical Swedes*," as they call them in Norfolk. A part of his crop is on ridges *five* feet apart, with *two rows* on the ridge, a part on *four* feet ridges with *one* row on the ridge. I cannot see that anything is

Spring ploughing in rural England.

gained in weight, by the double rows. I think, that there may be nearly twenty tons to the acre. Another piece Mr. WINNAL transplanted after vetches. They are very fine; and, altogether, he has a crop that any one, but a "*loyal*" farmer might envy him. This is really the *radical* system of husbandry. *Radical* means, *belonging to the root; going to the root*. And the main principle of this system (first taught by *Tull*) is, that the *root* of the plant is to be fed by *deep tillage*, while it is growing; and, to do this we must have our *wide distances*. Our system of husbandry is happily illustrative of our system of politics. Our lines of movement are fair and straightforward. We destroy all weeds, which, like tax-eaters, do nothing but devour the sustenance that ought to feed the valuable plants. Our plants are all *well fed*; and our nations of Swedes and of cabbages present a happy uniformity of enjoyments and of bulk, and not, as in the broad-cast system of Corruption, here and there one of enormous size, surrounded by thousands of poor little starveling things, scarcely distinguishable by the keenest eye, or, if seen, seen only to inspire a contempt of the husbandman. The Norfolk boys are, therefore, right in calling their Swedes *Radical Swedes*.

Bollitree,
Wednesday, 14th Nov.

There is one farmer, in the North of Hampshire, who has nearly eight thousand

30

acres of land in his hands; who grows fourteen hundred acres of wheat and two thousand acres of barley! He occupies what was formerly 40 farms! Is it any wonder that *paupers increase*? And is there not here cause enough for the increase of *poor*, without resorting to the doctrines of the barbarous and impious MALTHUS[2] and his assistants, the *feelosofers* of the Edinburgh Review, those eulogists and understrappers of the Whig-Oligarchy? "This farmer has done nothing *unlawful*," some one will say. I say he has; for there is a law to forbid him thus to monopolise land. But, no matter; the laws, the management of the affairs of a nation, *ought to be such as to prevent the existence of the temptation to such monopoly*. And, even now, the evil ought to be remedied, and could be remedied, in the space of half a dozen years. The disappearance of the paper-money[3] would do the thing in time; but this might be assisted by legislative measures.

Old Hall,
Thursday, 15 Nov.

We came this morning from Bollitree to *Ross-Market*, and, thence, to this place. Ross is an old-fashioned town; but it is very beautifully situated, and, if there is little of *finery* in the appearance of the inhabitants, there is also little of *misery*. It is a good, plain country town, or settlement of tradesmen, whose business is that of supplying the wants of the cultivators of the soil. It presents to us nothing of rascality and rouguishness of look, which you see on almost every visage in the *borough-towns*, not excepting the visages of the women. I remember, and I never shall forget, the horrid looks of the villains in Devonshire and Cornwall. Some people say, "O, *poor fellows!* It is not *their* fault." No? Whose fault is it, then? The miscreants who bribe them? True, that these deserve the halter (and some of them may have it yet); but, are not the takers of the bribes *equally* guilty? If we be so very lenient here, pray let us ascribe to the *Devil* all the acts of thieves and robbers: so we do; but we *hang* the thieves and robbers, nevertheless. It is no very unprovoking reflection, that from these sinks of atrocious villany come a very considerable part of the men to fill places of emolument and trust. What a clog upon a Minister to have people, bred in such scenes, forced upon him! And why does this curse continue? However, its natural consequences are before us, and are coming on pretty fast upon each other's heels. There are the landlords and farmers in a state of absolute ruin: there is the Debt, pulling the nation down like as a stone pulls a dog under water. The system seems to have fairly wound itself up; to have tied itself hand and foot with cords of its own spinning!—This is the town to which POPE has given an interest in our minds by his eulogium on the "*Man of Ross*," a portrait of whom is hanging up in the house in which I now am.—The market at Ross was very *dull*. No wheat in demand. No buyers. It must *come down*.

---

[2] The Revd Thomas Robert Malthus, author of the *Essay on Population* (1798), predicting inevitable famine unless the population ceased increasing.

[3] Paper currency was a permanent bee in Cobbett's bonnet. He wrote a pamphlet against it while in prison 1810–11.

Robert Jenkinson, 2nd Earl of Liverpool, a most unpopular minister who was responsible for the 'Pains and Penalties' Bill against Queen Caroline. He was Home Secretary under Pitt, and acted as leader of the House of Commons until his eventual elevation to the House of Lords. Cobbett said that he made excuses for the distress of the country in 1822, blaming it on the 'sudden transition from war to peace'.

Lord Liverpool's *remedy*, a bad harvest, has assuredly failed. Fowls 2*s.* a couple; a goose from 2*s.* 6*d.* to 3*s.*; a turkey from 3*s.* to 3*s.* 6*d.* Let a turkey come down to *a shilling*, as in France, and then we shall soon be to rights.

Friday, 16 Nov.

A whole day most delightfully passed a hare-hunting, with a pretty pack of hounds kept here by Messrs. Palmer. They put me upon a horse that seemed to have been made on purpose for me, strong, tall, gentle and bold; and that carried me either over or through every thing. I, who am just the weight of a four-bushel sack of good wheat, actually sat on his back from daylight in the morning to dusk (about nine hours), without once setting my foot on the ground. Our ground was at Orcop, a place about four miles distance from this place. We found a hare in a few minutes after throwing off; and, in the course of the day, we had to find four, and were never more than ten minutes in finding. A steep and naked ridge, lying between two flat valleys, having a mixture of pretty large fields and small woods, formed our ground. The hares crossed the ridge forward and backward, and gave us numerous views and very fine sport.—I never rode on such steep ground before; and, really, in going up and down some of the craggy places, where the rains had washed the earth from the rocks, I did think, once or twice of my neck, and how Sidmouth[4] would like to see me.—As to the *cruelty*, as some pretend, of this sport, that point I have, I think, settled, in one of the Chapters of my "*Year's Residence in America.*" As to the expense, a pack, even a full pack of harriers, like this, costs less than two bottles of wine a day with their inseparable concomitants. And, as to the *time* thus spent, hunting is inseparable from *early rising;* and, with habits of early rising, who ever wanted time for any business?

Oxford,
Saturday, 17 Nov.

We left OLD HALL (where we always breakfasted by candle light) this morning after breakfast; returned to Bollitree; took the Hereford coach as it passed about noon; and came in it through Gloucester, Cheltenham, Northleach, Burford, Whitney, and on to this city, where we arrived about ten o'clock. At *Gloucester* (as there were no meals on the road) we furnished ourselves with nuts and apples, which, first a handful of nuts and then an apple, are, I can assure the reader, excellent and most wholesome fare. They say, that nuts of all sorts are unwholesome; if they had been, I should never have written Registers, and if they were now, I should have ceased to write ere this; for, upon an average, I have eaten a pint a day since I left home. In short, I could be very well content to live on nuts, milk, and home-baked bread.—*Cheltenham* is a nasty, ill-looking place, half clown and half cockney. The town is one street about a mile long; but, then, at some distance from this street,

---

[4] Henry Addington, Prime Minister 1801–4, created Viscount Sidmouth 1805, one of Cobbett's pet aversions.

'A West Prospect of the City of Oxford.'

there are rows of white tenements, with green balconies, like those inhabited by the tax-eaters round London. Indeed, this place appears to be the residence of an assemblage of tax-eaters.

Soon after quitting this resort of the lame and the lazy, the gormandising and guzzling, the bilious and the nervous, we proceeded on, between stone walls, over a country little better than that from Cirencester to Burlip-hill.—A very poor, dull, and uninteresting country all the way to Oxford.

Burghclere (Hants),
Sunday, 18 Nov.

Upon beholding the masses of buildings, at Oxford, devoted to what they call "*learning*," I could not help reflecting on the drones that they contain and the wasps they send forth! However, malignant as some are, the great and prevalent characteristic is *folly*: emptiness of head; want of talent; and one half of the fellows who are what they call *educated* here, are unfit to be clerks in a grocer's or mercer's shop.—As I looked up at what they called *University Hall*, I could not help reflecting that what I had written, even since I left Kensington on the 29th of October, would produce more effect, and do more good in the world, than all that had, for a hundred years, been written by all the members of this University, who devour, perhaps, not less than *a million pounds a year*, arising from property,

34

completely at the disposal of the "Great Council of the Nation."

We got about three o'clock to this nice, snug little farm-house, and found our host, Mr. Budd,[5] at home.

Burghclere,
Monday, 19 Nov.

A thorough wet day, the only day the greater part of which I have not spent out of doors, since I left home.

Burghclere,
Wednesday, 21 Nov.

We intended to have a hunt; but the fox-hounds came across and rendered it impracticable. As an instance of the change which rural customs have undergone, since the hellish paper-system has been so furiously at work, I need only mention the fact, that, forty years ago, there were *five* packs of *foxhounds* and *ten* packs of *harriers* kept within *ten miles* of Newbury; and that now, there is *one* of the former (kept, too, by *subscription*) and *none* of the latter, except the few couple of dogs kept by Mr. Budd! "So much the better," says the shallow fool, who cannot duly estimate the difference between a resident *native* gentry, attached to the soil, known to every farmer and labourer from their childhood, frequently mixing with them in those pursuits where all artificial distinctions are lost, practising hospitality without ceremony, from habit and not on calculation; and a gentry, only now-and-then residing at all, having no relish for country-delights, foreign in their manners, distant and haughty in their behaviour, looking to the soil only for its rents, viewing it as a mere object of speculation, unacquainted with its cultivators, despising them and their pursuits, and relying, for influence, not upon the good will of the vicinage, but upon the dread of their power. The war and paper-system has brought in nabobs,[6] negro-drivers, generals, admirals, governors, commissaries, contractors, pensioners, sinecurists, commissioners, loan-jobbers, lottery-dealers, bankers, stock-jobbers; not to mention the long and *black list* in gowns and three-tailed wigs. You can see but few good houses, not in possession of one or the other of these.

Kensington,
Friday, 23 Nov.

Got home by the coach.

———

[5] See note 6 on page 23.

[6] A popular term for those who made fortunes in the East India Company.

KENTISH JOURNAL: FROM KENSINGTON TO DARTFORD,
ROCHESTER, CHATHAM, AND FAVERSHAM.

Tuesday, December 4, 1821,
Elverton Farm, near Faversham, Kent.

This is the first time, since I went to France, in 1792, that I have been on this side of
Shooter's Hill. The land, generally speaking, from Deptford to Dartford is poor,
and the surface ugly by nature, to which ugliness there has been made, just before
we came to the latter place, a considerable addition by the inclosure of a common,
and by the sticking up of some shabby-genteel houses, surrrounded with dead
fences, and things called gardens, in all manner of ridiculous forms, making, all
together, the bricks, hurdlerods and earth say, as plainly as they can speak, ''Here
dwell *vanity* and *poverty*.'' This is a little excrescence that has grown out of the
immense sums which have been drawn from other parts of the kingdom, to be
expended on Barracks, Magazines, Martello-Towers,[1] Catamarans, and all the
excuses for lavish expenditure, which the war for the Bourbons gave rise to. All
things will return; these rubbishy flimsy things, on this common, will first be
deserted, then crumble down, then be swept away, and the cattle, sheep, pigs and
geese will once more graze upon the common, which will again furnish heath,
furze, and turf for the labourers on the neighbouring lands.—After you leave
Dartford the land becomes excellent. Along through Gravesend towards Rochester
the country presents a sort of gardening scene.

Wednesday, 5 Dec.

The land on quitting Chatham is chalk at bottom; but, before you reach
Sittingbourne, there is a vein of gravel and sand under, but a great depth of loam
above. About Sittingbourne the chalk bottom comes again, and continues on to
this place, where the land appears to me, to be as good as it can possibly be. You
frequently see a field of fifty acres, level as a die, clean as a garden, and as rich. In
short, this is a country of hop-gardens, cherry, apple, pear and filbert orchards,
and quickset hedges. But, alas! what, in point of *beauty*, is a country without
woods and lofty trees! And here there are very few indeed. I declare, that I, a
million times to one, prefer, as a spot to *live on*, the heaths, the miry coppices, the
wild woods and the forests of Sussex and Hampshire.

Saturday, 8 Dec.

Kent is in a deplorable way. The farmers are skilful and intelligent, generally
speaking. But, there is infinite *corruption* in Kent, owing partly to the swarms of
West Indians, Nabobs, Commissioners, and others of nearly the same description,
that have selected it, for the place of their residence; but, owing still more to the

---

[1] Martello Towers, built along the South Coast when Napoleon's invasion was expected, regarded by Cobbett
as a useless extravagance.

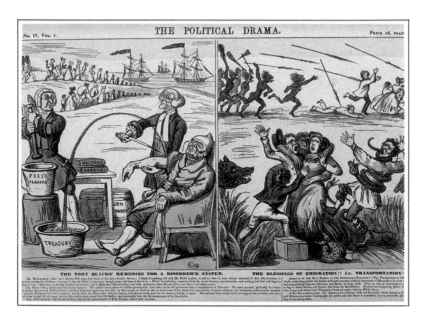

A cartoon attacking the Tory answer to the troubles of the 1820s—emigration.

Emigration to South Australia, a watercolour by R. Hillingford.

Coursing in Hatfield Park. The traditional country sports were an important and long-established part of rural life.

immense sums of public money that have, during the last thirty years, been expended in it. This county, so blessed by Providence, has been cursed by the System in a peculiar degree. It has been the *receiver* of immense sums, raised on the other counties. This has puffed its *rents* to an unnatural height; and now that the drain of other counties is stopped, it feels like a pampered pony, turned out in winter, to live upon a common.

NORFOLK AND SUFFOLK JOURNAL.

Bergh-Apton, near Norwich,
Monday, 10 Dec. 1821.

From the *Wen*[1] to Norwich, from which I am now distant seven miles, there is nothing in Essex, Suffolk, or this county, that can be called a *hill*. Essex, when you get beyond the immediate influence of the gorgings and disgorgings of the Wen; that is to say, beyond the demand for crude vegetables, and repayment in manure, is by no means a fertile county. There appears generally to be a bottom of *clay;* not *soft chalk*, which they persist in calling clay in Norfolk. It was not till I got nearly to SUDBURY that I saw much change for the better. Here the bottom of chalk, the soft dirty-looking chalk, that the Norfolk people call clay, begins to be the bottom, and this, with very little exception (as far as I have been) is the bottom of all the lands, of these two fine counties of Suffolk and Norfolk.—The land all along, to Bury Saint Edmund's is very fine; but no trees worth looking at. *Bury*, formerly the seat of an Abbot, the last of whom, was, I think, hanged, or somehow put to death, by that matchless tyrant, Henry VIII., is a very pretty place; extremely clean and neat: no ragged or dirty people to be seen, and women (*young* ones I mean) very pretty and very neatly dressed. The farming all along to Norwich, is very good. The land clean, and everything done in a masterly manner.

Saturday, 15 Dec.

Spent the evening amongst the Farmers, at their Market Room at Holt; and very much pleased at them I was. We talked over the *cause of the low prices*, and I, as I have done every where, endeavoured to convince them, that prices must fall a great deal lower yet; and, that no man, who wishes not to be ruined, ought to keep or take a farm, unless on a calculation of best wheat at 4*s.* a bushel and a best South Down ewe at 15*s.* or even 12*s.* They heard me patiently, and, I believe, were well convinced of the truth of what I said.

---

[1] It was Cobbett who first called London "the Great Wen."

Bergh Apton,
22nd Dec. (night).

Norwich is a very fine city, and the Castle, which stands in the middle of it, on a hill, is truly majestic. The meat and poultry and vegetable market is beautiful. It is kept in a large open square in the middle, or nearly so, of the City. The ground is a pretty sharp slope, so that you see all at once.

Kensington,
Monday, 24 Dec.

Went from Bergh Apton to Norwich in the morning, and from Norwich to London during the day, carrying with me great admiration of, and respect for, this county of *excellent farmers*, and hearty, open and spirited men. The Norfolk people are quick and smart in their motions and in their speaking. Very neat and *trim* in all their farming concerns, and very skilful. Their land is good, their roads are level, and the bottom of their soil is dry, to be sure; and these are great advantages; but, they are diligent, and make the most of every thing. Their management of all sorts of stock is most judicious; they are careful about manure; their teams move quickly; and, in short, it is a county of most excellent cultivators.

———

SUSSEX JOURNAL: TO BATTLE, THROUGH BROMLEY, SEVEN-OAKS, AND TUNBRIDGE.

Battle,
Wednesday, 2 Jan. 1822.

Came here to-day from Kensington, in order to see what goes on at the Meeting to be held here to-morrow, of the "Gentry, Clergy, Freeholders, and Occupiers of Land in the Rape[1] of Hastings, to take into consideration the distressed state of the Agricultural interest." I shall, of course, give an account of this meeting after it has taken place.—You come through part of *Kent* to get to *Battle* from the Great *Wen* on the Surrey side of the Thames. The first town is Bromley, the next Seven-Oaks, the next Tunbridge, and between Tunbridge and this place you cross the boundaries of the two counties.—From the Surrey Wen to Bromley, the land is generally a deep loam on a gravel, and you see few trees except elm. The agricultural state of the country or, rather, the quality of the land, from Bromley to Battle, may be judged of, from the fact, that I did not see, as I came along, more than thirty acres of Swedes, during the fifty-six miles! In Norfolk I should, in the same distance, have seen five hundred acres!

---

[1] Rape, a traditional land-division in Sussex.

SUSSEX

Battle,
Thursday (night), 3 Jan. 1822.

To-day there has been a *Meeting* here of the landlords and farmers in this part of Sussex, which is called the *Rape of Hastings*. The object was to agree on a petition to parliament praying for *relief!* Good God! Where is this to *end?* We now see the effects of those *rags*[2] which I have been railing against for the last twenty years. Here were collected together not less than 300 persons, principally landlords and farmers, brought from their homes by their distresses and by their alarms for the future! Never were such things heard in any country before; and, it is useless to hope, for terrific must be the consequences, if an effectual remedy be not speedily applied. The town, which is small, was in a great bustle before noon; and the Meeting (in a large room in the principal inn) took place about one o'clock. Lord Ashburnham was called to the chair, and there were present Mr. Curteis, one of the county members, Mr. Fuller, who formerly used to cut *such a figure* in the House of Commons, Mr. Lambe, and many other gentlemen of landed property within the Rape, or district, for which the Meeting was held. Mr. Curteis, after Lord Ashburnham had opened the business, addressed the Meeting.

Mr. Fuller then tendered some Resolutions, describing the fallen state of the landed interest, and proposing to pray, *generally*, for relief. Mr. Britton complained that it was not proposed to pray for some *specific measure*, and insisted, that the cause of the evil was the rise in the value of money, without a corresponding reduction in the taxes. — A Committee was appointed, to draw up a petition, which was next produced. It merely described the distress, and prayed generally for relief. Mr. Holloway proposed an addition, containing an imputation of the distress to restricted currency, and unabated taxation, and praying for a reduction of taxes. A discussion now arose upon two points: first, whether the addition were admissible at all! and, second, whether Mr. Holloway was qualified to offer it to the Meeting. Both the points having been, at last, decided in the affirmative, the addition, or amendment, was put, and *lost;* and then the original petition was adopted.

After the business of the day was ended, there was a dinner in the inn, in the same room where the Meeting had been held. I was at this dinner; and Mr. Britton having proposed my health, and Mr. Curteis, who was in the Chair, having given it, I thought it would have looked like mock-modesty, which is, in fact, only another term for hypocrisy, to refrain from expressing my opinions, upon a point or two, connected with the business of the day. I shall now insert a substantially correct sketch of what the company was indulgent enough to hear from me at the dinner: which I take from the report, contained in the *Morning Chronicle* of Saturday last.

---

[2] Rags: Cobbett's word for paper money. Bankers were "rag-merchants".

The following is a part of the speech so reported :—

'I am decidedly of opinion, Gentlemen, that a Corn Bill of no description, no matter what its principles or provisions, can do either tenant or landlord any good; and I am not less decidedly of opinion, that though prices are now low, they must, all the present train of public measures continuing, be yet lower, and continue lower upon an average of years and of seasons.—As to a Corn Bill; a law to prohibit or check the importation of human food, is a perfect novelty in our history, and ought, therefore, independent of the reason, and the recent experience of the case, to be received and entertained with great suspicion. Heretofore, *premiums* have been given for the exportation, and at other times, for the importation, of corn; but, of laws, to prevent the importation of human food, our ancestors knew nothing. And what says recent experience? When the present Corn Bill was passed, I, then a farmer, unable to get my brother farmers to join me, *petitioned singly* against this Bill! and I stated to my brother farmers, that such a Bill, could do us no good, while it would not fail to excite against us, the ill-will of the other classes of the community; a thought by no means pleasant. Thus has it been. The distress of agriculture was considerable in magnitude then; but what is it now? And yet the Bill was passed; that Bill which was to remunerate, and protect, is still in force; the farmers got what they prayed to have granted them; and their distress, with a short interval of tardy pace, has proceeded rapidly increasing from that day to this. What, in the way of Corn Bill, can you have, Gentlemen, beyond absolute prohibition? And, have you not, since about April, 1819, had absolute prohibition? Since that time, no corn has been imported, and then, only thirty millions of bushels, which, supposing it all to have been wheat, was a quantity much too insignificant to produce any sensible depression in the price of the immense quantity of corn, raised in this kingdom, since the last bushel was imported. If your produce had fallen in this manner, if your prices had come down very low, immediately after the importation had taken place, there might have been some colour of reason, to impute the fall to the importation; but it so happens, and as if for the express purpose of contradicting the crude notions of Mr. Webb Hall, that your produce has fallen in price, at a greater rate, in proportion as time has removed you from the point of importation; and, as to the circumstance, so ostentatiously put forward by Mr. Hall and others, that there is still some of the imported corn *unsold*, what does it prove, but the converse of what those Gentlemen aim at, that is to say, that the holders *cannot afford* to sell it at present prices; for, if they could gain, but ever so little by the sale, would they keep it wasting, and costing money in warehouse? There appears with some persons to be a notion, that the importation of corn is a *new thing*. They seem to forget, that, during the last war, when agriculture was so *prosperous*, the *ports were always open*: that prodigious quantities of corn were imported during the war; that, so far from importation being prohibited, high *premiums* were given, paid out of the taxes, partly raised upon English Farmers, to induce men to import corn. All this seems to be forgotten as much as if it had never taken place; and now the distress of the English farmer is imputed to a cause which was never before an object of his attention, and a desire is expressed, to put an end to a branch of commerce, which the nation has always freely carried on. I think, Gentlemen, that here are reasons quite sufficient to make any man, but Mr. Webb Hall, slow to impute the present distress to the importation of corn; but, at any rate, what can you have, beyond absolute efficient prohibition? No law, no duty, however high; nothing that the Parliament can do, can go beyond this; and this you now have, in effect, as completely as if this were the only country, beneath the sky. For these reasons, Gentlemen, (and to state more would be a waste of your time and an affront to your understandings), I am convinced, that, in the way of Corn Bill, it is impossible for the Parliament to afford you any, even the smallest, portion of relief. As to the other point, Gentlemen, the tendency which the present measures, and course of things, have to carry prices *lower*, and considerably lower than they now are, and to keep them for a permanency, at that low rate, this is a matter worthy of the serious attention of all connected with the land, and particularly of that of the renting farmer. During the *war* no importations distressed the farmer. It was not till peace came, that the cry of distress was heard. But, during the war, there was a boundless issue of paper money. Those issues were instantly narrowed by the peace, the law being, that the Bank should pay in cash, six months after the peace should take place. This was the cause of that distress which led to the present Corn Bill. The disease occasioned by the preparations for cash-payments, has been brought to a crisis by Mr. Peel's Bill,[3] which has, in effect, doubled, if not tripled, the real amount of the taxes, and violated all contracts for time; given triple gains to every lender, and placed every borrower in jeopardy.'

Kensington, Friday, 4 Jan. 1822.

Got home from *Battle*. I had no time to see the town, having entered the Inn on Wednesday in the dusk of the evening, having been engaged all day yesterday in the Inn, and having come out of it, only to get into the coach this morning.

———

JOURNAL: HERTFORDSHIRE AND BUCKINGHAMSHIRE: TO ST.
ALBANS, THROUGH EDGEWARE, STANMORE, AND WATFORD,
RETURNING BY REDBURN, HEMPSTEAD, AND CHESHAM.

Saint Albans, June 19, 1822.

From Kensington to this place, through Edgeware, Stanmore, and Watford, the crop is almost entirely hay, from fields of permanent grass, manured by dung and other matter brought from the *Wen*. Near the Wen, where they have had the *first haul* of the Irish and other perambulating labourers, the hay is all in rick. Some

---

[3] For the resumption of gold payments (1819), suspended since 1797.

miles further down it is nearly all in. Towards Stanmore and Watford, a third, perhaps of the grass remains to be cut. It is curious to see how the thing regulates itself. We saw, all the way down, squads of labourers, of different departments, migrating from tract to tract; leaving the cleared fields behind them and proceeding on towards the work to be yet performed; and, then, as to the classes of labourers, the *mowers* with their scythes on their shoulders, were in front, going on towards the standing crops, while the *hay-makers* were coming on behind towards the grass already cut or cutting. The weather is fair and warm; so that the public-houses on the road are pouring out their beer pretty fast, and are getting a good share of the wages of these thirsty souls. It is an exchange of beer for sweat; but the tax-eaters get, after all, the far greater part of the sweat; for, if it were not for the tax, the beer would sell for three-halfpence a pot, instead of fivepence. Of this threepence-halfpenny, the Jews and Jobbers get about twopence-halfpenny. It is curious to observe how the different labours are divided as to the *nations*. The mowers are all *English*; the haymakers all *Irish*. Scotchmen toil hard enough in Scotland; but when they go from home, it is not to *work*, if you please. They are found in gardens, and especially in gentlemen's gardens. Tying up flowers, picking dead leaves off exotics, peeping into melon-frames, publishing the banns of marriage between the*"male"* and *"female"* blossoms, tap-tap-tapping against a wall with a hammer that weighs half an ounce. They have backs as straight and shoulders as square as heroes of Waterloo; and who can blame them? The digging, the mowing, the carrying of loads; all the break-back and sweat-extracting work, they leave to be performed by those who have less *prudence* than they have. The great purpose of human art, the great end of human study, is to obtain *ease*, to throw the burden of labour from our own shoulders, and fix it on those of others. The crop of hay is very large, and that part which is in, is in very good order. We shall have hardly any hay that is not fine and sweet; and we shall have it, carried to London, at less, I dare say, than £3 a load, that is 18 cwt. So that here the *evil* of *"over-production"* will be great indeed! Whether we shall have any projects for taking hay into *pawn* is more than any of us can say; for, after what we have seen, need we be surprised, if we were to hear it proposed to take butter and even milk into pawn? In after times, the mad projects of these days will become proverbial. The Oracle and the over-production men will totally supplant the *March hare*. This is, all along here, and especially as far as Stanmore, a very dull and ugly country; flat, and all grass-fields and elms. Few *birds* of any kind, and few *constant* labourers being wanted; scarcely any cottages and gardens, which form one of the great beauties of a country. Stanmore is on a hill; but it looks over a country of little variety, though rich. What a difference between the view here and those which carry the eye over the coppices, the corn-fields, the hop-gardens and the orchards of Kent!

Kensington, June 24, 1822.

Set out at four this morning for Redbourn, and then turned off to the Westward to go to High Wycombe, through Hempstead and Chesham. The *wheat* is good all the way. The custom is in this part of Hertfordshire (and, I am told it continues into Bedfordshire) to leave a *border* round the ploughed part of the fields to bear grass, and to make hay from, so that, the grass being now made into hay, every corn field has a closely mowed grass walk about ten feet wide all round it, between the corn and the hedge. This is most beautiful! The hedges are now full of the shepherd's rose, honeysuckles, and all sorts of wild flowers; so that you are upon a grass walk, with this most beautiful of all flower gardens and shrubberies on your one hand, and with the corn on the other. And thus you go from field to field (on foot or on horseback), the sort of corn, the sort of underwood and timber, the shape and size of the fields, the height of the hedge-rows, the height of the trees, all continually varying. Talk of *pleasure-grounds* indeed! All along the country that I have come, the labourers' dwellings are good. They are made of what they call *brick-nog* (that is to say, a frame of wood, and a single brick thick, filling up the vacancies between the timber). They are generally covered with tile. Not *pretty* by any means; but they are good; and you see here, as in Kent, Sussex, Surrey and Hampshire, and, indeed, in almost every part of England, that most interesting of all objects, that which is such an honour to England, and that which distinguishes it from all the rest of the world, namely, *those neatly kept and productive little gardens round the labourers' houses*, which are seldom unornamented with more or less of flowers. We have only to look at these to know what sort of people English labourers are: these gardens are the answer to the *Malthuses* and the *Scarletts*. Shut your mouths, you Scotch Economists; cease bawling, Mr. Brougham,[1] and you Edinburgh Reviewers, till *you* can show us something, not *like*, but approaching towards a likeness of *this!*

The orchards all along this country are by no means bad. Not like those of Herefordshire and the north of Kent; but a great deal better than in many other parts of the kingdom. The cherry-trees are pretty abundant and particularly good. There are not many of the *merries*, as they call them in Kent and Hampshire; that is to say, the little black cherry, the name of which is a corruption from the French, *merise*, in the singular, and *merises* in the plural. I saw the little boys, in many places, set to keep the birds off the cherries, which reminded me of the time when I followed the same occupation, and also of the toll that I used to take in payment. The children are all along here, I mean the little children, locked out of the doors, while the fathers and mothers are at work in the fields. I saw many little groups of this sort; and this is one advantage of having plenty of room on the outside of a house. I never saw the country children better clad, or look cleaner and fatter than

---

[1] Henry Peter, Lord Brougham (1778–1868), a founder of the *Edinburgh Review*, and Lord Chancellor, frequently the object of Cobbett's keenest satire, being styled ''the shallow and noisy man,'' ''bawler,'' ''barker,'' ''ramper,'' and ''swamper.'' The strong dislike which Cobbett entertained for Brougham arose from reasons of a personal nature. Brougham charged Cobbett ''with direct incitements to the invasion of private property,'' to plunder, and to incendiarism, and indeed he appeared to take every opportunity for speaking vindictively of him. P.C.

they look here, and I have the very great pleasure to add, that I do not think I saw three acres of *potatoes* in this whole tract of fine country, from St. Albans to Redbourn, from Redbourn to Hempstead, and from Hempstead to Chesham. In all the houses where I have been, they use the roasted rye instead of coffee or tea, and I saw one gentleman who had sown a piece of rye (a grain not common in this part of the country) for the express purpose. It costs about three farthings a pound, roasted and ground into powder.

The pay of the labourers varies from eight to twelve shillings a-week. Grass mowers get two shillings a-day, two quarts of what they call strong beer, and as much small beer as they can drink.

I have traversed to-day, what I think may be called, an average of England as to corn-crops. Some of the best, certainly; and pretty nearly some of the worst. My observation as to the wheat is, that it will be a fair and average crop, and extremely early; because, though it is not a heavy crop, though the ears are not long they will be full; and the earliness seems to preclude the possibility of blight, and to ensure plump grain. The barley and oats must, upon an average, be a light crop. The peas a light crop; and as to beans, unless there have been rains where beans are mostly grown, they cannot be half a crop; for they will not endure heat. This fine summer, though it may not lead to a good crop of turnips, has already put safe into store such a crop of hay, as I believe England never saw before. Looking out of the window, I see the harness of the Wiltshire waggon-horses (at this moment going by) covered with the chalk-dust of that county; so that the fine weather continues in the West. Such a summer is a great blessing; and the only draw-back is, the dismal apprehension of not seeing such another for many years to come. It is favourable for poultry, for colts, for calves, for lambs, for young animals of all descriptions, not excepting the game. The partridges will be very early. They are now getting into the roads with their young ones, to roll in the dust. The first broods of partridges in England are very frequently killed by the wet and cold; and this is one reason why the game is not so plenty here, as it is in countries more blest with sun. This will not be the case this year; and, in short, this is one of the finest years that I ever knew.

Wm. COBBETT.

RURAL RIDE, OF 104 MILES, FROM KENSINGTON TO UPHUSBAND.

Chilworth, near Guildford, Surrey,
Wednesday, 25th Sept., 1822.

This morning I set off, in rather a drizzling rain, from Kensington, on horseback, accompanied by my son,[1] with an intention of going to Uphusband, near Andover, which is situated in the North West corner of Hampshire. It is very true that I could have gone to Uphusband by travelling only about 66 miles, and in the space

---

[1] James Paul, Cobbett's third son (1803–81), Editor of the second, enlarged, edition of *Rural Rides*, 1853.

of about eight hours. But, my object was, not to see inns and turnpike-roads, but to see the *country:* to see the farmers at home, and to see the labourers in the fields; and to do this you must go either on foot or on horse-back. With a gig you cannot get about amongst bye-lanes and across fields, through bridle-ways and hunting-gates; and to *tramp it* is too slow, leaving the labour out of the question, and that is not a trifle.

This county of Surrey presents to the eye of the traveller a greater contrast than any other county in England. It has some of the very best and some of the worst lands, not only in England, but in the world. We were here upon those of the latter description. For five miles on the road towards Guildford the land is a rascally common, covered with poor heath, except where the gravel is so near the top as not to suffer even the heath to grow.

To come to Chilworth, which lies on the south side of St. Martha's Hill, most people would have gone along the level road to Guildford and come round through Shawford under the hills; but we, having seen enough of streets and turnpikes, took across over Merrow Down, where the Guildford race-course is, and then mounted the "Surrey Hills," so famous for the prospects they afford. Here we looked back over Middlesex, and into Buckinghamshire and Berkshire, away towards the North West, into Essex and Kent towards the East, over part of Sussex to the South, and over part of Hampshire to the West and South West.

Lea, near Godalming, Surrey, Thursday, 26 Sept.

We started from Chilworth this morning, came down the vale, left the village of Shawford to our right, and that of Wonersh to our left, and crossing the river Wey, got into the turnpike-road between Guildford and Godalming, went on through Godalming, and got to Lea, which lies to the north-east snugly under Hind-Head, about 11 o'clock. This was coming only about eight miles, a sort of rest after the 32 miles of the day before. Coming along the road, a farmer overtook us, and as he had known me from seeing me at the Meeting at Epsom last year, I had a part of my main business to perform, namely, to talk politics. He was going to *Haslemere* Fair. Upon the mention of that sink-hole of a Borough, which sends, *"as clearly as the sun at noonday,"*[2] the celebrated Charles Long, and the scarcely less celebrated Robert Ward, to the celebrated House of Commons,[3] we began to talk, as it were, spontaneously, about Lord Lonsdale and the Lowthers. The farmer wondered why the Lowthers, that were the owners of so many farms, should be for a system which was so manifestly taking away the estates of the landlords and the capital of the farmers, and giving them to Jews, loan-jobbers, stock-jobbers, placemen, pensioners, sinecure people, and people of the "dead weight."[4] But, his wonder

---

[2] A phrase used in the Commons in 1809, referring to the shameless sale of Parliamentary seats.

[3] Charles Long, Paymaster-General 1810–26, 1st Baron Farnborough 1820. Robert Ward, author of three society novels.

[4] A phrase coined by Lord Castlereagh to describe placemen or pensioners who were automatic government supporters.

ceased; his eyes were opened; and "his heart seemed to burn within him as I talked to him on the way," when I explained to him the nature of *Crown-Lands* and *"Crown-Tenants,"* and when I described to him certain districts of property in Westmoreland and other parts. I had not the book in my pocket, but my memory furnished me with quite a sufficiency of matter to make him perceive, that, in supporting the present system, the Lowthers were by no means so foolish as he appeared to think them. From the Lowthers I turned to Mr. Poyntz,[5] who lives at Midhurst in Sussex, and whose name as a *"Crown-Tenant"* I find in a Report lately laid before the House of Commons, and the particulars of which I will state another time for the information of the people of Sussex. I used to wonder myself what made Mr. Poyntz call me a Jacobin. I used to think that Mr. Poyntz must be a fool to support the present system. What I have seen in that Report convinces me that Mr. Poyntz is no fool, as far as relates to his own interest, at any rate. There is a mine of wealth in these *"Crown Lands."* Here are farms, and manors, and mines, and woods, and forests, and houses, and streets, incalculable in value. What can be so proper as to apply this public property towards the discharge of a part, at least, of that public debt, which is hanging round the neck of this nation like a mill-stone? Mr. Ricardo[6] proposes to seize upon a part of the private property of every man, to be given to the stock-jobbing race. At an act of injustice like this the mind revolts. The foolishness of it, besides, is calculated to shock one. But, in the *public property* we see the suitable thing. And who can possibly object to this, except those, who, amongst them, now divide the possession or benefit of this property? I have once before mentioned, but I will repeat it, that *Marlborough House* in Pall Mall, for which the Prince of Saxe Coburg pays a rent to the Duke of Marlborough of three thousand pounds a-year, is rented of this generous public by that most Noble Duke at the rate of less than *forty pounds* a-year. There are three houses in Pall Mall, the whole of which pay a rent *to the public* of about fifteen pounds a-year, I think it is. I myself, twenty-two years ago, paid three hundred pounds a-year for one of them, to a man that I thought was the owner of them; but I now find that these houses belong to the public. The Duke of Buckingham's house in Pall Mall,[7] which is one of the grandest in all London, and which is not worth less than seven or eight hundred pounds a-year, belongs to the public. The Duke is the tenant; and I think he pays for it much less than twenty pounds a-year. I speak from memory here all the way along; and therefore not positively; I will, another time, state the particulars from the books. The book that I am now referring to is also of a date of some years back; but, I will mention all the particulars another time. Talk of *reducing rents*, indeed! Talk of *generous landlords!* It is the public that is the generous landlord. It is the public that lets its houses and manors and mines

---

[5] William Stephen Poyntz (1770–1840) a moderate Whig.
[6] David Ricardo (1772–1823) author of *Principles of Political Economy* (1817).
[7] Now Buckingham Palace.

and farms at a cheap rate. It certainly would not be so good a landlord if it had a Reformed Parliament to manage its affairs, nor would it suffer so many snug *Corporations* to carry on their snugglings in the manner that they do, and therefore it is obviously the interest of the rich tenants of this poor public, as well as the interest of the snugglers in Corporations, to prevent the poor public from having such a Parliament.

Winchester, Sunday Morning, 29 Sept.

I am going to place myself down at Uphusband, in excellent free-quarter, in the midst of all the great fairs of the West, in order, before the winter campaign begins, that I may see as many farmers as possible, and that they may hear my opinions, and I theirs. I wish to see many people, and to talk to them: and there are a great many people who wish to see and to talk to me. What better reason can be given for a man's going about the country and dining at fairs and markets?

Uphusband, Sunday Evening, 29 Sept. 1822.

We came along the turnpike-road, through Wherwell and Andover, and got to this place about 2 o'clock.

This country, though so open, has its beauties. The homesteads in the sheltered bottoms, with fine lofty trees about the houses and yards, form a beautiful contrast with the large open fields. The little villages, running straggling along the dells (always with lofty trees and rookeries) are very interesting objects, even in the winter. You feel a sort of satisfaction, when you are out upon the bleak hills yourself, at the thought of the shelter, which is experienced in the dwellings in the valleys.

Andover is a neat and solid market-town. It is supported entirely by the agriculture around it; and how the makers of *population returns* ever came to think of classing the inhabitants of such a town as this, under any other head than that of *"persons employed in agriculture,"* would appear astonishing to any man who did not know those population return makers as well as I do.

The village of Uphusband, the legal name of which is Hurstbourn Tarrant is, as the reader will recollect, a great favourite with me, not the less so certainly on account of the excellent free-quarter that it affords.

THROUGH HAMPSHIRE, BERKSHIRE, SURREY, AND SUSSEX.

11th October.

WENT to Weyhill-fair, at which I was about 46 years ago, when I rode a little pony, and remember how proud I was on the occasion; but I also remember that my brothers, two out of three of whom were older than I, thought it unfair that my father selected me; and my own reflections upon the occasion have never been

A country horse fair. Fairs were important occasions for meeting, discussing news and exchanging information as well as for commercial transactions.

forgotten by me. The 11th of October is the Sheep-fair. About £300,000 used, some few years ago, to be carried home by the sheep-sellers, to-day, perhaps less than £70,000, and yet the *rents* of these sheep-sellers are, perhaps, as high, on an average, as they were then. The countenances of the farmers were descriptive of their ruinous state. I never, in all my life, beheld a more mournful scene. There is a horse-fair upon another part of the Down; and there I saw horses keeping pace in depression with the sheep. A pretty numerous group of the tax-eaters,[1] from Andover and the neighbourhood were the only persons that had smiles on their faces. I was struck with a young farmer trotting a horse backward and forward to show him off to a couple of gentlemen, who were bargaining for the horse, and one of whom finally purchased him. These *gentlemen* were two of our "*dead-weight*," and the horse was that on which the farmer had pranced in the *Yeomanry Troop!*

---

[1] Cobbett's term for parasites.

Here is a turn of things! Distress; pressing distress; dread of the bailiffs alone could have made the farmer sell his horse. If he had the firmness to keep the tears out of his eyes, his heart must have paid the penalty. What then, must have been his feelings, if he reflected, as I did, that the purchase-money for the horse had first gone from his pocket into that of the *dead-weight!* And further, that the horse had pranced about for years for the purpose of subduing all opposition to those very measures which had finally dismounted the owner!

From this dismal scene, a scene formerly so joyous, we set off back to Uphusband pretty early, were overtaken by the rain, and got a pretty good soaking. Met with a farmer who said he must be ruined, unless another "good war" should come! This is no uncommon notion. They saw high prices *with* war, and they thought that the war was the *cause.*

12 to 16 of October.

THE fair was too dismal for me to go to it again. My sons went two of the days, and their account of the hop-fair was enough to make one gloomy for a month, particularly as my townsmen of Farnham were, in this case, amongst the sufferers. On the 12th I went to dine with, and to harangue the farmers at Andover. Great attention was paid to what I had to say. The crowding to get into the room was a proof of nothing, perhaps, but *curiosity;* but there must have been a *cause* for the curiosity, and that cause would, under the present circumstances, be matter for reflection with a wise government.

17 October.

WENT to Newbury to dine with, and to harangue the farmers. It was a fair-day. It rained so hard that I had to stop at Burghclere to dry my clothes, and to borrow a great coat to keep me dry for the rest of the way; so as not to have to sit in wet clothes. At Newbury the company was not less attentive or less numerous than at Andover. Some one of the tax-eating crew had, I understand, called me an "incendiary." The day is passed for those tricks. They deceive no longer. Here, at Newbury, I took occasion to notice the base accusation of *Dundas*, the Member for the County.[2] I stated it as something that I had heard of, and I was proceeding to charge him conditionally, when Mr. Tubb of Shillingford rose from his seat, and said, "I myself, sir, heard him say the words." I had heard of his vile conduct long before; but I abstained from charging him with it till an opportunity should offer for doing it in his own country. After the dinner was over I went back to Burghclere.

22 October.

Went to dine with the farmers at Salisbury, and got back to Uphusband by ten

---

[2] Charles Dundas (1751–1832) falsely accused Cobbett of complicity in Arthur Thistlewood's Cato Street Conspiracy to assassinate the Cabinet (1820).

o'clock at night, two hours later than I have been out of bed for a great many months.

The company at Salisbury was very numerous; not less than 500 farmers were present. They were very attentive to what I said, and, which rather surprised me, they received very docilely what I said against squeezing the labourers.

9 November.

Started at day-break in a hazy frost, for Reading. The horses' manes and ears covered with the hoar before we got across Windsor Park, which appeared to be a blackguard soil, pretty much like Hounslow Heath, only not flat. A very large part of the Park is covered with heath or rushes, sure sign of execrable soil. But the roads are such as might have been made by Solomon. "A greater than Solomon is here!" some one may exclaim. Of that I know nothing. I am but a traveller; and the roads in this park are beautiful indeed. My servant, whom I brought from amongst the hills and flints of Uphusband, must certainly have thought himself in Paradise as he was going through the Park. If I had told him that the buildings and the labourers' clothes and meals, at Uphusband, were the *worse* for those pretty roads with edgings cut to the line, he would have wondered at me, I dare say. It would, nevertheless, have been perfectly true; and this is *feelosofee* of a much more useful sort, than that which is taught by the Edinburgh Reviewers.

A road as smooth as a die, a real stock-jobber's road, brought us to Reading by eleven o'clock. We dined at one; and very much pleased I was with the company. I have seldom seen a number of persons assembled together, whose approbation I valued more than that of the company of this day. This has been a fine meeting at Reading, I feel very proud of it.

I came on horse-back forty miles, slept on the road, and finished my harangue[3] at the end of *twenty-two hours* from leaving Kensington; and, I cannot help saying, that is pretty well for "*Old* Cobbett." I am delighted with the people that I have seen at Reading. Their kindness to me is nothing in my estimation compared with the sense and spirit which they appear to possess. It is curious to observe how things have *worked* with me. That combination, that sort of *instinctive* union, which has existed for so many years, amongst all the parties, to *keep me down* generally, and particularly, as the *County-Club* called it, to keep me out of Parliament "*at any rate*," this combination has led to the present *haranguing* system, which, in some sort, supplies the place of a seat in Parliament. It may be said, indeed, that I have not the honour to sit in the same room with those great Reformers, Lord John Russell, Sir Massey Lopez, and his guest, Sir Francis Burdett;[4] but man's happiness here below is never perfect; and there may be,

---

[3] Referring to Cobbett's "Rustic Harangue" (omitted in this edition) at Winchester, 28 September 1822, denouncing tithes.

[4] Lord John Russell (1792–1878), Prime Minister 1846 and 1865. Sir Manasseh Masseh Lopez (1755–1831), Radical M.P. for Barnstaple until imprisoned for bribery 1819, but Conservative M.P. for Westbury 1823–9. Sir Francis Burdett 1770–1844, Radical M.P. for Westminster 1807–37, twice imprisoned for "sedition". Became Conservative M.P. for North Wilts 1837–44.

There is but one man in the Country who can extricate it from difficulties why dont you send Him to Parliament?

William Cobbett successfully contested the seat for Oldham in 1832 after the First Reform Act made illegal the system of rotten boroughs and extended the right to vote to the middle classes.

besides, people to believe, that a man ought not to break his heart on account of being shut out of such company, especially when he can find such company, as I have this day found at Reading.

11 November.

Uphusband *once more*, and, for the sixth time this year, over the North Hampshire Hills, which, notwithstanding their everlasting flints, I like very much. As you ride along, even in a *green lane*, the horses' feet make a noise like *hammering*. It seems as if you were riding on a mass of iron. Yet the soil is good, and bears some of the best wheat in England. All these high, and indeed, all chalky lands, are excellent for sheep. But on the top of some of these hills, there are as fine meadows as I ever saw. Pasture richer, perhaps, than that about Swindon in the North of Wiltshire. And the singularity is, that this pasture is on the *very tops* of these lofty hills, from which you can see the Isle of Wight. There is a stiff loam, in some places twenty feet deep, on a bottom of chalk. Though the grass grows so finely, there is no apparent wetness in the land. The wells are more than three hundred feet deep. The main part of the water, for all uses, comes from the clouds; and, indeed, these are pretty constant companions of these chalk hills, which are very often enveloped in clouds and wet, when it is sunshine down at Burghclere or Uphusband. They manure the land here by digging *wells* in the fields, and bringing up the chalk, which they spread about on the land; and which, being free-chalk, is reduced to powder by the frosts. A considerable portion of the land is covered with wood; and as, in the clearing of the land, the clearers followed the good soil, without regard to shape of fields, the forms of the woods are of endless variety, which, added to the never-ceasing inequalities of the surface of the whole, makes this, like all the others of the same description, a very pleasant country.

17 November.

Set off from Uphusband for Hambledon. The first place I had to get to was Whitchurch. On my way, and at a short distance from Uphusband, down the valley, I went through a village called *Bourn*, which takes its name from the water that runs down this valley. A *bourn*, in the language of our forefathers, seems to be a river, which is, part of the year, *without water*. There is one of these bourns down this pretty valley. It has, generally, no water till towards Spring, and then it runs for several months.

The little village of *Bourn*, therefore, takes its name from its situation. Then there are two *Hurstbourns*, one above and one below this village of Bourn. *Hurst* means, I believe, a Forest. There were, doubtless, one of those on each side of Bourn; and when they became villages, the one above was called *Up*-hurstbourn, and the one below, *Down*-hurstbourn; which names have become *Uphusband* and *Downhusband*.

Whitchurch is a small town, but famous for being the place where the paper has been made for the *Borough-Bank!* I passed by the *mill* on my way to get out upon the Downs to go to Alresford, where I intended to sleep. I hope the time will come, when a monument will be erected where that mill stands, and when on that monument will be inscribed *the curse of England*. This spot ought to be held accursed in all time henceforth and for evermore. It has been the spot from which have sprung more and greater mischief than ever plagued mankind before. However, the evils now appear to be fast recoiling on the merciless authors of them; and, therefore, one beholds this scene of papermaking with a less degree of rage than formerly.

Nov. 24, Sunday.

Set off from Hambledon to go to Thursley in Surrey, about five miles from Godalming. Here I am at Thursley, after as interesting a day as I ever spent in all my life. They say that "*variety* is charming," and this day I have had of scenes and of soils a variety indeed!

Off we set over the downs (crossing the bottom sweep of Old Winchester Hill) from West-End to East-Meon. We came down a long and steep hill that led us winding round into the village, which lies in a valley that runs in a direction nearly east and west, and that has a rivulet that comes out of the hills towards

Salisbury Cathedral from Bishop's Ground, a painting by John Constable, 1823, 'that beautiful and matchless spire'.

A boy tending sheep on Mousehold Heath, near Norwich, by John Crome the Elder.

Petersfield. If I had not seen any thing further to-day, I should have dwelt long on the beauties of this place. Here is a very fine valley, in nearly an elliptical form, sheltered by high hills sloping gradually from it; and not far from the middle of this valley there is a hill nearly in the form of a goblet-glass with the foot and stem broken off and turned upside down. And this is clapped down upon the level of the valley, just as you would put such goblet upon a table. The hill is lofty, partly covered with wood, and it gives an air of great singularity to the scene.

"The History and Antiquities of Selborne," (or something of that sort) written, I think by a parson of the name of *White*,[5] brother of Mr. *White*, so long a Bookseller in Fleet-street was mentioned to me as a work of great curiosity and interest. But, at that time, the THING was biting *so very sharply* that one had no attention to bestow on antiquarian researches. Wheat as 39*s.* a quarter, and South-Down ewes at 12*s.* 6*d.* have so weakened the THING's jaws and so filed down its teeth, that I shall now certainly read this book if I can get it. By-the-bye if *all the parsons* had, for the last thirty years, employed their leisure time in writing the histories of their several parishes, instead of living, as many of them have, engaged in pursuits that I need not here name, neither their situation, nor that of their flocks would, perhaps, have been the worse for it at this day.

Nov. 25.
Thursley (Surrey).

Could you see and hear what I have seen and heard during this Rural Ride, you would no longer say, that the House "works well." Mrs. Canning and your children are dear to you;[6] but, Sir, not more dear, than are to them the wives and children, of perhaps, two hundred thousand men, who, by the Acts of this same House, see those wives and children doomed to beggary, and to beggary, too, never thought of, never regarded as more likely than a blowing up of the earth or a falling of the sun. It was reserved for this "working well" House to make the fire-sides of farmers scenes of gloom. These fire-sides, in which I have always so delighted, I now approach with pain. And, does this House, then, "work well?" How many men, of the most industrious, the most upright, the most exemplary, upon the face of the earth, have been, by this one Act of this House, driven to despair, ending in madness or self-murder, or both! Nay, how many scores! And, yet, are we to be banished for life, if we endeavour to show, that this House does not "work well?"—However, banish or banish not, these facts are notorious: *the House* made all the *Loans* which constitute the debt: *the House* contracted for the

---

[5] The Revd Gilbert White (1720–93) author of *The Natural History and Antiquities of Selborne*, published 1794 by his brother Benjamin, the bookseller here mentioned.

[6] This "Ride" takes the form of a letter to George Canning (1770–1827) then Foreign Secretary, of whose sympathy Cobbett entertained some hopes.

A north-east view of Selborne in Hampshire, home of the naturalist Gilbert White.

Dead Weight: *the House* put a stop to gold-payments in 1797: *the House* unanimously passed Peel's Bill. Here are *all* the causes of the ruin, the misery, the anguish, the despair, and the madness and self-murders. Here they are *all*. They have all been acts of this House; and yet, we are to be banished if we say, in words suitable to the subject, that this House does not "*work well!*"

This one Act, I mean this *Banishment Act*, would be enough with posterity, to characterize this House. When they read (and can believe what they read) that it actually passed a law to banish for life any one who should write, print, or publish anything having a *tendency* to bring it into *contempt*;[7] when posterity shall read this, and believe it, they will want nothing more to enable them to say what sort of an assembly it was! It was delightful, too, that they should pass this law just after they had passed *Peel's Bill!* Oh, God! thou art *just!* As to *reform*, it *must come*. Let what else will happen, it must come. Whether before, or after, all the estates be transferred, I cannot say. But, this I know very well; that the later it come, the *deeper* will it go.

I shall, of course, go on remarking, as occasion offers, upon what is done by and said in this present House; but I know that it can do nothing efficient for the relief of the country. I have seen some men of late, who seem to think, that even a reform, enacted, or begun, by this House, would be an evil; and that it would be better to let the whole thing go on, and produce its natural consequence. I am not of this opinion: I am for a reform as soon as possible, even though it be not, at first,

---

[7] Referring to one of the Six Acts of 1819. (See note 1, page 14.)

'A Memento of the Great Public Question of Reform.' A mezzotint of 1832. By redistributing parliamentary seats, abolishing rotten boroughs and lowering property qualifications for voters, the 1832 Reform Act avoided revolution and increased the electorate by a half—approximately two-thirds of a million.

The Reform Bill of 1832 receiving King George IV's assent by Royal Commission in the House of Lords.

precisely what I could wish; because, if the debt blow up before the reform take place, confusion and uproar there must be; and I do not want to see confusion and uproar. I am for a reform of *some sort*, and *soon;* but, when I say of *some sort*, I do not mean of Lord John Russell's sort; I do not mean a reform in the Lopez way. In short, what I want, is, to see the *men* changed. I want to see *other men* in the House; and as to *who* those other men should be, I really should not be very nice. I want to see a change *in the men*. These have done enough in all conscience; or, at least, they have done enough to satisfy me. I want to see some fresh faces, and to hear a change of some sort or other in the sounds. A *"hear, hear,"* coming everlastingly from the same mouths, is what I, for my part, am tired of.

I am aware that this is not what the *"great reformers"* in the House mean. They mean, on the contrary, no such thing as a change of men. They mean that *Lopez* should sit there for ever; or, at least, till succeeded by a legitimate heir. I believe that Sir Francis Burdett, for instance, has not the smallest idea of an Act of Parliament ever being made without his assistance, if he chooses to assist, which is not very frequently the case. I believe that he looks upon a seat in the House as being his property; and that the other seat is, and ought to be, held as a sort of leasehold or copyhold under him. My idea of reform, therefore; my change of faces and of names and of sounds will appear quite horrible to him. However, I think the nation begins to be very much of my way of thinking; and this I am very sure of, that we shall never see that change in the management of affairs, which we most of us want to see, unless there be a pretty complete change of men.

Some people will blame me for speaking out so broadly upon this subject. But I think it the best way to disguise nothing; to do what is *right;* to be sincere; and to let come what will.

Godalming.
November 26 to 28.

I came here to meet my son, who was to return to London when we had done our business.

This is a very pretty country. You see few prettier spots than this. The chain of little hills that run along to the South and South-East of Godalming, and the soil, which is a good loam upon a sand stone bottom, run down on the South side, into what is called the *Weald*. This Weald is a bed of clay, in which nothing grows well but oak trees. It is first the Weald of Surrey, and then the Weald of Sussex. It runs along on the South of Dorking, Reigate, Bletchingley, Godstone, and then winds away down into Kent.

November 29.

Went on to Guildford, where I slept. Everybody, that has been from Godalming to Guildford, knows, that there is hardly another such a pretty four miles in all England. The road is good; the soil is good; the houses are neat; the people are neat; the hills, the woods, the meadows, all are beautiful. Nothing wild and bold,

Guildford, looking down the High Street in 1790.

to be sure, but exceedingly pretty; and it is almost impossible to ride along these four miles without feelings of pleasure, though you have rain for your companion, as it happened to be with me.

Dorking, November 30.

This pretty valley of Chilworth has a run of water which comes out of the high hills, and which, occasionally, spreads into a pond; so that there is in fact a series of ponds connected by this run of water. This valley, which seems to have been created by a bountiful providence, as one of the choicest retreats of man; which seems formed for a scene of innocence and happiness, has been, by ungrateful man, so perverted as to make it instrumental in effecting two of the most damnable of purposes; in carrying into execution two of the most damnable inventions that ever sprang from the minds of man under the influence of the devil! namely, the making of *gunpowder* and of *bank-notes!* Here in this tranquil spot, where the

Henry, 1st Baron Brougham and Vaux, from a cartoon by Cruikshank in 1825. Brougham was prominent in public life over a period of nearly sixty years, particularly in law, literature, politics and science. He was especially active in the field of education, and was largely responsible for the establishment of London University.

A cartoon of 1826, against the evils of over-speculation in often spurious companies, which led to considerable suffering by the credulous investor.

nightingales are to be heard earlier and later in the year than in any other part of England; where the first bursting of the bud is seen in Spring, where no rigour of seasons can ever be felt; where every thing seems formed for precluding the very thought of wickedness; here has the devil fixed on as one of the seats of his grand manufactory; and perverse and ungrateful man not only lends him his aid, but lends it cheerfully! As to the gunpowder, indeed, we might get over that. In some cases that may be innocently, and, when it sends the lead at the hordes that support a tyrant, meritoriously employed. The alders and the willows, therefore, one can see, without so much regret, turned into powder by the waters of this

64

Foxhunting — the hounds going to cover.

Partridge shooting.

Opposite above:
Agricultural distress in 1829. The sufferings of the rural poor in the first half of the nineteenth century roused Cobbett and other Radicals like him to fury.

Opposite below:
Until the invention of the 'spinning Jenny' by James Hargreaves in 1764, the spinning wheel was an essential piece of equipment in every cottage.

FARMER GILES'S ESTABLISHMENT!!! Christmas 1829

William Heath

An engraving of *c.* 1830 showing a labourer at home. The herring on a pipe in front of the fire was a sign of extreme and squalid poverty.

valley; but, the *Bank-notes!* To think that the springs which God has commanded to flow from the sides of these happy hills, for the comfort and the delight of man; to think that these springs should be perverted into means of spreading misery over a whole nation; and that, too, under the base and hypocritical pretence of promoting its *credit* and maintaining its *honour* and its *faith!* There was one circumstance, indeed, that served to mitigate the melancholy excited by these reflections; namely, that a part of these springs have, at times, assisted in turning rags into *Registers!* Somewhat cheered by the thought of this, but, still, in a more melancholy mood than I had been for a long while, I rode on with my friend towards *Albury*, up the valley, the sand-hills on one side of us and the chalk-hills on the other. Albury is a little village consisting of a few houses, with a large house or two near it. At the end of the village we came to a park, which is the residence of Mr. Drummond. — Having heard a great deal of this park, and of the gardens, I

Henry Drummond, magistrate of Surrey and founder of the Professorship of Political Economy at Oxford, was a Conservative MP until his death in 1860.

wished very much to see them. My way to Dorking lay through Shire,[8] and it went along on the outside of the park. I *guessed*, as the Yankees say, that there must be a way through the park to Shire; and I fell upon the scheme of going into the park as far as Mr. Drummond's house, and then asking his leave to go out at the other end of it. This scheme, though pretty barefaced, succeeded very well. It is true that I was aware that I had not a *Norman* to deal with; or I should not have ventured upon the experiment. I sent in word that, having got into the park, I should be exceedingly obliged to Mr. Drummond if he would let me go out of it on the side next to Shire. He not only granted this request, but, in the most obliging manner, permitted us to ride all about the park, and to see his gardens, which, without any exception, are, to my fancy, the prettiest in England; that is to say, that I ever saw in England.

They say that these gardens were laid out for one of the Howards, in the reign of Charles the Second, by Mr. Evelyn, who wrote the *Sylva*.[9] The mansion-house, which is by no means magnificent, stands on a little flat by the side of the parish church, having a steep, but not lofty, hill rising up on the south side of it. It looks right across the gardens, which lie on the slope of a hill which runs along at about a quarter of a mile distant from the front of the house. The gardens, of course, lie facing the south. At the back of them, under the hill, is a high wall; and there is also a wall at each end, running from north to south. Between the house and the gardens there is a very beautiful run of water, with a sort of little wild narrow sedgy meadow. The gardens are separated from this by a hedge, running along from east to west. From this hedge there go up the hill, at right angles, several other hedges, which divide the land here into distinct gardens, or orchards. Along at the top of these there goes a yew hedge, or, rather, a row of small yew trees, the trunks of which are bare for about eight or ten feet high, and the tops of which form one solid head of about ten feet high, while the bottom branches come out on each side of the row about eight feet horizontally. This hedge, or row, is *a quarter of a mile long*. There is a nice hard sand-road under this species of umbrella; and, summer and winter, here is a most delightful walk! Behind this row of yews, there is a space, or garden (a quarter of a mile long you will observe) about thirty or forty feet wide, as nearly as I can recollect. At the back of this garden, and facing the yew-tree row, is a wall probably ten feet high, which forms the breastwork of a *terrace;* and it is this terrace which is the most beautiful thing that I ever saw in the gardening way. It is a quarter of a mile long, and, I believe, between thirty and forty feet wide; of the finest green sward, and as level as a die.

Take it altogether, this, certainly, is the prettiest garden that I ever beheld. There was taste and sound judgment at every step in the laying out of this place. Every where utility and convenience is combined with beauty. The terrace is by

---

[8] Shere.

[9] John Evelyn (1620–1706) the diarist. His *Sylva* or *Discourse on Forest Trees* would have specially appealed to Cobbett.

Albury Park in Surrey, whose gardens Cobbett considered 'the prettiest in England'.

far the finest thing of the sort that I ever saw, and the whole thing altogether is a great compliment to the taste of the times in which it was formed. I know there are some ill-natured persons, who will say, that I want a revolution that would turn Mr. Drummond out of this place and put me into it. Such persons will hardly believe me, but upon my word I do not. From everything that I hear, Mr. Drummond is very worthy of possessing it himself, seeing that he is famed for his justice and his kindness *towards the labouring classes*, who, God knows, have very few friends amongst the rich. If what I have heard be true, Mr. Drummond is singularly good in this way; for, instead of hunting down an unfortunate creature who has exposed himself to the lash of the law; instead of regarding a crime committed as proof of an inherent disposition to commit crime; instead of rendering the poor creatures desperate by this species of *proscription*, and forcing them on to the *gallows*, merely because they have once merited the *Bridewell;* instead of this, which is the common practice throughout the country, he rather seeks for such unfortunate creatures to take them into his employ, and thus to reclaim them, and to make them repent of their former courses. If this be true, and I am credibly informed that it is, I know of no man in England so worthy of his estate. I saw, in the gardens at Albury Park, what I never saw before in all my life; that is, some plants of the *American Cranberry*. I never saw them in America; for there they grow in those swamps, into which I never happened to go at the time of their bearing fruit. I may have seen the plant, but I do not know that I ever did.

71

Here it not only grows, but bears; and, there are still some cranberries on the plants now. I tasted them, and they appeared to me to have just the same taste as those in America. They grew in a long bed near the stream of water which I have spoken about, and therefore it is clear that they may be cultivated with great ease in this country.

––––––––––

Thus, Sir, have I led you about the country. All sorts of things have I talked of, to be sure; but there are very few of these things which have not their interest of one sort or another. At the end of a hundred miles or two of travelling, stopping here and there; talking freely with every body. Hearing what gentlemen, farmers, tradesmen, journeymen, labourers, women, girls, boys, and all have to say; reasoning with some, laughing with others, and observing all that passes; and especially if your manner be such as to remove every kind of reserve from every class; at the end of a tramp like this, you get impressed upon your mind a true picture, not only of the state of the country, but of the state of the people's minds throughout the country. And, Sir, whether you believe me or not, I have to tell you, that it is my decided opinion, that the people, high and low, with one unanimous voice, except where they live upon the taxes, *impute their calamities to the House of Commons*. Whether they be right or wrong is not so much the question, in this case. That such is the fact I am certain; and, having no power to make any change myself, I must leave the making or the refusing of the change to those who have the power. I repeat, and with perfect sincerity, that it would give me as much pain as it would give to any man in England, to see a change *in the form of the Government*. With *King*, *Lords*, and *Commons*, this nation enjoyed many ages of happiness and of glory. *Without Commons*, my opinion is, it never can again see any thing but misery and shame; and when I say Commons I *mean* Commons, and, by Commons, I mean, men elected by the free voice of the untitled and unprivileged part of the people, who, in fact as well as in law, are the Commons of England.

I am, Sir, your most obedient and most humble servant,

WM. COBBETT.

––––––––––

JOURNAL: RIDE FROM KENSINGTON TO WORTH, IN SUSSEX.

Monday, May 5, 1823.

From London to Reigate, through Sutton, is about as villanous a tract as England contains. The soil is a mixture of gravel and clay, with big yellow stones in it, sure sign of really bad land. At Reigate they are (in order to save a few hundred yards length of road,) cutting through a hill. They have lowered a little hill on the London side of Sutton. Thus is the money of the country actually thrown away:

the produce of labour is taken from the industrious, and given to the idlers. Mark the process; the town of Brighton, in Sussex, 50 miles from the Wen, is on the seaside, and is thought by the stock-jobbers, to afford a *salubrious air*. It is so situated that a coach, which leaves it not very early in the morning, reaches London by noon; and, starting to go back in two hours and a half afterwards, reaches Brighton not very late at night. Great parcels of Stock-jobbers stay at Brighton with the women and children. They skip backward and forward on the coaches, and actually carry on stock-jobbing, in 'Change Alley, though they reside at Brighton. This place is, besides, a place of great resort with the *whiskered* gentry. There are not less than twenty coaches that leave the Wen every day for this place; and, there being three or four different roads, there is a great rivalship for the custom. This sets the people to work to shorten and to level the roads; and here you see hundreds of men and horses constantly at work to make pleasant and quick travelling for the jews and jobbers. The jews and jobbers pay the turnpikes, to be sure; but, they get the money from the land and labourer. They drain these, from John-a-Groat's House to the Land's End, and they lay out some of the money on the Brighton roads! More and more new houses are building as you leave the Wen to come on this road. *Whence come* the means of building these new houses and keeping the inhabitants? Do they came out of *trade* and *commerce?* Oh, no! they come from *the land*. When you quit Reigate to go towards Crawley, you enter on what is called the *Weald of Surrey*. It is a level country, and the soil a very, very strong loam, with clay beneath to a great depth. The fields are small, and about a third of the land covered with oak-woods and coppice-woods. This is a country of wheat and beans; the latter of which are about three inches high, the former about seven, and both looking very well. I did not see a field of bad-looking wheat from Reigate-hill foot to Crawley, nor from Crawley across to this place, where, though the whole country is but poorish, the wheat looks very well; and, if this weather hold about twelve days, we shall recover the lost time. They have been stripping trees (taking the bark off) about five or six days. The nightingales sing very much, which is a sign of warm weather. The house-martins and the swallows are come in abundance; and they seldom do come until the weather be set in for mild.

FROM THE WEN [LONDON]ACROSS THE WEST OF SUSSEX, AND INTO THE SOUTH EAST OF HAMPSHIRE.

Horsham (Sussex),
Thursday, 31 July.

When you get down into this town, you are again in the Weald of Sussex. I believe that *Weald* meant *clay*, or low, wet, stiff land. This is a very nice, solid, country town. Very clean, as all the towns in Sussex are. The people very clean. The Sussex women are very nice in their dress and in their houses. The men and boys wear smock-frocks, more than they do in some counties. When country people do not, they always look dirty and comfortless. This has been a pretty good day; but there was a little rain in the afternoon; so that St. Swithin keeps on as yet, at any rate. The hay has been spoiled here, in cases where it has been cut; but, a great deal of it is not yet cut. I speak of the meadows; for the clover-hay was all well got in. The grass which is not cut is receiving great injury. It is, in fact, in many cases, rotting upon the ground.

Billingshurst (Sussex),
Friday Morning, 1 Aug.

This village is 7 miles from Horsham, and I got here to breakfast about seven o'clock. A very pretty village, and a very nice breakfast, in a very neat little parlour of a very decent public-house. The landlady sent her son to get me some cream, and he was just such a chap as I was at his age, and dressed just in the same sort of way, his main garment being a blue smock-frock, faded from wear, and mended with pieces of *new* stuff, and, of course, not faded. The sight of this smock-frock brought to my recollection many things very dear to me. This boy will, I dare say, perform his part at Billingshurst, or at some place not far from it. If accident had not taken me from a similar scene, how many villains and fools, who have been well teased and tormented, would have slept in peace at night, and have fearlessly swaggered about by day!

Petworth (Sussex)
Friday Evening, 1st Aug.

As I was coming into this town I saw a new-fashioned sort of stone-cracking. A man had a sledge-hammer, and was cracking the heads of the big stones that had been laid on the road a good while ago. This is a very good way; but this man told me, that he was set at this, because the farmers had *no employment* for many of the men. "Well," said I, "but they pay you to do this!" "Yes," said he. "Well, then," said I, "is it not better for them to pay you for working *on their land?*" "I can't tell, indeed, Sir, how that is." But, only think; here is half the haymaking to do: I saw, while I was talking to this man, fifty people in one hay-field of Lord Egremont, making and carrying hay; and yet, at a season like this, the farmers are so poor, as to be unable to pay the labourers to work on the land! From this cause there will certainly be some falling off in production. This will, of course, have a tendency to keep prices from falling so low as they would do if there were no falling off. But, can this *benefit* the farmer and landlord? The poverty of the farmers is seen in their diminished stock. The animals are sold *younger* than formerly. Last year was a year of great slughtering. There will be less of every thing produced; and the quality of each thing will be worse. It will be a lower and more mean concern altogether. It is, upon the whole, a most magnificent seat, and the Jews will not be able to get it from the *present* owner; though, if he live many years, they will give even him a *twist*. If I had time, I would make an actual survey of one whole county, and find out how many of the old gentry have lost their estates, and have been supplanted by the Jews, since Pitt began his reign. I am sure I should prove that, in number, they are one-half extinguished. But, it is *now*, that they go. The little ones are, indeed, gone; and the rest will follow in proportion as the present farmers are exhausted. These will keep on giving rents, as long as they can beg or borrow the money, to pay rents with. But, a little more time will so completely exhaust them, that they will be unable to pay; and, as that takes place, the landlord will lose their estates. Indeed, many of them, and even a large portion of them, have, in fact, no estates now. They are *called* theirs; but the mortgagees and annuitants receive the rents. As the rents fall off, sales must take place, unless in cases of entails; and, if this thing go on, we shall see acts passed to *cut off entails*, in order that the Jews may be put into full possession. Such, thus far, will be the result of our "glorious victories" over the French! Such will be, in part, the price of the deeds of Pitt, Addington, Perceval[1] and their successors. For having applauded such deeds; for having boasted of the Wellesleys;[2] for having bragged of battles, won by *money* and by money *only*, the nation deserves that which it will receive; and, as to the landlords, they, above all men living, deserve punishment. They put the power into the hands of Pitt and his crew to torment the people; to keep the people down; to raise soldiers and to build barracks for this purpose. They would fain have us believe, that the calamities they endure do not arise from the acts of the Government. What do they arise from, then? The Jacobins did not contract the *Debt* of £800,000,000, sterling. The Jacobins did not create a *Dead Weight* of £150,000,000. The Jacobins did not cause a pauper-charge of £200,000,000, by means of "new inclosure bills," "vast improvements," paper-money, potatoes, and other "proofs of prosperity." The Jacobins did not do these things. And will the Government pretend that "Providence" did it? That would be "blasphemy" indeed. — Poh! These things are the price of efforts to crush freedom in France, *lest the example of France should produce a reform in England*. These things are the price of that undertaking; which, however, has not yet been crowned with *success;* for the question is *not yet decided*. They boast of their victory over the French. The Pitt crew, boast of their achievements in the war. They boast of the battle of Waterloo. Why! what fools could not get the same, or the like, if they had as much *money* to get it with? Shooting with *a silver gun* is a saying amongst game-eaters. That is to say, *purchasing* the game. A waddling, fat fellow, that does not know how to prime and load, will, in this way, beat the best shot in the country. And, this is the way that our crew "beat" the people of France. They laid out, in the first place, six hundred millions which they borrowed, and for which they mortgaged the revenues of the nation. Then they contracted for a "dead weight" to the amount of one hundred and fifty millions. Then they stripped the labouring classes of the commons, of their kettles, their bedding, their beer-barrels; and, in short, made

---

[1] William Pitt the Younger (1759–1806), Prime Minister 1784–1801 and 1803–6. Addington, see note 4 on page 33. Spencer Perceval (1762–1812), Prime Minister 1809 until his assassination in 1812.

[2] Arthur, Duke of Wellington (1769–1852) and Richard Colley (1760–1842), Earl of Mornington and Marquis Wellesley, Governor-General of India (1797–1805).

them all paupers, and thus fixed on the nation a permanent annual charge of about 8 or 9 millions, or, a gross debt of £200,000,000. By these means, by these anticipations, our crew did what they thought would keep down the French nation for ages; and what they were sure would, for the present, enable them to keep up the *tithes* and other things of the same sort in England. But, the crew did not reflect on the *consequences* of the anticipations! Or, at least the landlords, who gave the crew their power, did not thus reflect. These consequences are now come, and are coming; and that must be a base man indeed, who does not see them with pleasure.

Singleton (Sussex), Saturday, 2 Aug.

Ever since the middle of March, I have been trying remedies for the *hooping-cough*, and have, I believe, tried everything, except riding, wet to the skin, two or three hours amongst the clouds on the South Downs. This remedy is now under trial. As Lord Liverpool said, the other day, of the Irish Tithe Bill, it is "under experiment." I am treating my disorder (with better success I hope) in somewhat the same way, that the pretty fellows at Whitehall treat the disorders of poor Ireland. There is one thing in favour of this remedy of mine, I shall *know* the effect of it, and that, too, in a short time.

It is very pretty to look down upon this little village, as you come winding up the hill.

From this hill I ought to have had a most extensive view. I ought to have seen the Isle of Wight, and the sea before me; and to have looked back to Chalk Hill at Reigate, at the foot of which I had left some bonnet-grass bleaching. But, alas! *Saint Swithin* had begun his work for the day, before I got to the top of the hill. Soon after the two turnip-hoers had assured me that there would be no rain, I saw, beginning to poke up over the South Downs (then right before me) several parcels of those white, curled clouds, that we call *Judges' Wigs*. And they are just like Judges' wigs. Not the *parson-like* things which the Judges wear, when they have to listen to the dull wrangling and duller jests of the lawyers; but, those *big* wigs which hang down about their shoulders, when they are about to tell you a little of *their intentions*, and when their very looks say, *"Stand clear!"* These clouds (if rising from the South-West) hold precisely the same language to the greatcoatless traveller. Rain is *sure* to follow them. The sun was shining very beautifully when I first saw these Judges' wigs rising over the hills. At the sight of them he soon began to hide his face! and, before I got to the top of the hill of Donton, the white clouds had become black, had spread themselves all around, and a pretty decent and sturdy rain began to fall.

As I came along between Upwaltham and Eastdean, I called to me a young man, who, along with other turnip-hoers, was sitting under the shelter of a hedge at breakfast. He came running to me with his victuals in his hand; and, I was glad to see, that his food consisted of a good lump of household bread, and not a very small piece of *bacon*. I did not envy him his appetite, for I had, at that moment, a very

Right:
A view of Weymouth Bay by John Constable.

Below:
A political cartoon showing 'The Reformers Attack on the Old Rotten Tree.' As a result of the Reform Act, which put an end to the system of rotten boroughs, ie boroughs which could 'elect' Members of Parliament without any voters, Cobbett was elected MP for Oldham in 1832.

good one of my own; but, I wanted to know the distance I had to go before I should get to a good public-house. In parting with him, I said, "You do get some *bacon* then?" "Oh, yes! Sir," said he, and with an emphasis and a swag of the head, which seemed to say, "We *must* and *will* have *that*." I saw, and with great delight, a pig at almost every labourer's house. The houses are good and warm; and the gardens some of the very best, that I have seen in England.

This is really a soaking day, thus far. I got here at nine o'clock. I stripped off my coat, and put it by the kitchen fire. In a parlour just eight feet square, I have another fire, and have dried my shirt on my back. We shall see what this does for a hooping cough. The clouds fly so low as to be seen passing by the sides of even little hills on these downs. The devil is said to be busy in a *high* wind; but, he really appears to be busy now in this South-west wind. The Quakers will, next market day, at Mark-lane, be as busy as he. They and the Ministers and St. Swithin and Devil, all seem to be of a mind.

Fareham (Hants,) Saturday, 2 August.

Now I come to one of the great objects of my Journey: that is to say, to see the state of the corn along at the South foot, and on the South side, of Portsdown-hill. It is impossible that there can be, any where, a better corn country than this. The hill is eight miles long, and about three-fourths of a mile high, beginning at the road that runs along at the foot of the hill. On the hill-side the corn land goes rather better than half way up; and, on the sea side, the corn land is about the third (it may be half) a mile wide. Portsdown-hill is very much in the shape of an oblong tin cover to a dish. From Bedhampton, which lies at the Eastern end of the hill, to Fareham, which is at the Western end of it, you have brought under your eye not less than eight square miles of corn fields, with scarcely a hedge or ditch of any consequence, and being, on an average, from twenty to forty acres each in extent. The land is excellent. The situation good for manure. The spot the *earliest in the whole kingdom*. Here, if the corn were backward, then the harvest must be backward. We were talking at Reigate of the prospect of a backward harvest. I observed, that it was a rule, that, if no *wheat were cut* under Portsdown-hill on the hill *fair-day*, 26th July, the harvest must be generally backward. When I made this observation, the fair-day was passed; but I determined in my mind to come and see how the matter stood. When, therefore, I got to the village of Bedhampton, I began to look out pretty sharply. I came on to Wymering, which is just about the mid-way along the foot of the hill, and there I saw, at a good distance from me, five men reaping in a field of wheat of about 40 acres. I found, upon inquiry, that they began this morning, and that the wheat belongs to Mr. Boniface, of Wymering. Here the first sheaf is cut that is cut in England: that the reader may depend upon.

Opposite:
A caricature of 'Cousin' Robert Peel in 1829. He was responsible for the eventual repeal of the iniquitous Corn Laws which restricted the import of cheap corn and caused severe hardship to the poor, and was regarded by the working and middle classes with gratitude and respect.

A Quaker meeting. Cobbett held strong views against these rigid Nonconformists, calling them a 'villainous tribe . . . none of whom ever work, and all of whom prey upon the rest of the community'. In 1928, however, the Test Act was repealed, giving full rights for Nonconformists.

It was never known, that the average even of Hampshire was less than ten days behind the average of Portsdown-hill. The corn under the hill is as good as I ever saw it, except in the year 1813. No beans here. No peas. Scarcely any oats. Wheat, barley, and turnips. The Swedish turnips not so good as on the South Downs and near Funtington; but the wheat full as good, rather better; and the barley as good as it is possible to be. In looking at these crops, one wonders whence are to come the hands to clear them off.

I have now come, if I include my *boltings*, for the purpose of looking at farms and woods, a round hundred miles from the Wen to this town of Fareham; and, in the whole of the hundred miles, I have not seen one single wheat rick, though I have come through as fine corn countries as any in England, and by the homesteads of the richest of farmers. Not one single wheat rick have I seen, and not one rick of any sort of corn. I never saw, nor heard of the like of this before; and, if I had not witnessed the fact with my own eyes, I could not have believed it.

————

THROUGH THE SOUTH-EAST OF HAMPSHIRE, BACK THROUGH THE
SOUTH-WEST OF SURREY, ALONG THE WEALD OF SURREY, AND
THEN OVER THE SURREY HILLS DOWN TO THE WEN.

Botley (Hampshire), 5th August 1823.

Before I got to my friend's house, I passed by a farm where I expected to find a wheat-rick standing. I did not, however; and this is the strongest possible proof, that the stock of corn is gone out of the hands of the farmers. I set out from Titchfield at 7 o'clock in the evening, and had seven miles to go to reach Botley. It rained, but I got myself well furnished forth as a defence against the rain. I had not gone two hundred yards before the rain ceased; so that I was singularly fortunate as to rain this day; and I had now to congratulate myself on the success of the remedy for the hooping-cough which I used the day before on the South Downs; for really, though I had a spell or two of coughing on Saturday morning, when I set out from Petworth, I have not had, up to this hour, any spell at all since I got wet upon the South Downs.

Easton (Hampshire),
Wednesday Evening, 6th August.

Whiteflood is at the foot of the first of a series of hills over which you come to get to the top of that lofty ridge called Morning Hill. The farmer came to the top of the first hill along with me; and he was just about to turn back, when I, looking away to the left, down a valley which stretched across the other side of the Down, observed a rather singular appearance, and said to the farmer, "What is that coming up that valley? is it smoke, or is it a cloud?" The day had been very fine hitherto; the sun was shining very bright where we were. The farmer answered, "Oh, it's smoke; it comes from Ouselberry, which is down in that bottom behind

81

those trees.'' So saying, we bid each other good day; he went back, and I went on. Before I had got a hundred and fifty yards from him, the cloud which he had taken for the Ouselberry smoke, came upon the hill and wet me to the skin. He was not far from the house at Whiteflood; but I am sure that he could not entirely escape it. It is curious to observe how the clouds sail about in the hilly countries, and particularly, I think, amongst the chalk-hills. I have never observed the like amongst the sand-hills, or amongst rocks.

Selborne (Hants),
Thursday, 7th August, Noon.

The village of Selborne is precisely what it is described by Mr. White. A straggling irregular street, bearing all the marks of great antiquity, and showing, from its lanes and its vicinage generally, that it was once a very considerable place. I went to look at the spot where Mr. White supposes the convent formerly stood. It is very beautiful. Nothing can surpass in beauty these dells and hillocks and hangers, which last are so steep that it is impossible to ascend them except by means of a serpentine path. I found here deep hollow ways, with beds and sides of solid white stone; but not quite so white and so solid, I think, as the stone which I found in the roads at Hawkley. The churchyard of Selborne is most beautifully situated. The land is good, all about it. The trees are luxuriant and prone to be lofty and large. I measured the yew-tree in the church-yard, and found the trunk to be, according to my measurement, twenty-three feet, eight inches, in circumference. The trunk is very short, as is generally the case with yew-trees; but the head spreads to a very great extent, and the whole tree, though probably several centuries old, appears to be in perfect health. Here are several hop-plantations in and about this village; but, for this once, the prayers of the over-production men will be granted, and the devil of any hops there will be. The bines are scarcely got up the poles; the bines and the leaves are black, nearly, as soot; full as black as a sooty bag or dingy coal-sack, and covered with lice.[1] I have never seen such quantities of grapes upon any vines as I see upon the vines in this village, badly pruned as all the vines have been. To be sure, this is a year for grapes, such, I believe, as has been seldom known in England, and the cause is, the perfect ripening of the wood by the last beautiful summer. I am afraid, however, that the grapes come in vain; for this summer has been so cold, and is now so wet, that we can hardly expect grapes, which are not under glass to ripen. The hops are of considerable importance to the village, and their failure must necessarily be attended with consequences very inconvenient to the whole of a population so small as this. Upon inquiry, I find that the hops are equally bad at Alton, Froyle, Crondall, and even at Farnham. I saw them bad in Sussex; I hear that they are bad in Kent; so, that hop-planters, at any rate, will be, for once, free from the dreadful evils of abundance.

---

[1] The hop-fly, a species of aphis.

Kentish hop gardens, showing the traditional oast houses which are still a distinctive part of the landscape.

Thursley (Surrey),
Thursday, 7th August.

The day has been fine; notwithstanding I saw the Judge's terrific wigs as I came up upon the turnpike-road from the village of Itchen.

At Churt I had, upon my left, three hills out upon the common called the *Devil's Jumps*. The Unitarians will not believe in the Trinity, because they cannot account for it. Will they come here to Churt, go and look at these "Devil's Jumps," and account to me for the placing of those three hills, in the shape of three rather squat sugar-loaves, along in a line upon this heath, or the placing of a rock-stone upon the top of one of them as big as a Church tower? For my part I cannot account for this placing of these hills. That they should have been formed by mere chance is hardly to be believed. How could waters rolling about have formed such hills? How could such hills have bubbled up from beneath? But, in short, it is all wonderful alike: the stripes of loam running down through the chalk-hills; the circular parcels of loam in the midst of chalk-hills; the lines of flint running parallel with each other horizontally along the chalk-hills; the flints placed in circles as true as a hair in the chalk-hills; the layers of stone at the bottom of hills of loam; the chalk first soft, then some miles further on, becoming chalk-stone; then, after another distance, becoming burr-stone, as they call it; and at last, becoming hard white stone, fit for any buildings; the sand-stone at Hindhead becoming harder, and harder, till it becomes very nearly iron in Herefordshire, and quite iron in Wales; but, indeed, they once dug iron out of this very Hindhead. The clouds, coming and settling upon the hills, sinking down and creeping along, at last coming out again in springs, and those becoming rivers. Why, it is all equally wonderful, and as to not believing in this or that, because the thing cannot be proved by logical deduction, why is any man to believe in the existence of a God, any more than he is to believe in the doctrine of the Trinity?

I got to Thursley about sunset, and without experiencing any inconvenience from the wet.

I am very happy to hear that that beautiful little bird, the American partridge, has been introduced with success to this neighbourhood, by Mr. Leech at Lea. I am told that they have been heard whistling this summer; that they have been frequently seen, and that there is no doubt that they have broods of young ones. I tried several times to import some of these birds; but I always lost them, by some means or other, before the time arrived for turning them out. They are a beautiful little partridge, and extremely interesting in all their manners. Some persons call them *quail*. If anyone will take a quail and compare it with one of these birds, he will see that they cannot be of the same sort. Quails assemble in flocks like larks, starlings or rooks. Partridges keep in distinct coveys; that is to say, the brood lives distinct from all other broods until the ensuing spring, when it forms itself into pairs and separates. Nothing can be a distinction more clear than this. Our own partridges stick to the same spot from the time that they are hatched to the time that they pair off, and these American partridges do the same. These, therefore,

Hop pickers—an idealized view of what was a harsh way of life.

which have been brought to Thursley, are partridges; and, if they be suffered to live quietly for a season or two, they will stock the whole of that part of the country, where the delightful intermixture of corn-fields, coppices, heaths, furze-fields, ponds and rivulets, is singularly favourable to their increase.[2]

Reigate (Surrey),
Friday, 8th August.

At the end of a long, twisting-about ride, but a most delightful ride, I got to this place about nine o'clock in the evening. From Thursley I came to Brook, and there crossed the turnpike-road from London to Chichester through Godalming and Midhurst. Thence I came on, turning upon the left upon the sand-hills of Hambledon (in Surrey, mind). On one of these hills is one of those precious jobs, called *"Semaphores."* For what reason this pretty name is given to a sort of Telegraph house, stuck up at public expense upon a high hill; for what reason this outlandish name is given to the thing, I must leave the reader to guess; but as to the thing itself; I know that it means this: a pretence for giving a good sum of the public money away every year to some one that the Borough-system has condemned this labouring and toiling nation to provide for.

Wen, Sunday, 10th August.

I STAID at Reigate yesterday, and came to the Wen to-day, every step of the way in a rain; as good a soaking as any devotee of St. Swithin ever underwent for his sake. I promised that I would give an account of the effect which the soaking on the South-Downs, on Saturday the 2nd instant, had upon the hooping-cough. I do not recommend the remedy to others; but this I will say, that I had a spell of the hooping-cough, the day before I got that soaking, and that I have not had a single spell since; though I have slept in several different beds, and got a second soaking in going from Botley to Easton. The truth is, I believe, that rain upon the South-Downs, or at any place near the sea, is by no means the same thing with rain in the interior. No man ever catches cold from getting wet with sea-water; and, indeed, I have never known an instance of a man catching cold at sea. The air upon the South-Downs is saltish, I daresay; and the clouds may bring something a little partaking of the nature of sea-water.

Thus I have concluded this "rural ride," from the Wen and back again to the Wen, being, taking in all the turnings and windings, as near as can be, two hundred miles in length. My objects were to ascertain the state of the crops, both of hops and of corn. The hop-affair is soon settled, for there will be no hops. As to the corn, my remark is this: that on all the clays, on all the stiff lands upon the chalk, on all the rich lands, indeed, but more especially on all the stiff lands, the

---

[2] These birds are generally called Virginian colins; they are abundant in most parts of North America, in some places being called quails, and in others partridges. In size they are between the quail and the partridge; the plumage is brownish red and the under parts whitish. Great numbers are killed by guns and taken in snares. They are easily domesticated, and seem well fitted for the poultry yard. P.C.

wheat is as good as I recollect ever to have seen it, and has as much straw. On all the light lands and poor lands, the wheat is thin, and, though not short, by no means good. The oats are pretty good almost every where; and I have not seen a bad field of barley during the whole of my ride; though there is no species of soil in England, except that of the fens, over which I have not passed. The state of the farmers is much worse than it was last year, notwithstanding the ridiculous falsehoods of the London newspapers, and the more ridiculous delusion of the jolter-heads. In numerous instances the farmers, who continue in their farms, have ceased to farm for themselves, and merely hold the land for the landlords. The delusion caused by the rise of the price of corn has pretty nearly vanished already; and if St. Swithin would but get out of the way with his drippings for about a month, this delusion would disappear, never to return. In the mean while, however, the London newspapers are doing what they can to keep up the delusion; and, in a paper called *Bell's Weekly Messenger* edited, I am told, by a place-hunting lawyer; in that stupid paper of this day, I find the following passage:—"So late as January last, the average price of wheat was 39s. per quarter, and on the 29th ult. it was above 62s. As it has been rising ever since, it may *now be quoted as little under* 65s. So that in this article alone, there is a rise of more than *thirty-five* per cent. Under these circumstances, it is not likely that we shall hear anything of *agricultural distress*. A writer of considerable talents, but no prophet, had *frightened* the kingdom by a confident prediction, that wheat, after the 1st of May, would sink to 4s. per bushel, and that under the effects of Mr. Peel's bill, and the payments in cash by the Bank of England, it would *never again exceed that price!* Nay, so assured was Mr.Cobbett of the mathematical certainty of his deductions on the subject, that he did not hesitate to make use of the following language: 'And farther, if what I say do not come to pass, I will give any one leave to broil me on a gridiron, and for that purpose I will get one of the best gridirons I can possibly get made, and it shall be hung out as near to my premises as possible, in the Strand, so that it shall be seen by everybody as they pass along.' The 1st of May has now passed, Mr. Peel's bill has not been repealed, and the Bank of England has paid its notes in cash, and yet wheat has risen nearly 40 per cent."

Here is a tissue of falsehoods! But, only think of a country being "*frightened*" by the prospect of a low price of provisions! When such an idea can possibly find its way even into the shallow brain of a cracked-skull lawyer; when such an idea can possibly be put into print, at any rate, there must be something totally wrong in the state of the country. Here is this lawyer telling his readers that I had frightened the kingdom, by saying that wheat would be sold at four shillings a bushel. As to the rest of this article, it is a tissue of downright lies. The writer says that the price of wheat is sixty-five shillings a quarter. The fact is, that, on the second instant, the price was fifty-nine shillings and seven-pence: and it is now about two shillings less than that. Then again, this writer must know, that I never said that wheat would not rise above four shillings a bushel; but that, on the contrary, I always expressly said that the price would be affected by the seasons, and that I thought, that the price would vibrate between three shillings a bushel and seven shillings a bushel. Then again, Peel's Bill has, in part, been repealed; if it had not, there could have been no small notes in circulation at this day. So that this lawyer is "*All Lie.*"

The quantity of the harvest will be great. If the quality be bad, owing to wet weather, the price will be still lower than it would have been in case of dry weather. The price, therefore, must come down; and if the newspapers were conducted by men who had any sense of honour or shame, those men must be covered with confusion.

RIDE THROUGH THE NORTH-EAST PART OF SUSSEX, AND ALL
ACROSS KENT, FROM THE WEALD OF SUSSEX, TO DOVER.

Worth (Sussex),
Friday, 29 August, 1823.

I have so often described the soil and other matters, appertaining to the country between the Wen, and this place, that my readers will rejoice at being spared the repetition here. As to the harvest, however, I find that they were deluged here on Tuesday last, though we got but little, comparatively, at Kensington. Between Mitcham and Sutton they were making wheat-ricks. The corn has not been injured here worth notice. Now and then an ear in the butts *grown;* and grown wheat is a sad thing! You may almost as well be without wheat altogether. However, very little harm has been done here as yet.

Tonbridge Wells (Kent),
Saturday, 30 August.

I came from Worth about seven this morning, passed through East Grinstead, over Holthigh Common, through Ashurst, and thence to this place. The morning was very fine, and I left them at Worth, making a wheat-rick. There was no show for rain till about one o'clock, as I was approaching Ashurst. The shattering that came at first I thought nothing of; but the clouds soon grew up all round, and the rain set in for the afternoon. The buildings at Ashurst (which is the first parish in Kent on quitting Sussex) are a mill, an alehouse, a church, and about six or seven other houses. I stopped at the alehouse to bait my horse, and, for want of bacon, was compelled to put up with bread and cheese for myself. I waited in vain for the rain to cease or to slacken, and the *want of bacon* made me fear as to a *bed*. So, about five o'clock, I, without greatcoat, got upon my horse, and came to this place, just as fast and no faster than if it had been fine weather. A very fine soaking! If the South Downs have left any little remnant of the hooping-cough, *this* will take it away to be sure. I made not the least haste to get out of the rain, I stopped, here and there, as usual, and asked questions about the corn, the hops, and other things. But, the moment I got in, I got a good fire, and set about the work of drying in good earnest. It costing me nothing for drink, I can afford to have plenty of fire. I have not been in the house an hour; and all my clothes are now as dry as if they had never been wet. It is not getting wet that hurts you, if you keep moving, while you are wet. It is the suffering of yourself to be *inactive*, while the wet clothes are on your back.

Tenterden (Kent), Sunday, 31 August.

Here I am after a most delightful ride of twenty-four miles through Frant, Lamberhurst, Goudhurst, Milkhouse-Street, Benenden, and Rolvenden. By making a great stir in rousing waiters and "boots" and maids, and by leaving behind me the name of "a — noisy, troublesome fellow," I got clear of "*the Wells*," and out of the contagion of its Wen-engendered inhabitants, time enough to meet the first rays of the sun, on the hill that you come up in order to get to Frant, which is a most beautiful little village at about two miles from "*the Wells*."

Coming through the village of Benenden, I heard a man at my right, talking very loud about *houses! houses! houses!* It was a Methodist parson, in a house close by the roadside. I pulled up, and stood still, in the middle of the road, but looking, in silent soberness, into the window (which was open) of the room in which the preacher was at work. I believe my stopping rather disconcerted him; for he got into shocking *repetition*. "Do you *know*," said he, laying great stress on the word *know*: "do you *know*, that you have ready for you houses, houses I say; I say do you know; do you know that you have houses in the heavens, not made with hands? Do you know this from *experience*? Has the blessed Jesus *told you so*?" And, on he went to say, that, if Jesus had told them so, they would be saved, and that if he had not, and did not, they would be damned. Some girls whom I saw in the room, plump and rosy as could be, did not seem at all daunted by these menaces; and indeed, they appeared to me to be thinking much more about getting houses for themselves *in this world first;* just to *see a little* before they entered, or endeavoured to enter, or even thought much about, those "*houses*" of which the parson was speaking: *houses* with pig-styes and little snug gardens attached to them, together with all the other domestic and conjugal circumstances, these girls seemed to me to be preparing themselves for. The truth is, these fellows have no power on the minds of any but the miserable.

Scarcely had I proceeded a hundred yards from the place where this fellow was bawling, when I came to the very situation which he ought to have occupied, I mean the *stocks*, which the people of Benenden have, with singular humanity, fitted up with a *bench*, so that the patient, while he is receiving the benefit of the remedy, is not exposed to the danger of catching cold by sitting, as in other places, upon the ground, always damp, and sometimes actually wet. But, I would ask the people of Benenden what is the *use* of this humane precaution, and, indeed, what is the use of the stocks themselves, if, while a fellow is ranting and bawling in the manner just described, at the distance of a hundred yards from the stocks, the stocks (as is here actually the case) are almost hidden by grass and nettles? This,

The gamekeeper, an important figure in rural life.

however, is the case all over the country; not nettles and grass indeed smothering the stocks, but, I never see any feet peeping through the holes, anywhere, though I find Methodist parsons everywhere, and though *the law compels the parishes to keep up* all the pairs of stocks that exist in all parts of them; and, in some parishes, they have to keep up several pairs.[1] I am aware, that a good part of the use of the stocks is the *terror* they ought to produce. I am not supposing, that they are of no use because not continually furnished with legs. But, there is a wide difference between *always* and *never;* and it is clear, that a fellow, who has had the stocks under his eye all his lifetime, and has *never* seen a pair of feet peeping through them, will stand no more in awe of the stocks than rooks do of an old shoy-hoy, a

---

[1] The keeping of stocks in every village, though still a legal obligation since 1376, was rapidly falling into disuse.

mere mockery; a thing laughed at by those whom it is intended to keep in check. It is time that the stocks were again *in use*, or that the expense of keeping them up were put an end to.

This mild, this gentle, this good-humoured sort of correction is *not enough* for our present rulers. But, mark the consequence; gaols ten times as big as formerly; houses of correction; tread-mills; the hulks; and the country filled with *spies* of one sort and another, *game-spies*, or other spies, and if a hare or pheasant come to an untimely death, *police-officers* from the Wen are not unfrequently called down to find out and secure the bloody offender![2] *Mark this*, Englishmen! Mark how we take to those things, which we formerly ridiculed in the French; and take them up too just as that brave and spirited people have shaken them off!

This Tenterden is a market town, and a singularly bright spot. It consists of one street, which is, in some places, more, perhaps, than two hundred feet wide. On one side of the street the houses have gardens before them, from 20 to 70 feet deep. The town is upon a hill; the afternoon was very fine, and, just as I rose the hill and entered the street, the people had come out of church and were moving along towards their houses. It was a very fine sight. *Shabbily-dressed people do not go to church*. I saw, in short, drawn out before me, the dress and beauty of the town; and a great many very, very pretty girls I saw; and saw them, too, in their best attire.

The church at this place is a very large and fine old building. The tower stands upon a base thirty feet square. Like the church at Goudhurst, it will hold three thousand people. And, let it be observed, that, when these churches were built, people had not yet thought of cramming them with *pews*, as a stable is filled with stalls. Those who built these churches, had no idea that worshipping God meant, going to *sit* to hear a man talk out what he called preaching. By *worship*, they meant very different things; and, above all things, when they had made a fine and noble building, they did not dream of disfiguring the inside of it by filling its floor with large and deep boxes, made of deal boards. In short, the floor was the place for the worshippers to stand or to kneel; and there was *no distinction;* no *high* place and no *low* place; all were upon a level *before God* at any rate. Some were not stuck into pews lined with green or red cloth, while others were crammed into corners to stand erect, or sit on the floor. These odious distinctions are of Protestant origin and growth. This lazy lolling in pews we owe to what is called the *Reformation*. A place filled with benches and boxes looks like an eating or a drinking place; but certainly not like a place of worship. A Frenchman, who had been driven from St. Domingo to Philadelphia by the Wilberforces of France,[3] went to church along with me one Sunday. He had never been in a Protestant place of *worship* before. Upon looking round him, and seeing every body comfortably seated, while a couple of good stoves were keeping the place as warm as a slack oven, he

---

[2] A reference to the savage Game Laws.

[3] Presumably a slave-owner who had fled from San Domingo when the slaves were emancipated in French colonies during the Revolution.

exclaimed: "*Pardi! On sert Dieu bien à son aise ici!*" That is: "Egad! they serve God very much at their ease here!" I always think of this, when I see a church full of pews; as, indeed, is now always the case with our churches.[4]

This evening I have been to the Methodist Meeting-house. I was attracted, fairly drawn all down the street, by the *singing*. When I came to the place the parson was got into prayer. His hands were clenched together and held up, his face turned up and back so as to be nearly parallel with the ceiling, and he was bawling away, with his "do thou," and "mayest thou," and "may we," enough to stun one. Noisy, however, as he was, he was unable to fix the attention of a parcel of girls in the gallery, whose eyes were all over the place, while his eyes were so devoutly shut up. After a deal of this rigmarole called prayer, came the *preachy*, as the negroes call it; and a *preachy* it really was. Such a mixture of whining cant and of foppish affectation I scarcely ever heard in my life. The text was (I speak from memory) 1st St. Peter iv. 18. The words were to this amount: that, *as the righteous would be saved with difficulty, what must become of the ungodly and the sinner?* After as neat a dish of nonsense and of impertinences as one could wish to have served up, came the distinction between the *ungodly* and the *sinner*. The sinner was one who did moral wrong; the ungodly, one who did no moral wrong, but who was not regenerated. *Both*, he positively told us, were to be damned. One was just as bad as the other. Moral rectitude was to do nothing in saving the man. He was to be damned, unless born again, and how was he to be born again, unless he came to the regeneration-shop, and gave the fellows money? He distinctly told us, that a man perfectly moral, might be damned; and that "the vilest of the vile, and the basest of the base" (I quote his very words) "would be saved if they became regenerate; and that colliers, whose souls had been as black as their coals, had by regeneration, become bright as the saints that sing before God and the Lamb." And will the *Edinburgh Reviewers* again find fault with me for cutting at this bawling, canting crew? Monstrous it is to think that the Clergy of the Church really encourage these roving fanatics. The Church seems aware of its loss of credit and of power. It seems willing to lean even upon these men; who, be it observed, seem, on their part, to have taken the Church under their protection. They always pray for the *Ministry;* I mean the ministry at *Whitehall*. They are most "loyal" souls. The THING protects *them;* and they lend their aid *in upholding the* THING. What silly; nay, what base creatures those must be, who really give their money, give their pennies, which ought to buy bread for their own children; who thus give their money to these lazy and impudent fellows, who call themselves ministers of God, who prowl about the country living easy and jovial lives upon the fruit of the labour of other people. However, it is, in some measure, these people's fault. If they did not give, the others could not receive. I wish to see every labouring man well fed and well

---

[4] Cobbett had a High-Church prejudice against the use of churches as places to hear sermons rather than as places of prayer and worship.

One of Cobbett's favourite villains, the 'Master Parson with a Good Living.'

clad; but, really, the man who gives any portion of his earnings to these fellows, deserves to want: he deserves to be pinched with hunger: misery is the just reward of this worst species of prodigality.

The *singing* makes a great part of what passes in these meeting-houses. A number of women and girls singing together make very sweet sounds. Few men there are who have not felt *the power* of sounds of this sort. Men are sometimes pretty nearly bewitched without knowing how. *Eyes* do a good deal, but *tongues* do more. We may talk of sparkling eyes and snowy bosoms as long as we please; but, what are these with a croaking, masculine voice? The parson seemed to be fully aware of the importance of this part of the "service." The subject of his hymn was something about *love*: Christian love; love of Jesus; but, still it was about *love;* and the parson read, or gave out, the verses, in a singularly *soft* and *sighing* voice, with his head on one side, and giving it rather a swing. I am satisfied, that the singing forms great part of the *attraction*. Young girls like to sing; and young men like to hear them. Nay, old ones too; and, as I have just said, it was the singing that *drew* me three hundred yards down the street at Tenterden, to enter this meeting-house. By-the-by, I wrote some Hymns myself, and published them in "*Twopenny Trash*." I will give any Methodist parson leave, to put them into his hymn-book.

Folkestone (Kent),
Monday (Noon), 1 Sept.

At three miles from Appledore I came through Snargate, a village with five houses, and with a church capable of containing two thousand people! The vagabonds tell us, however, that we have a wonderful increase of population! These vagabonds will be hanged by-and-by, or else justice will have fled from the face of the earth.

At Brenzett (a mile further on) I with great difficulty got a rasher of bacon for breakfast. The few houses that there are, are miserable in the extreme. The church here (only a *mile* from the last) nearly as large; and nobody to go to it. What! will the *vagabonds* attempt to make us believe, that these churches were *built for nothing! "Dark ages"* indeed those must have been, if these churches were erected without there being any more people than there are now. But, *who* built them? Where did the *means*, where did the hands come from? This place presents another proof of the truth of my old observation: *rich land* and *poor labourers*.

Opposite above:
Portrait of Sir George O'Brien Wyndham, 3rd Earl of Egremont, by Thomas Phillips. A generous man, he turned Petworth House, the family home, into a nursery of art and college of agriculture. He was Lord-lieutenant of Sussex from 1819–35. A patron of Turner, he introduced many fine art treasures to Petworth House, where he died, unmarried, in 1837, aged eighty-six.

Opposite below:
The Market Cross and Abbey Church of Malmesbury in Gloucestershire, by Amelia Long. According to Cobbett, even in his day the Abbey was remarkably 'well preserved', and of the Market Cross, he says it is a sight 'worth a journey of hundreds of miles.'

Rustic figures. The smock worn by the men was at that time commonly worn by rural labourers in all parts of the country.

'Stag Drinking', one of the series of Turner landscapes at Petworth House in Sussex.

At this Old Romney there is a church (two miles only from the last, mind!) fit to contain one thousand five hundred people, and there are, for the people of the parish to live in, twenty-two, or twenty-three houses! And yet the *vagabonds* have the impudence to tell us, that the population of England has vastly increased;[5] Curious system that depopulates Romney Marsh and peoples Bag-shot Heath! It is an unnatural system. It is the *vagabond's* system. It is a system that must be destroyed, or that will destroy the country.

I had baited my horse at New Romney, and was coming jogging along very soberly, now looking at the sea, then looking at the cattle, then the corn, when, my eye, in swinging round, lighted upon a great round building, standing upon the beach. I had scarcely had time to think about what it could be, when twenty or thirty others, standing along the coast, caught my eye; and, if any one had been behind me, he might have heard me exclaim, in a voice that made my horse bound, "The *Martello Towers* by ————!" Oh, Lord! To think that I should be destined to behold these monuments of the wisdom of Pitt and Dundas and Perceval! Good G—. Here they are, piles of bricks in a circular form about three hundred feet (*guess*) circumference at the base, about forty feet high, and about one hundred and fifty feet circumference at the top. There is a door-way, about midway up, in each, and each has two windows. Cannons were to be fired from the top of these things, in order to defend the country against the French Jacobins!

I think I have counted along here upwards of thirty of these ridiculous things, which, I dare say, cost five, perhaps, ten, thousand pounds each; and one of which was, I am told, *sold* on the coast of Sussex, the other day, for two hundred pounds! There is, they say, a chain of these things all the way to Hastings! I dare say they cost millions. But, far indeed are these from being all, or half, or a quarter of the squanderings along here. Hythe is half *barracks;* the hills are covered with barracks; and barracks most expensive, most squandering, fill up the side of the hill. Here is a canal (I crossed it at Appledore) made for the length of thirty miles (from Hythe, in Kent, to Rye, in Sussex) to *keep out the French;* for, those armies who had so often crossed the Rhine, and the Danube, were to be kept back by a canal, made by Pitt, thirty feet wide at the most! All along the coast there are works of some sort or other; incessant sinks of money; walls of immense dimensions; masses of stone brought and put into piles. Then you see some of the walls and buildings falling down; some that have never been finished. The whole thing, all taken together, looks as if a spell had been, all of a sudden, set upon the workmen; or, in the words of the Scripture, here is the *"desolation of abomination, standing in high places."* However, all is right. These things were made with the hearty good will of those who are now coming to ruin in consequence of the Debt, contracted for the purpose of making these things! This is all *just.* The load will come, at last, upon the right shoulders.

---

[5] Cobbett often argued, fallaciously, that a large church in a small village must be evidence of a fall in population.

Between Hythe and Sandgate (a village at about two miles from Hythe) I first saw the French coast. The chalk cliffs at Calais are as plain to the view as possible, and also the land which they tell me is near Boulogne.

Before I got into Folkstone I saw no less than eighty-four men, women, and boys and girls gleaning or leasing, in a field of about ten acres. The people all along here complain most bitterly of the *change of times*. The truth is, that the squandered millions are gone! The nation has now to suffer for this squandering. The money served to silence some; to make others bawl; to cause the good to be oppressed; to cause the bad to be exalted; to "crush the Jacobins:" and what is the *result*? What is the *end*? The *end* is not yet come: but as to the result thus far, go, ask the families of those farmers, who, after having, for so many years, threatened to shoot Jacobins, have, in instances not a few, shot themselves! Go, ask the ghosts of Pitt and of Castlereagh what has, thus far, been the *result!* Go, ask the Hampshire farmer, who, not many months since, actually blowed out his own brains with one of those very pistols which he had long carried in his Yeomanry Cavalry holsters, to be ready "to keep down the Jacobins and Radicals!" Oh, God! inscrutable are thy ways; but thou art just, and of thy justice what a complete proof have we in the case of these very Martello Towers! They were erected to keep out the Jacobin French, lest they should come and assist the Jacobin English. The *loyal* people of this coast were fattened by the building of them. Pitt and his loyal *Cinque Ports* waged interminable war against Jacobins. These very towers are now used to keep these *loyal* Cinque Ports themselves in order. These towers are now used to lodge men, whose business it is to sally forth, not upon Jacobins, but upon *smugglers?* Thus, after having sucked up millions of the nation's money, these loyal Cinque Ports are squeezed again: kept in order, kept down, by the very towers, which they rejoiced to see rise to keep down the Jacobins.

Dover, Monday, Sept. 1st, Evening.

I got here this evening about six o'clock, having come to-day thirty-six miles: but I must defer my remarks on the country between Folkestone and this place; a most interesting spot, and well worthy of particular attention. What place I shall date from after Dover, I am by no means certain; but, be it from what place it may, the continuation of my Journal shall be published, in due course. If the Atlantic Ocean could not cut off the communication between me and my readers, a mere strip of water, not much wider than an American river, will hardly do it.[6] I am, in real truth, undecided, as yet, whether I shall go on to France, or back to the *Wen*. I think I shall, when I go out of this Inn, toss the bridle upon my horse's neck, and let him decide for me. I am sure he is more fit to decide on such a point than our Ministers are to decide on any point connected with the happiness, greatness, and honour of this kingdom.

---

[6] A reference to Cobbett's having edited his *Political Register* by remote control, when in America 1817–19.

98

RURAL RIDE FROM DOVER, THROUGH THE ISLE OF THANET, BY
CANTERBURY AND FAVERSHAM, ACROSS TO MAIDSTONE, UP TO
TONBRIDGE, THROUGH THE WEALD OF KENT AND OVER THE HILLS
BY WESTERHAM AND HAYS, TO THE WEN.

Dover,
Wednesday, Sept. 3, 1823 (Evening).

On Monday I was balancing in my own mind whether I should go to France or not. To-day I have decided the question in the negative, and shall set off this evening for the Isle of Thanet; that spot so famous for corn.

I broke off without giving an account of the country between Folkestone and Dover, which is a very interesting one in itself, and was peculiarly interesting to me on many accounts. I have often mentioned, in describing the parts of the country over which I have travelled; I have often mentioned the *chalk-ridge* and also the *sand-ridge*, which I had traced, running parallel with each other from about Farnham, in Surrey, to Sevenoaks, in Kent. Here, at Folkestone, the sand-ridge tapers off in a sort of flat towards the sea. The land is like what it is at Reigate, a very steep hill; a hill of full a mile high, and bending exactly in the same manner as the hill at Reigate does. The land to the south of the hill begins a poor, thin, white loam upon the chalk, soon gets to be a very fine rich loam upon the chalk, goes on till it mingles the chalky loam with the sandy loam, and thus it goes on down to the sea-beach, or to the edge of the cliff. It is a beautiful bed of earth here.

From the hill, you keep descending all the way to Dover, a distance of about six miles, and it is absolutely six miles of down hill. On your right, you have the lofty land which forms a series of chalk cliffs, from the top of which you look into the sea; on your left, you have ground that goes rising up from you in the same sort of way. The turnpike-road goes down the middle of a valley, each side of which, as far as you can see, may be about a mile and a half. It is six miles long, you will remember; and here, therefore, with very little interruption, very few chasms, there are *eighteen square miles of corn*. It is a patch such as you very seldom see, and especially of corn so good as it is here.

The town of Dover is like other sea-port towns; but really much more clean, and with less blackguard people in it than I ever observed in any sea-port before. It is a most picturesque place, to be sure. On one side of it rises, upon the top of a very steep hill, the Old Castle, with all its fortifications. On the other side of it there is another chalk-hill, the side of which is pretty nearly perpendicular, and rises up from sixty to a hundred feet higher than the tops of the houses, which stand pretty nearly close to the foot of the hill.

I got into Dover rather late. It was dusk when I was going down the street towards the quay. I happened to look up, and was quite astonished to perceive cows grazing upon a spot apparently fifty feet above the tops of the houses, and measuring horizontally not, perhaps, more than ten or twenty feet from a line which would have formed a continuation into the air. I went up to the same spot,

Pevensey Bay from Crowhurst Park.

the next day, myself; and you actually look down upon the houses, as you look out of a window, upon people in the street. The valley that runs down from Folkestone, is, when it gets to Dover, crossed by another valley that runs down from Canterbury, or, at least, from the Canterbury direction. It is in the gorge of this cross valley that Dover is built. The two chalk-hills jut out into the sea, and the water that comes up between them forms a harbour for this ancient, most interesting, and beautiful place. On the hill to the North, stands the Castle of Dover, which is fortified in the ancient manner, except on the sea-side, where it has the steep *Cliff* for a fortification. On the South side of the town, the hill is, I

100

believe, rather more lofty than that on the North side; and here is that Cliff, which is described by Shakespeare, in the Play of King Lear. It is fearfully steep, certainly. Very nearly perpendicular for a considerable distance. The grass grows well, to the very tip of the cliff; and you see cows and sheep grazing there with as much unconcern, as if grazing in the bottom of a valley.[1]

It was not, however, these natural curiosities that took me over *this* hill; I went to see, with my own eyes, something of the sorts of means that had been made use of to squander away countless millions of money. Here is a hill containing, probably, a couple of square miles or more, hollowed like a honey-comb. Here are line upon line, trench upon trench, cavern upon cavern, bomb-proof upon bomb-proof; in short the very sight of the thing convinces you that either madness the most humiliating, or profligacy the most scandalous must have been at work here for years. The question that every man of sense asks, is: What reason had you to suppose that the *French would ever come to this hill* to attack it, while the rest of the country was so much more easy to assail? However, let any man of good plain understanding, go and look at the works that have here been performed, and that are now all tumbling into ruin. Let him ask what this cavern was for; what that ditch was for; what this tank was for; and why all these horrible holes and hiding-places at an expense of millions upon millions? Let this scene be brought and placed under the eyes of the people of England, and let them be told that Pitt and Dundas and Perceval had these things done to prevent the country from being conquered; with voice unanimous the nation would instantly exclaim: Let the French or let the devil take us, rather than let us resort to means of defence like these. This is, perhaps, the only set of fortifications in the world ever framed for mere *hiding*. There is no appearance of any intention to annoy an enemy.[2] It is a parcel of holes made in a hill, to hide Englishmen from Frenchmen. Just as if the Frenchmen would come to this hill! And for a purpose like this; for a purpose so stupid, so senseless, so mad as this, and withal, so scandalously disgraceful, more brick and stone have been buried in this hill than would go to build a neat new cottage for every labouring man in the counties of Kent and of Sussex!

Dreadful is the scourge of such Ministers. However, those who supported them

---

[1] Twenty years before this date, Mr. Perceval, as Attorney General, when prosecuting the Author for libel, contemptuously exclaimed, "Who is Mr. Cobbett? Is he a man of family in this country? Is he a man writing purely from motives of patriotism? Quis homo hic est? Quo patre natus? He seems to imagine himself a species of Censor who, elevated to the solemn seat of judgment, is to deal about his decisions, for the instruction of mankind! He casts his eye downward like the character represented by the poet of nature, from Dover Cliff, and looks upon the inferior world below, as pigmies beneath him." P.C.

[2] The Author is here speaking, not without a certain knowledge of military science. While in his regiment in Nova Scotia and New Brunswick he made some large plans of military fortifications, drawn with pen and ink, most exact in every line and geometrically accurate. He thus describes his "chef-d'œuvre" on fortification:— "My plan was a regular sexagon, with every description of outwork; then I set to work to lay down the plan of a siege, made my line of circumvallation, fixed my batteries and cantonments, opened my trenches, made my approaches, covered by my gabions and fascines—at last effected a mine, and had all prepared for blowing up the citadel." P.C.

will now have to suffer. The money must have been squandered purposely, and for the worst ends. Fool as Pitt was; unfit as an old hack of a lawyer, like Dundas, was, to judge of the means of defending the country, stupid as both these fellows were, and as their brother lawyer, Perceval, was too: unfit as these lawyers were to judge in any such a case, they must have known that this was an useless expenditure of money. They must have known that; and, therefore, their general folly, their general ignorance is no apology for their conduct. What they wanted, was to prevent the landing, not of Frenchmen, but of French principles; that is to say, to prevent the example of the French from being alluring to the people of England. They wanted to keep out of England those principles which had a natural tendency to destroy borough-mongering, and to put an end to peculation and plunder. No matter whether by the means of Martello Towers, making a great chalk-hill a honey-comb, cutting a canal thirty feet wide to stop the march of the armies of the Danube and the Rhine: no matter how they squandered the money, so that it silenced some and made others bawl, to answer their great purpose of preventing French example from having an influence in England. And what have they done? It is impossible to be upon this honey-combed hill; upon this enormous mass of anti-jacobin expenditure, without seeing the chalk-cliffs of Calais and the corn-fields of France. At this season, it is impossible to see those fields without knowing that the farmers are getting in their corn there as well as here; and it is impossible to think of that fact without reflecting, at the same time, on the example which the farmers of France hold out to the farmers of England. Looking down from this very anti-jacobin hill, this day, I saw the parsons' shocks of wheat and barley left in the field after the farmer had taken his away. Turning my head, and looking across the channel, "There," said I, pointing to France, "There the spirited and sensible people have ridded themselves of this burden, of which our farmers so bitterly complain." It is impossible not to recollect here, that, in numerous petitions, sent up, too, by the *loyal*, complaints have been made that the English farmer has to carry on a competition against the French farmer who has *no tithes to pay!* Well, *loyal gentlemen*, why do not you petition, then, to be relieved from tithes? What do you mean else? Do you mean to call upon our big gentlemen at Whitehall for them to compel the French to pay tithes? Oh, you loyal fools! Better hold your tongues about the French not paying tithes. Better do that, at any rate; for never will they pay tithes again.

Here is a large tract of *land* upon these hills at Dover, which is the property of the public, having been purchased at an enormous expense. This is now let out as pasture land to people of the town. I daresay that the letting of this land is a curious affair. If there were a Member for Dover who would do what he ought to do, he would soon get before the public a list of the tenants, and of the rents paid by them. I should like very much to see such list. However, there is nothing of this sort that can, in the present state of things, be deemed to be of any real consequence. As long as the people at Whitehall can go on paying the interest of the debt in full, so long will there be no change worth the attention of any rational man. In the meanwhile, the French nation will be going on rising over us; and our Ministers will be cringing and crawling to every nation upon earth, who is known to possess a cannon or a barrel of powder.

Sandwich, Wednesday, 3 Sept. Night.

I got to this place about half an hour after the ringing of the eight o'clock bell, or Curfew, which I heard at about two miles' distance from the place. From the town of Dover you come up the Castle-Hill, and have a most beautiful view from the top of it. You have the sea, the chalk cliffs of Calais, the high land at Boulogne, the town of Dover just under you, the valley towards Folkestone, and the much more beautiful valley towards Canterbury; and, going on a little further, you have the Downs and the Essex or Suffolk coast in full view, with a most beautiful corn country to ride along through. The corn was chiefly cut between Dover and Walmer. The barley almost all cut and tied up in sheaf. Nothing but the beans seemed to remain standing along here.

Deal is a most villanous place. It is full of filthy-looking people. Great desolation of abomination has been going on here; tremendous barracks, partly pulled down and partly tumbling down, and partly occupied by soldiers. Every thing seems upon the perish. I was glad to hurry along through it, and to leave its inns and public-houses to be occupied by the tarred, and trowsered, and blue-and-buff crew whose very vicinage I always detest. From Deal you come along to Upper Deal, which, it seems, was the original village; thence upon a beautiful road to Sandwich, which is a rotten Borough. Rottenness, putridity is excellent for land, but bad for Boroughs. This place, which is as villanous a hole as one would wish to see, is surrounded by some of the finest land in the world. Along on one side of it, lies a marsh. On the other side of it is land which they tell me bears *seven quarters* of wheat to an acre. It is certainly very fine; for I saw large pieces of radish-seed on the road side; this seed is grown for the seedmen in London; and it will grow on none but rich land. All the corn is carried here except some beans and some barley.

Canterbury
Thursday Afternoon, 4th Sept.

When I got upon the corn land in the Isle of Thanet, I got into a garden indeed. There is hardly any fallow; comparatively few turnips. It is a country of corn. The labourers' houses all along through this island, beggarly in the extreme. The people dirty, poor-looking; ragged, but particularly *dirty*. The men and boys with dirty faces, and dirty smock-frocks, and dirty shirts; and, good G—! what a difference between the wife of a labouring man here, and the wife of a labouring man in the forests and woodlands of Hampshire and Sussex! Invariably have I observed, that the richer the soil, and the more destitute of woods; that is to say, the more purely a corn country, the more miserable the labourers. The cause is this, the great, the big bull frog grasps all. In this beautiful island every inch of land is appropriated by the rich. No hedges, no ditches, no commons, no grassy

103

lanes: a country divided into great farms; a few trees surround the great farm-house. All the rest is bare of trees; and the wretched labourer has not a stick of wood, and has no place for a pig or cow to graze, or even to lie down upon. The rabbit countries are the countries for labouring men. There the ground is not so valuable. There it is not so easily appropriated by the few. Here, in this island, the work is almost all done by the horses. The horses plough the ground; they sow the ground; they hoe the ground; they carry the corn home; they thresh it out; and they carry it to market: nay, in this island, they *rake* the ground; they rake up the straggling straws and ears; so that they do the whole, except the reaping and the mowing. It is impossible to have an idea of anything more miserable than the state of the labourers in this part of the country.

After coming by Margate, I passed a village called Monckton, and another called Sarr. At Sarr I began to cross the marsh, and had, after this, to come through the village of Up-street, and another village called Steady, before I got to Canterbury. At Up-street I was struck with the words written upon a board which was fastened upon a pole, which pole was standing in a garden near a neat little box of a house. The words were these. "PARADISE PLACE. *Spring guns and steel traps are set here.*"[3] A pretty idea it must give us of Paradise, to know that spring guns and steel traps are set in it! This is doubtless some stockjobber's place; for, in the first place, the name is likely to have been selected by one of that crew; and, in the next place, whenever any of them go to the country, they look upon it that they are to begin a sort of warfare against every thing around them. They invariably look upon every labourer as a thief.

As you approach Canterbury, from the Isle of Thanet, you have another instance of the squanderings of the lawyer Ministers. Nothing equals the ditches, the caverns, the holes, the tanks, and hiding places of the hill at Dover; but, considerable as the City of Canterbury is, that city, within its gates, stands upon less ground than those horrible erections, the barracks of Pitt, Dundas, and Perceval. Here are horse-barracks, foot-barracks, artillery-barracks, engineer-barracks: a whole country of barracks; but, only here and there a soldier. The thing is actually perishing. It is typical of the state of the great Thing of things. It gave me inexpressible pleasure to perceive the gloom that seemed to hang over these barracks, which once swarmed with soldiers and their blythe companions, as a hive swarms with bees. These barracks now look like the environs of a hive in winter.

This fine old town, or, rather city, is remarkable for cleanliness and niceness, notwithstanding it has a Cathedral in it. The country round it is very rich, and this year, while the hops are so bad in most other parts, they are not so very bad just about Canterbury.

---

[3] These were made illegal in 1827.

Turner's view of a cottage interior in the early nineteenth century.

An early nineteenth-century country fair.

Opposite above:
The Corn Bill of 1815, which prevented cheap corn from entering the country, caused riots in the year of Napoleon's surrender.

Opposite below:
Chichester Canal by Turner.

'The Beach at Old Folkestone' by Samuel Prout.

Elverton Farm, near Faversham,
Friday Morning, Sept. 5.

In going through Canterbury, yesterday, I gave a boy sixpence to hold my horse, while I went into the Cathedral, just to thank St. Swithin for the trick that he had played my friends, the Quakers. Led along by the wet weather till after the harvest had actually begun, and then to find the weather turn fine all of a sudden! This must have soused them pretty decently; and I hear of one, who, at Canterbury, has made a bargain by which he will certainly lose two thousand pounds.

In 1821 I gave Mr. William Waller, who lives here, some American apple-cuttings; and he has now some as fine Newtown Pippins as one would wish to see. They are very large of their sort; very free in their growth; and they promise to be very fine apples of the kind. Mr. Waller had cuttings from me of several sorts, in 1822. These were cut down last year; they have, of course, made shoots this summer; and great numbers of these shoots have fruit-spurs, which will have blossom, if not fruit, next year. This very rarely happens, I believe; and the state of Mr. Waller's trees clearly proves to me that the introduction of these American trees would be a great improvement.

Merryworth,
Friday evening, 5th Sept.

From Maidstone to this place (Merryworth) is about seven miles, and these are the finest seven miles that I have ever seen in England or anywhere else. The Medway is to your left, with its meadows about a mile wide. You cross the Medway, in coming out of Maidstone, and it goes and finds its way down to Rochester, through a break in the chalk-ridge. From Maidstone to Merryworth, I should think that there were hop-gardens on one half of the way, on both sides of the road. Then looking across the Medway, you see hop-gardens and orchards two miles deep, on the side of a gently rising ground: and this continues with you all the way from Maidstone to Merryworth. The orchards form a great feature of the country; and plantations of ashes and of chestnuts add greatly to the beauty. These gardens of hops are kept very clean, in general, though some of them have been neglected this year owing to the bad appearance of the crop. The culture is sometimes mixed: that is to say, apple-trees or cherry-trees or filbert-trees and hops, in the same ground. This is a good way, they say, of raising an orchard. I do not believe it; and I think that nothing is gained by any of these mixtures. They plant apple-trees or cherry-trees in rows here; they then plant a filbert-tree close to each of these large fruit-trees; and then they cultivate the middle of the ground by planting potatoes. This is being too greedy. It is impossible that they can gain by this. What they gain one way they lose the other way; and I verily believe, that the most profitable way would be, never to mix things at all.

Tonbridge,
Saturday morning, 6th Sept.

This Tonbridge is but a common country town, though very clean, and the people looking very well. The climate must be pretty warm here; for in entering the town, I saw a large Althea Frutex in bloom, a thing rare enough, any year, and particularly a year like this.[4]

Westerham,
Saturday, noon, 6th Sept.

Instead of going on to the Wen along the turnpike road through Sevenoaks, I turned to my left when I got about a mile out of Tonbridge, in order to come along that tract of country called the Weald of Kent; that is to say, the solid clays, which have no bottom, which are unmixed with chalk, sand, stone, or anything else; the country of dirty roads and of oak trees. I stopped at Tonbridge only a few minutes; but in the Weald, I stopped to breakfast at a place called Leigh. From Leigh, I came to Chittingstone causeway, leaving Tonbridge Wells six miles over the hills to my left. From Chittingstone, I came to Bough-beach, thence to Four Elms, and thence to this little market-town of Westerham, which is just upon the border of Kent. Indeed, Kent, Surrey, and Sussex form a joining very near to this town. Westerham, exactly like Reigate and Godstone, and Sevenoaks, and Dorking, and Folkestone, lies between the sand-ridge and the chalk-ridge. The valley is here a little wider than at Reigate, and that is all the difference there is between the places. As soon as you get over the sand hill to the south of Reigate, you get into the Weald of Surrey; and here, as soon as you get over the sand hill to the south of Westerham, you get into the Weald of Kent.

Coming through the Weald I found the corn very good; and, low as the ground is, wet as it is, cold as it is, there will be very little of the wheat, which will not be housed before Saturday night. I have had a most beautiful ride through the Weald. The day is very hot; but I have been in the shade; and my horse's feet very often in the rivulets and wet lanes. In one place I rode above a mile completely arched over by boughs of the underwood, growing in the banks of the lane. What an odd taste that man must have who prefers a turnpike-road to a lane like this.

Very near to Westerham there are hops: and I have seen now and then a little bit of hop garden, even in the Weald. Hops will grow well where lucerne will grow well; and lucerne will grow well where there is a rich top and a dry bottom. When therefore you see hops in the Weald, it is on the side of some hill, where there is sand or stone at bottom, and not where there is real clay beneath. There appear to be hops, here and there, all along from nearly at Dover to Alton, in Hampshire. You find them all along Kent; you find them at Westerham; across at Worth, in Sussex; at Godstone, in Surrey; over to the north of Merrow Down, near Guildford; at

---

[4] This plant is of the hollyhock and marsh mallow tribe; its botanical name is Hibiscus. P.C.

Godalming; under the Hog's-back, at Farnham; and all along that way to Alton. But there, I think, they end. The whole face of the country seems to rise, when you get just beyond Alton, and to keep up. Whether you look to the north, the south, or west, the land seems to rise, and the hops cease, till you come again away to the north-west, in Herefordshire.

Kensington, Saturday night, 6 Sept.

Here I close my day, at the end of forty-four miles.

After getting up the hill from Westerham, I had a general descent to perform all the way to the Thames. When you get to Beckenham, which is the last parish in Kent, the country begins to assume a cockney-like appearance; all is artificial, and you no longer feel any interest in it. I was anxious to make this journey into Kent, in the midst of harvest, in order that I might *know* the real state of the crops. The result of my observations, and my inquiries, is, that the crop is a *full average* crop of everything except barley, and that the barley yields a great deal more than an average crop.

Now then, we shall see how all this tallies with the schemes, with the intentions and expectations of our matchless gentlemen at Whitehall.

Mark the curious fact, that all the vile press of London; the whole of that infamous press; that newspapers, magazines, reviews; the whole of the base thing; and a baser surely this world never saw; that the whole of this base thing rejoiced, exulted, crowed over me, and told an impudent lie, in order to have the crowing; crowed, for what? *Because wheat and bread were become dear!* Now, it is notorious, that, heretofore, every periodical publication in this kingdom was in the constant habit of lamenting, when bread became dear, and of rejoicing, when it became cheap. This is notorious. Nay it is equally notorious, that this infamous press was everlastingly assailing bakers, and millers, and butchers, for not selling bread, flour, and meat cheaper than they were selling them. In how many hundreds of instances has this infamous press, caused attacks to be made by the mob, upon tradesmen of this description![5] All these things are notorious. Moreover, notorious it is that, long previous to every harvest, this infamous, this execrable, this beastly press, was engaged in stunning the public with accounts of the *great crop* which was just coming forward! There was always, with this press, a prodigiously large crop. This was invariably the case. It was never known to be contrary.

Now these things are perfectly well known to every man in England. How comes it, then, reader, that the profligate, the trading, the lying, the infamous press of London, has now totally changed its tone and bias? The base thing never now tells us that there is a great crop or even a good crop. It never now wants cheap bread, and cheap wheat, and cheap meat. It never now finds fault of bakers

---

[5] A little unfair, since Cobbett was himself a free trader, on the grounds that what mattered to the poor was cheap food.

and butchers. It now always endeavours to make it appear that corn is dearer than it is. The base "*Morning Herald*," about three weeks ago, not only suppressed the fact of the fall of wheat, but asserted that there had been a rise in the price. Now *why is all this?* That is a great question, reader. That is a very interesting question. Why has this infamous press, which always pursues that which it thinks its own interest; why has it taken this strange turn? This is the reason: stupid as the base thing is, it has arrived at a conviction, that if the price of the produce of the land cannot be kept up to something approaching ten shillings a bushel for good wheat, the system of funding must be blown up. The infamous press has arrived at a conviction, that that cheating, that fraudulent system by which this press lives, must be destroyed unless the price of corn can be kept up. The infamous traders of the press are perfectly well satisfied, that the interest of the Debt must be reduced, unless wheat can be kept up to nearly ten shillings a bushel. Stupid as they are, and stupid as the fellows down at Westminster are, they know very well, that the whole system, stock-jobbers, Jews, cant and all, go to the devil at once, as soon as a deduction is made from the interest of the Debt. Knowing this, they want wheat to sell high; because it has, at last, been hammered into their skulls, that the interest cannot be paid in full, if wheat sells low.

Is it not a novelty in the world to see a Government, and in ordinary seasons, too, having its whole soul absorbed in considerations, relating to the price of corn? There are our neighbours, the French, who have got a Government engaged in taking military possession of a great neighbouring kingdom to free which from these very French, we have recently expended a *hundred and fifty millions of money*.[6] Our neighbours have got a Government that is thus engaged, and we have got a Government that employs itself in making incessant "inquiries in all the qualified quarters" relative to the price of wheat! Curious employment for a Government! Singular occupation for the Ministers of the Great George! They seem to think nothing of Spain, with its eleven millions of people, being in fact added to France. Wholly insensible do they appear to concerns of this sort, while they sit thinking, day and night, upon the price of the bushel of wheat!

However, they are not, after all, such fools as they appear to be. Despicable, indeed, must be that nation, whose safety or whose happiness does, in any degree, depend on so fluctuating a thing as the price of corn. This is a matter that we must take as it comes. The seasons will be what they will be; and all the calculations of statesmen must be made wholly independent of the changes and chances of seasons. This has always been the case, to be sure. What nation could ever carry on its affairs, if it had to take into consideration the price of corn? Nevertheless, such is the situation of *our Government*, that its very existence, in its present way, depends upon the price of corn. We laugh at a Government employing itself in making calculations about the price of corn, and in employing its press to put forth

---

[6] The French were threatening to intervene in the Spanish Revolution of 1820–23, that is, in the country freed from them by so much British blood and money in the Peninsular War.

Queen Caroline of Brunswick, the consort of George IV, in 1804. Cobbett felt that she had been 'deeply injured' by Lord Liverpool's efforts to deprive her of her rights and title of Queen when the Prince Regent succeeded to the throne in 1821.

market puffs. We laugh at these things; but we should not laugh, if we considered, that it is on the price of wheat, that the duration of the power and the profits of these men depends.

Ours is a Government that now seems to depend very much upon the *weather*. Pitt, when he had just made a monstrous issue of paper, and had, thereby, actually put the match which blowed up the old She Devil in 1797—Pitt, at that time, congratulated the nation, that the wisdom of Parliament had established a solid system of finance. Any thing but solid it assuredly was; but his system of finance was as worthy of being called solid, as that system of Government which now manifestly depends upon the weather and the winds.

I thus conclude, for the present, my remarks relative to the harvest and the price of corn. It is the great subject of the day. As to the infamous London press, the moment the wheat comes down to forty shillings; that is to say, an average

Government Return of forty shillings, I will spend ten pounds in placarding this infamous press, after the manner in which we used to placard the base and detestable enemies of the QUEEN.[7]

RURAL RIDE: FROM KENSINGTON, ACROSS SURREY, AND ALONG THAT COUNTY.

Reigate, Thursday Evening,
20th October 1825.[1]

Having done my business at Hartswood to-day about eleven o'clock, I went to a sale at a farm, which the farmer is quitting. Here I had a view of what has long been going on all over the country. The farm, which belongs to *Christ's Hospital*, has been held by a man of the name of Charington, in whose family the lease has been, I hear, a great number of years. The house is hidden by trees. It stands in the Weald of Surrey, close by the *River Mole*, which is here a mere rivulet, though just below this house the rivulet supplies the very prettiest flour-mill I ever saw in my life.

Everything about this farm-house was formerly the scene of *plain manners* and *plentiful living*. Oak clothes-chests, oak bedsteads, oak chests of drawers, and oak tables to eat on, long, strong, and well supplied with joint stools. Some of the things were many hundreds of years old. But all appeared to be in a state of decay and nearly of *disuse*. There appeared to have been hardly any *family* in that house, where formerly there were, in all probability, from ten to fifteen men, boys, and maids: and, which was the worst of all, there was a *parlour*. Aye, and a *carpet* and *bell-pull* too! One end of the front of this once plain and substantial house had been moulded into a *"parlour;"* and there was the mahogany table, and the fine chairs, and the fine glass, and all as bare-faced upstart, as any stock-jobber in the kingdom can boast of. And, there were the decanters, the glasses, the "dinner-set" of crockery-ware, and all just in the true stock-jobber style. And I daresay it has been *'Squire* Charington and the *Miss* Charingtons; and not plain Master Charington, and his son Hodge, and his daughter Betty Charington, all of whom this accursed system has, in all likelihood, transmuted into a species of mock gentlefolks, while it has ground the labourers down into real slaves. Why do not farmers now *feed* and *lodge* their work-people, as they did formerly? Because they cannot keep them *upon so little* as they give them in wages. This is the real cause of the change. There needs no more to prove that the lot of the working classes, has become worse than it formerly was. This fact alone is quite sufficient to settle this point. All the world

---

[7] Cobbett had been an ardent supporter of Queen Caroline when her husband George IV refused to give her proper recognition. Cobbett had in fact drafted her Letter of Remonstrance to the king.

[1] There were no Rural Rides in 1824. On this one Cobbett was accompanied by his youngest son, Richard (1814–75).

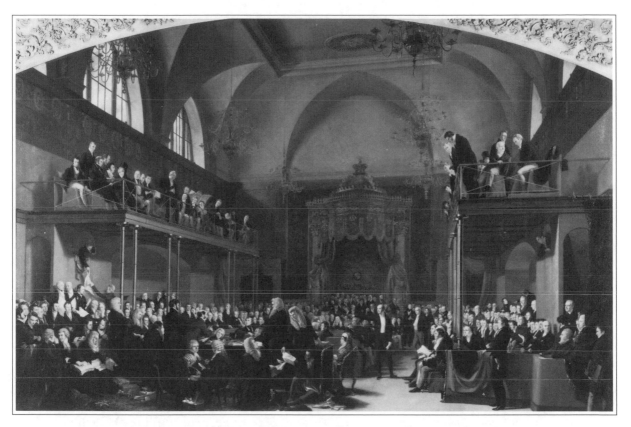

Queen Caroline being tried for adultery in the House of Lords, 1820. Lord Brougham's brilliant defence and the overwhelming support Caroline had from the public caused the Divorce Bill to be abandoned. She fully assumed the rank of royalty but was refused coronation.

knows, that a number of people, boarded in the same house, and at the same table, can, with as good food, be boarded much cheaper than those persons divided into twos, threes, or fours, can be boarded. This is a well-known truth: therefore, if the farmer now shuts his pantry against his labourers, and pays them wholly in money, is it not clear, that he does it because he thereby gives them a living, *cheaper* to him; that is to say, a *worse* living than formerly? Mind, he has *a house* for them; a kitchen for them to sit in, bedrooms for them to sleep in, tables, and stools, and benches, of everlasting duration. All these he has: all these *cost him nothing;* and yet so much does he gain by pinching them in wages, that he lets all these things remain as of no use, rather than feed labourers in the house. Judge, then, of the *change* that has taken place in the condition of these labourers! And, be astonished, if you can, at the *pauperism* and the *crimes* that now disgrace this once happy and moral England.

The land produces, on an average, what it always produced; but, there is a new distribution of the produce. This 'Squire Charington's father used, I dare say, to sit at the head of the oak-table along with his men, say grace to them, and cut up the meat and the pudding. He might take a cup of *strong beer* to himself, when they had none; but, that was pretty nearly all the difference in their manner of living. So that *all* lived well. But, the *'Squire* had many *wine-decanters and wine-glasses* and "a *dinner set*" and a "*breakfast set*," and "*desert knives;*" and these evidently imply carryings on and a consumption, that must of necessity have greatly robbed the long oak table, if it had remained fully tenanted. That long table could not share in the work of the decanters and the dinner set. Therefore, it became almost untenanted; the labourers retreated to hovels, called cottages; and, instead of board and lodging, they got money; so little of it as to enable the employer to drink wine; but, then, that he might not reduce them to *quite starvation*, they were enabled to come to him, in the *king's name*, and demand food *as paupers*. And, now, mind, that which a man receives in the *king's name*, he knows well he has *by force;* and it is not in nature that he should *thank* anybody for it, and least of all the party *from whom it is forced*. Then, if this sort of force be insufficient to obtain him enough to eat and to keep him warm, is it surprising, if he think it no great offence against God (who created no man to starve) to use another sort of FORCE more within his own control? Is it, in short, surprising, if he resort to *theft* and *robbery?*

This is not only the *natural* progress, but it *has been* the progress in England. The blame is not justly imputed to 'Squire Charington and his like: the blame belongs to the infernal stock-jobbing system. There was no reason to expect, that farmers would not endeavour to keep pace, in point of show and luxury, with fund-holders, and with all the tribes that *war* and *taxes* created. Farmers were not the authors of the mischief; and *now* they are compelled to shut the labourers out of their houses, and to pinch them in their wages in order to be able to pay their own taxes; and, besides this, the manners and the principles of the working class are so changed, that a sort of self-preservation, bids the farmer (especially in some counties) to keep them from beneath his roof.

I could not quit this farm house without reflecting on the thousands of scores of bacon, and thousand of bushels of bread, that had been eaten from the long oak-table which, I said to myself, is now perhaps, going at last, to the bottom of a bridge that some stock-jobber will stick up over an artificial river in his cockney garden. "*By —— it shant,*" said I, almost in a real passion: and so I requested a friend to buy it for me; and if he do so, I will take it to Kensington, or to Fleet-street, and keep it for the good it has done in the world.

When the old farm-houses are down (and down they must come in time) what a miserable thing the country will be! Those that are now erected are mere painted shells, with a Mistress within, who is stuck up in a place she calls a *parlour*, with, if she have children, the "young ladies and gentlemen" about her: some showy chairs and a sofa (a *sofa* by all means): half a dozen prints in gilt frames hanging up: some swinging book-shelves with novels and tracts upon them: a dinner brought in by a girl that is perhaps better "educated" than she: two or three nick-nacks to eat instead of a piece of bacon and a pudding: the house too neat for a dirty-shoed carter to be allowed to come into; and everything proclaiming to every sensible beholder, that there is here a constant anxiety to make a *show* not warranted by the reality. The children (which is the worst part of it) are all too clever to *work*: they are all to be *gentlefolks*. Go to plough! Good G——! What, "young gentlemen" go to plough! They become *clerks*, or some skimmy-dish thing or other. They flee from the dirty *work*, as cunning horses do from the bridle. What misery is all this! What a mass of materials for producing that general and *dreadful convulsion* that must, first or last, come and blow this funding and jobbing and enslaving and starving system to atoms!

Chilworth, Friday Evening,
21st Oct.

It has been very fine to-day. Yesterday morning there was *snow* on Reigate Hill, enough to look white from where we were in the valley. We set off about half-past one o'clock, and came all down the valley, through Buckland, Betchworth, Dorking, Sheer and Aldbury, to this place. Very few prettier rides in England, and the weather beautifully fine.

To-morrow we intend to move on towards the West; to take a look, just a look, at the Hampshire Parsons again. The turnips seem fine; but they cannot be large. All other things are very fine indeed. Every thing seems to prognosticate a hard winter. All the country people say that it will be so.

RIDE: FROM CHILWORTH, IN SURREY, TO WINCHESTER.

Thursley, four miles from
Godalming, Surrey,
Sunday Evening, 23rd October, 1825.

We set out from Chilworth to-day about noon.

We did not go to Guildford, nor did we cross the *River Wey*, to come through Godalming; but bore away to our left, and came through the village of Hambledon, going first to Hascomb, to show Richard the South Downs from that high land, which looks Southward over the *Wealds* of Surrey and Sussex, with all their fine and innumerable oak trees. Those that travel on turnpike roads know nothing of England.—From Hascomb to Thursley almost the whole way is across fields, or commons, or along narrow lands. Here we see the people without any disguise or affectation. Against a *great road* things are made for *show*. Here we see them *without any show*. And here we gain real knowledge as to their situation.

Thursley, Wednesday, 26th Oct.

Being out a-coursing to-day, I saw a queer-looking building upon one of the thousands of hills that nature has tossed up in endless variety of form round the skirts of the lofty Hindhead. This building is, it seems, called a *Semaphore*, or *Semiphare*, or something of that sort. What this word may have been hatched out of I cannot say; but it means *a job*, I am sure.[1] To call it an *alarm-post* would not have been so convenient; for, people not endued with Scotch *intellect*, might have wondered why the d— we should have to pay for alarm-posts; and might have thought, that, with all our "glorious victories," we had "brought our hogs to a fine market," if our dread of the enemy were such as to induce us to have alarm-posts all over the country! Such unintellectual people might have thought that we had "conquered France by the immortal Wellington," to little purpose, if we were still in such fear as to build alarm-posts; and they might, in addition, have observed, that, for many hundred of years, England stood in need of neither signal posts nor standing army of mercenaries; but relied safely on the courage and public spirit of the people themselves. By calling the thing by an outlandish name, these reflections amongst the unintellectual are obviated. *Alarm-post* would be a nasty name; and it would puzzle people exceedingly, when they saw one of these at a place like Ashe, a little village on the north side of the chalk-ridge (called the Hog's Back) going from Guildford to Farnham! What can this be *for*? Why are these expensive things put up all over the country? Respecting the movements of *whom* is wanted this *alarm-system*? Will no member ask this in Parliament? Not one! not

---

[1] The semaphore, begun 1816, consisted of wooden arms on high towers, five to ten miles apart, from Greenwich via the Admiralty to Portsmouth. The time-signal could be sent from Greenwich to Portsmouth and acknowledged within 45 seconds. Its installation was not necessarily a "job" in the pejorative sense.

a man: and yet it is a thing to ask about. Ah! it is in vain, THING, that you thus are *making your preparations;* in vain that you are setting your trammels! The DEBT, the blessed debt, that best ally of the people, will break them all; will snap them, as the hornet does the cob-web; and, even these very "Semaphores," contribute towards the force of that ever-blessed debt.

Farnham, Surrey,
Thursday, Oct. 27th.

We came hither by the way of Waverley Abbey and Moore Park. On the commons I showed Richard some of my old hunting scenes, when I was of his age, or younger, reminding him that I was obliged to hunt on foot. We got leave to go and see the grounds at Waverley, where all the old monks' garden walls are totally gone, and where the spot is become a sort of lawn. I showed him the spot where the strawberry garden was, and where I, when sent to gather *hautboys,* used to eat every remarkably fine one, instead of letting it go to be eaten by Sir Robert Rich.[2] I showed him a tree, close by the ruins of the Abbey, from a limb of which I once fell into the river, in an attempt to take the nest of a *crow,* which had artfully placed it upon a branch so far from the trunk, as not to be able to bear the weight of a boy eight years old. I showed him an old elm tree, which was hollow even then, into which I, when a very little boy, once saw a cat go, that was as big as a middle-sized spaniel dog, for relating which I got a great scolding, for standing to which I, at last got a beating; but stand to which I still did. I found the ruins not very greatly diminished; but, it is strange how small the mansion, and ground, and everything but the trees, appeared to me. They were all great to my mind when I saw them last; and that early impression had remained, whenever I had talked or thought of the spot; so that, when I came to see them again, after seeing the sea and so many other immense things, it seemed as if they had all been made small. This was not the case with regard to the trees, which are nearly as big here as they are any where else; and, the old cat-elm, for instance, which Richard measured with his whip, is about 16 or 17 feet round.

From Waverley we went to Moore Park, once the seat of Sir William Temple, and, when I was a very little boy, the seat of a Lady, or a Mrs. Temple. Here I showed Richard Mother Ludlum's Hole; but, alas! it is not the enchanting place that I knew it, nor that which Grose describes in his Antiquities![3] The semicircular paling is gone; the basins, to catch the never-ceasing little stream, are gone; the iron cups, fastened by chains, for people to drink out of, are gone; the pavement all broken to pieces; the seats, for people to sit on, on both sides of the cave, torn up, and gone; the stream that ran down a clean paved channel, now making a dirty

---

[2] Sir Robert Rich (1714–85), General, wounded at Culloden. Owner of Waverley Abbey during Cobbett's boyhood.
[3] Francis Grose (1731–91), *Richmond Herald,* published his *Antiquities of England and Wales,* 1773–87.

Mother Ludlum's Hole at Moore Park in Surrey, by S. H. Grimm.

gutter; and the ground opposite, which was a grove, chiefly of laurels, intersected by closely-mowed grass-walks, now become a poor, ragged-looking alder-coppice. Near the mansion, I showed Richard the hill, upon which Dean Swift tells us, he used to run for exercise, while he was pursuing his studies here;[4] and I would have showed him the garden-seat, under which Sir William Temple's heart was buried, agreeably to his will; but, the seat was gone, also the wall at the back of it; and the exquisitely beautiful little lawn in which the seat stood, was turned into a parcel of divers-shaped cockney-clumps, planted according to the strictest rules of artificial and refined vulgarity.

At Waverley, Mr. Thompson, a merchant of some sort, has succeeded (after the monks) the Orby Hunters and Sir Robert Rich. At Moore Park, a Mr. Laing, a West India planter or merchant, has succeeded the Temples; and at the castle of Farnham, which you see from Moore Park, Bishop Prettyman Tomline, has, at last, after perfectly regular and due gradations, succeeded William of Wykham![5] In coming up from Moore Park to Farnham town, I stopped opposite the door of a little old house, where there appeared to be a great parcel of children. ''There, Dick,'' said I, ''when I was just a little creature as that, whom you see in the door-

---

[4] Swift was secretary to Sir William Temple at Moor Park 1692–4.
[5] Sir George Pretyman-Tomline (1750–1827), Bishop of Winchester 1820–27, owed his ecclesiastical preferments to having been tutor, secretary and political adviser to the younger Pitt—hence Cobbett's sarcasm.

A view of Winchester Cathedral.

way, I lived in this very house with my grand-mother Cobbett." He pulled up his horse, and looked *very hard at it*, but said nothing, and on we came.

Winchester,
Sunday noon, Oct. 30.

This being Sunday, I heard, about 7 o'clock in the morning, a sort of a jangling, made by a bell or two in the *Cathedral*. We were getting ready to be off, to cross the country to Burghclere, which lies under the lofty hills at Highclere, about 22 miles from this city; but hearing the bells of the cathedral, I took Richard to show him that ancient and most magnificent pile, and particularly to show him the tomb of that famous bishop of Winchester, William of Wykham; who was the Chancellor and the Minister of the great and glorious King Edward III.; who sprang from poor parents in the little village of Wykham, three miles from Botley; and who, amongst other great and most munificent deeds, founded the famous College, or School, of Winchester, and also one of the Colleges at Oxford.[6] I told Richard about this as we went from the inn down to the cathedral; and when I showed *him the tomb* where the bishop lies on his back, in his Catholic robes, with his mitre on his head, his shepherd's crook by his side, with little children at his feet, their hands put together in a praying attitude, he looked with a degree of inquisitive earnestness that pleased me very much.

---

[6] New College, founded 1379.

RURAL RIDE: FROM WINCHESTER TO BURGHCLERE.

Burghclere, Monday Morning,
31st October, 1825.

We had, or I had, resolved not to breakfast at Winchester yesterday: and yet we were detained till nearly noon. But, at last off we came, *fasting*. The turnpike road from Winchester to this place comes through a village, called Sutton Scotney, and then through Whitchurch, which lies on the Andover and London road, through Basingstoke. We did not take the cross-turnpike till we came to Whitchurch. We went to King's Worthy; that is, about two miles on the road from Winchester to London; and then, turning short to our left, came up upon the downs to the north of Winchester race-course. Here, looking back at the city and at the fine valley above and below it, and at the many smaller valleys that run down from the high ridges into that great and fertile valley, I could not help admiring the taste of the ancient kings, who made this city (which once covered all the hill round about, and which contained 92 churches and chapels) a chief place of their residence. There are not many finer spots in England; and if I were to take in a circle of eight or ten miles of semi-diameter, I should say that I believe there is not one so fine.

After steering for some time, we came down to a very fine farm-house, which we stopped a little to admire; and I asked Richard whether *that* was not a place to be happy in. The village, which we found to be Stoke-Charity, was about a mile lower down this little vale. Before we got to it, we overtook the owner of the farm, who knew me, though I did not know him; but, when I found it was Mr. Hinton Bailey, of whom and whose farm I had heard so much, I was not at all surprised at the fineness of what I had just seen. I told him that the word *charity*, making, as it did, part of the name of this place, had nearly inspired me with boldness enough to go to the farm-house, in the ancient style, and ask for something to eat; for, that we had not yet breakfasted. He asked us to go back; but, at Burghclere we were *resolved to dine*. After, however, crossing the village, and beginning again to ascend the downs, we came to a labourer's (*once a farm house*), where I asked the man, whether he had any *bread and cheese*, and was not a little pleased to hear him say "*Yes.*" Then I asked him to give us a bit, protesting that we had not yet broken our fast. He answered in the affirmative, at once, though I did not talk of payment. His wife brought out the cut loaf, and a piece of Wiltshire cheese, and I took them in hand, gave Richard a good hunch, and took another for myself. I verily believe, that all the pleasure of eating enjoyed by all the feeders in London in a whole year, does not equal that which we enjoyed in gnawing this bread and cheese, as we rode over this old down, whip and bridle-reins in one hand, and the hunch in the other. Richard, who was purse bearer, gave the woman, by my direction, about enough to buy two quartern loaves: for she told me, that they had to buy their bread *at the mill*, not being able to bake themselves for *want of fuel;* and this, as I said before, is one of the draw-backs in this sort of country. I wish every one of these people had an *American fire-place*. Here they might, then, even in these bare countries have comfortable warmth. Rubbish of any sort would, by this means, give them warmth. I am now, at six o'clock in the morning, sitting in a room, where one of these fire-places, with very light *turf* in it, gives as good and steady a warmth as it is possible to feel, and which room has, too, been *cured of smoking* by this fire-place.

Before we got this supply of bread and cheese, we, though in ordinary times a couple of singularly jovial companions, and seldom going a hundred yards (except going very fast) without one or the other speaking, began to grow *dull* or rather *glum*. The way seemed long; and, when I had to speak in answer to Richard, the speaking was as brief as might be. Unfortunately, just at this critical period, one of the loops that held the straps of Richard's little portmanteau broke; and it became necessary (just before we overtook Mr. Bailey) for me to fasten the portmanteau on before me, upon my saddle. This, which was not the work of more than five minutes, would, had I had *a breakfast*, have been nothing at all, and, indeed, matter of laughter. But, *now*, it was *something*. It was his *"fault"* for capering and jerking about *"so."* I jumped off, saying, *"Here!* I'll carry it *myself."* And then I began to take off the remaining strap, pulling, with great violence and in great haste. Just at this time, my eyes met his, in which I saw *great surprise;* and, feeling the just rebuke, feeling heartily ashamed of myself, I instantly changed my tone and manner, cast the blame upon the saddler, and talked of the effectual means which we would take to prevent the like in future.

Now, if such was the effect produced upon me by the want of food for only two or three hours; me, who had dined well the day before and eaten toast and butter the over-night; if the missing of only one breakfast, and that, too, from my own whim, while I had money in my pocket, to get one at any public-house; and while I could get one only for asking for at any farm-house; if the not having breakfasted could, and under such circumstances, make me what you call *"cross"* to a child like this, whom I must necessarily love so much, and to whom I never speak but in the very kindest manner; if this mere absence of a breakfast could thus put me *out of temper*, how great are the allowances that we ought to make for the poor creatures, who, in this once happy and now miserable country, are doomed to lead a life of constant labour and of half-starvation. I suppose, that, as we rode away from the cottage, we gnawed up, between us, a pound of bread and a quarter of a pound of cheese. Here was about *five-pence* worth at present prices. Even this, which was only a mere *snap*, a mere *stay-stomach*, for us, would, for us two, come to 3*s.* a week all but a penny. How, then, gracious God! is a labouring man, his wife, and, perhaps, four or five small children, to exist upon 8s. or 9s. a week! Aye, and to find house-rent, clothing, bedding and fuel out of it? Richard and I ate here, at this snap, more, and much more, than the average of labourers, their wives and children, have to eat in a whole day, and that the labourer has to *work* on too!

When we got here to Burghclere, we were again as *hungry* as hunters. What, then, must be the life of these poor creatures? But is not the state of the country, is not the curse of the system, all depicted in this one disgraceful and damning fact, that the magistrates, who settle on what the *labouring poor* ought to have to live on, ALLOW THEM LESS THAN IS ALLOWED TO FELONS IN THE GAOLS, and allow them *nothing for clothing and fuel, and house rent!* And yet, while this is notoriously the case while the main body of the working class in England are fed and clad and even lodged worse than felons, and are daily becoming even worse and worse off, the King is advised to tell the Parliament, and the world, that we are in a state of *unexampled prosperity*, and that this prosperity must be *permanent*, because *all the* GREAT *interests are prospering!* THE WORKING PEOPLE ARE NOT, THEN, "A *GREAT* INTEREST!" THEY WILL BE FOUND TO BE ONE, BY-AND-BY. What is to be the *end* of this? What can be the *end* of it, but dreadful convulsion? What other can be produced by a system, which allows the *felon* better food, better clothing, and better lodging than the *honest labourer?*

Burgclere,
Sunday Morning, 6th November.

It has been fine all the week, until to-day, when we intended to set off for Hurstburn-Tarrant, vulgarly called Uphusband, but the rain seems as if it would stop us.

This rain has given me time to look at the newspapers of about a week old. The wise men of the newspapers are for a repeal of the *Corn Laws*. With all my heart. I will join any body in a petition for their repeal. But, this will not be done.[1] We shall stop short of this extent of "liberality," let what may be the consequence to the manufacturers. The Cotton Lords must all go, to the last man, rather than a repeal of these laws take place: and of this the newspaper wise men may be assured. The farmers can but just rub along now, with all their high prices and low wages. What would be their state, and that of their landlords, if the wheat were to come down again to 4, 5, or even 6 shillings a bushel? Universal agricultural bankruptcy would be the almost instant consequence. Many of them are now deep in debt from the effects of 1820, 1821, and 1822. One more year like 1822 would have broken the whole mass up, and left the lands to be cultivated, under the overseers, for the benefit of the paupers. Society would have been nearly dissolved, and the state of nature would have returned. The Small-Note Bill, co-operating with the Corn Laws, have given a respite, and nothing more. This Bill must remain *efficient*, paper-money must cover the country, and the corn-laws must remain in force; or an "equitable adjustment" must take place; or, to a state of nature this country must return. What, then, as *I want* a repeal of the corn-laws, and also *want* to get rid of the paper-money, I must want to see this return to a state of nature? By no means. I want the "equitable adjustment," and I am quite sure, that no adjustment can be *equitable*, which does not apply *every penny's worth of public property* to the payment of the fund-holders and dead-weight and the like. Clearly just and reasonable as this is, however, the very mention of it makes the

[1] It was not done until 1846.

124

FIRE-SHOVELS,[2] and some others, half-mad. It makes them storm and rant and swear like Bedlamites. But it is curious to hear them talk of the impracticability of it; when they all know that, by only two or three Acts of Parliament, Henry VIII. did ten times as much as it would now, I hope, be necessary to do. If the duty were imposed *on me*, no statesman, legislator or lawyer, but a simple citizen, I think I could, in less than twenty-four hours, draw up an Act, that would give satisfaction to, I will not say *every man;* but to, at least, ninety-nine out of every hundred; an Act that would put all affairs of money and of religion to rights at once; but that would, I must confess, soon take from us that amiable *modesty,* of which I have spoken above, and which is so conspicuously shown in our works of free trade and liberality.

The weather is clearing up; our horses are saddled, and we are off.

RIDE, FROM BURGHCLERE TO PETERSFIELD.

Hurstbourne Tarrant (or Uphusband),
Monday, 7th November, 1825.

It is about six miles from Burghclere to this place; and, we made it about twelve; not in order to avoid the turnpike-road; but, because we do not ride about to *see* turnpike-roads; and, moreover, because I had seen this most monstrously hilly turnpike-road before. We came through a village called Woodcote, and another, called Binley. I never saw any inhabited places more recluse than these. Yet into these, the all-searching eye of the taxing Thing reaches. Its Exciseman can tell it, what is doing even in the little odd corner of Binley; for even there I saw, over the door of a place, not half so good as the place in which my fowls roost, *"Licensed to deal in tea and tobacco."* Poor, half-starved wretches of Binley! The hand of taxation, the collection for the sinecures and pensions, must fix its nails even in them, who really appeared too miserable to be called by the name of *people.* Yet there was one whom the taxing Thing had licensed (good God! *licensed!*) to serve out cat-lap[1] to these wretched creatures! And, our impudent and ignorant newspaper scribes, talk of the *degraded state of the people of Spain!* Impudent imposters! Can they show a group so wretched, so miserable, so truly enslaved as this, in all Spain? These poor creatures that I behold here, *pass their lives amidst flocks of sheep;* but, never does a morsel of mutton enter their lips. A labouring man told me, at Binley, that he had not tasted meat since harvest; and his looks vouched for the statement. Old Fortescue[2] says that "the English are clothed in good

---

[2] Cobbett's term for Anglican parsons.
[1] Cobbett's term for tea.
[2] Sir John Fortescue (1394–1476), Lord Chief Justice, whose book *De Laudibus Legum Angliae* Cobbett much admired.

woollens throughout," and they have "plenty of flesh of all sorts to eat." Yes; but at this time, the nation was not mortgaged. The "enlightening" Patriots would have made Spain what England now is. The people must never more, after a few years, have tasted mutton, though living surrounded with flocks of sheep.

Easton, near Winchester,
Wednesday Evening, 9th Nov.

I had been three times at Uphusband before, and had, as my readers will, perhaps, recollect, described the bourn here, or the *brook*. It has, in general, no water at all in it, from August to March. There is the bed of a little river; but no water. In March, or thereabouts, the water begins to boil up, in thousands upon thousands of places, in the little narrow meadows, just above the village; that is to say a little higher up the valley. When the chalk hills are full; when the chalk will hold no more water; then it comes out at the lowest spots near these immense hills and becomes a rivulet first, and then a river. But, until this visit to Uphusband (or Hurstbourn Tarrant, as the map calls it), little did I imagine, that this rivulet, dry half the year, was the head of the river Teste, which, after passing through Stockbridge and Romsey, falls into the sea near Southampton.

Petersfield, Friday Evening,
11th November.

Before we got to Petersfield, we called at an old friend's and got some bread and cheese and small beer, which we preferred to strong. In approaching Petersfield we began to descend from the high chalk-country, which (with the exception of the valleys of the Itchen and the Teste) had lasted us from Uphusband (almost the north-west point of the country) to this place, which is not far from the south-east point of it. Here we quit flint and chalk and downs, and take to sand, clay, hedges, and coppices; and here, on the verge of Hampshire, we begin again to see those endless little bubble-formed hills that we before saw round the foot of Hindhead. We have got in in very good time, and got, at the Dolphin, good stabling for our horses. The waiters and people at inns *look so hard at us* to see us so liberal as to horse-feed, fire, candle, beds, and room, while we are so very very sparing in the article of *drink!* They seem to pity our taste. I hear people complain of the "exhorbitant charges" at inns; but, my wonder always is, how the people can live with charging so little. Except in one single instance, I have uniformly, since I have been from home, thought the charges too low for people to live by.

This long evening has given me time to look at the *Star* newspaper of last night; and I see, that, with all possible desire to disguise the fact, there is a great "*panic*" brewing. It is impossible that this thing can go on, in its present way, for any length of time. The talk about "speculations;" that is to say, "adventurous dealings," or rather, commercial gamblings; the talk about *these* having been the cause of the breakings and the other symptoms of approaching convulsion, is the most miserable nonsense that ever was conceived in the heads of idiots. These are *effect;* not *cause.* The cause is the *Small-note Bill,* that last brilliant effort of the joint mind of Van[3] and Castlereagh.[4] That Bill was, as I always called it, *a respite;* and it was, and could be, nothing more. It could only put off the evil hour; it could not prevent the final arrival of that hour. To have proceeded with Peel's Bill was, indeed, to produce total convulsion. The land must have been surrendered to the overseers for the use of the poor. That is to say, without an "Equitable Adjustment." But that adjustment, as prayed for by Kent, Norfolk, Hereford, and Surrey, might have taken place; it *ought* to have taken place; and it must, at last, take place, or convulsion must come. As to the *nature* of this "adjustment," is it not most distinctly described in the Norfolk Petition?[5] Is not that memorable petition now in the Journals of the House of Commons? What more is wanted than to act on the prayer of that very petition? Had I to draw up a petition again, I would not change a single word of that. It pleased Mr. Brougham's "best public instructor" to abuse that petition, and it pleased Daddy Coke and the Hickory Quaker, Gurney, and the wise barn orator, to calumniate its author.[6] They succeeded; but, their success was but shame to them; and that author is yet destined to triumph over them. I have seen no London paper for ten days, until to-day; and I should not have seen this, if the waiter had not forced it upon me. I know *very nearly* what will happen by *next May,* or thereabouts; and, as to the manner in which things will work in the meanwhile, it is of far less consequence to the nation, than it is what sort of weather I shall have to ride in tomorrow. One thing, however, I wish to observe, and that is, that, if any attempt be made to repeal the *Corn-Bill,* the main body of the farmers will be crushed into total ruin. I come into *contact* with few, who are not gentlemen, or very substantial farmers: but, I know the state of the *whole;* and I know, that, even with present prices, and with *honest labourers fed worse than felons,* it is *rub-and-go* with nineteen twentieths of the farmers; and of this fact I beseech the ministers to be well aware. And with this fact staring them in the face! with that other horrid fact, that, by the regulations of the *magistrates,* (who cannot avoid it, mind,) the honest labourer is fed worse than the convicted felon; with the breakings of merchants, so ruinous to confiding foreigners, so disgraceful to the name of England; with the thousands of industrious and care-taking creatures reduced to beggary by bank-paper; with panic upon panic, plunging thousands upon thousands into despair: with all this notorious as the

---

[3] Sir Nicholas Vansittart, Chancellor of the Exchequer 1812–23, responsible for the economic measures of 1819, so much reviled by Cobbett. The Small-note Bill (1822) permitted the use of one-pound paper notes.

[4] Robert Stewart, Viscount Castlereagh (1769–1822), best known for foreign policy but opposed resumption of cash payments in 1819.

[5] Petition adopted at Norwich in 1823 demanding the application of Church property and Crown lands to liquidation of the National Debt, reduction of the standing army and the abolition of all sinecures.

[6] Viz. Thomas William Coke ("Coke of Norfolk") of Holkham (1752–1842), agricultural reformer. "The Hickory Quaker" was Hudson Gurney (1775–1854), politician and antiquary. "The barn orator" was Edmund Wodehouse (1784–1855), M.P. for Norfolk, advocate of the "equitable adjustment of contracts", a phrase often ridiculed by Cobbett.

sun at noon-day, will they again advise their Royal Master to tell the Parliament and the world, that this country is "in a state of unequalled prosperity," and that this prosperity "must be permanent, because *all* the great interests are *flourishing?*" Let them! That will not alter the *result*. I had been, for several weeks, saying, that the *seeming prosperity* was *fallacious;* that the cause of it must lead to *ultimate* and shocking ruin; that it could not last, because it arose from causes so manifestly *fictitious;* that, in short, it was the fair-looking, but poisonous, fruit of a miserable expedient. I had been saying this for several weeks, when, out came the King's Speech, and gave me and my doctrines the *lie direct*, as to every point. Well: now, then, we shall *soon see*.

———

RURAL RIDE: FROM PETERSFIELD TO KENSINGTON.

Petworth, Saturday, 12th Nov. 1825.

We came this morning from Petersfield, with an intention to cross to Horsham, and go thence to Worth, and then into Kent; but Richard's horse seemed not to be fit for so strong a bout, and therefore we resolved to bend our course homewards, and first of all, to fall back upon our resources at Thursley, which we intend to reach to-morrow, going through North Chapel, Chiddingfold, and Brook.

At about four miles from Petersfield, we passed through a village, called Rogate. Just before we came to it, I asked a man who was hedging on the side of the road, how much he got a day. He said, 1*s.* 6*d.*: and he told me that the *allowed* wages was 7*d.* a day for the man *and a gallon loaf a week for the rest of his family;* that is to say, one pound and two and a quarter ounces of bread for each of them; and nothing more! And this, observe, is one-third short of the bread allowance of gaols, to say nothing of the meat and clothing and lodging of the inhabitants of gaols. If the man have full work; if he get his eighteen-pence a day, the whole nine shillings does not purchase a gallon loaf each for a wife and three children, and two gallon loaves for himself. In the gaols, the convicted felons have a pound and a half each of bread a day to begin with: they have some meat generally, and it has been found absolutely necessary to allow them meat when they work at the tread-mill. It is impossible to make them work at the tread-mill without it. However, let us take the bare allowance of bread allowed in the gaols. This allowance is, for five people, fifty-two pounds and a half in the week; whereas, the man's nine shillings will buy but fifty-two pounds of bread; and this, observe, is a vast deal better than the state of things in the north of Hampshire, where the day-labourer gets but eight shillings a week. I asked this man how much a day they gave to a young able man who had no family, and who was compelled to come to the parish-officers for work. Observe, that there are a great many young men in this situation, because the farmers will not employ single men *at full wages*, these full wages being wanted for the married man's family, just to keep them alive according to the calculation that we have just seen. About the borders of the north of Hampshire, they give to these single men two gallon loaves a week, or, in money, two shillings and eight-pence, and nothing more. Here, in this part of Sussex, they give the single man seven-pence a day, that is to say, enough to buy two pounds and a quarter of bread for six days in the week, and as he does not work on the Sunday, there is no seven-pence allowed for the Sunday, and of course nothing to eat: and this is the allowance, settled by the magistrates, for a young, hearty, labouring man; and that, too, in the part of England where, I believe, they live better than in any other part of it. The poor creature here has seven-pence a day for six days in the week to find him food, clothes, washing, and lodging! It is just seven-pence, less than one half of what the meanest foot soldier in the standing army receives; besides that the latter has clothing, candle, fire, and lodging into the bargain! Well may we call our happy state of things the "envy of surrounding nations, and the admiration of the world!" We hear of the efforts of Mrs. Fry, Mr. Buxton,[1] and numerous other persons, to improve the situation of felons in the gaols; but never, no never, do we catch them ejaculating one single pious sigh for these innumerable sufferers, who are doomed to become felons or to waste away their bodies by hunger.

When we came into the village of Rogate, I saw a little group of persons standing before a blacksmith's shop. The church-yard was on the other side of the road, surrounded by a low wall. The earth of the church-yard was about four feet and a half higher than the common level of the ground round about it; and you may see, by the nearness of the church windows to the ground, that this bed of earth has been made by the innumerable burials that have taken place in it. The group, consisting of the blacksmith, the wheelwright, perhaps, and three or four others, appeared to me to be in a deliberative mood. So I said, looking significantly at the church-yard, "It has taken a pretty many thousands of your fore-fathers to raise that ground up so high." "Yes, Sir," said one of them. "And," said I, "for about nine hundred years those who built that church thought about religion very differently from what we do." "Yes," said another. "And," said I, "do you think that all those who made that heap there are gone to the devil?" I got no answer to this. "At any rate," added I, "they never worked for a pound and a half of bread a day." They looked hard at me, and then looked hard at one another; and I, having trotted off, looked round at the first turning, and saw them looking after us still. I should suppose that the church was built about seven or eight hundred years ago, that is to say, the present church; for the first church built upon this spot was, I daresay, erected more than a thousand years ago. If I had had time, I should have told this group, that, before the Protestant Reformation, the labourers of Rogate received four-pence a day from Michaelmas to Lady-day; five-pence a day from Lady-day to Michaelmas, except in harvest and grass-mowing time, when able labourers had seven-pence a day; and that, at this time, bacon was *not so much as a*

---

[1] Mrs Elizabeth Fry (née Gurney) (1780–1845) and Sir Thomas Fowell Buxton (1786–1845), prison reformers.

halfpenny a pound: and, moreover, that the parson of the parish maintained out of the tithes all those persons in the parish that were reduced to indigence by means of old age or other cause of inability to labour.[2]

We got to Petworth pretty early in the day. On entering it you see the house of Lord Egremont,[3] which is close up against the park-wall, and which wall bounds this little vale on two sides. There is a sort of a town hall here, and on one side of it there is the bust of Charles the Second, I should have thought; but they tell me it is that of Sir William Wyndham, from whom Lord Egremont is descended. But there is *another building* much more capacious and magnificent than the town hall; namely, the Bridewell, which from the modernness of its structure, appears to be one of those "wauste improvements, Ma'am," which distinguish this *enlightened* age. This structure vies, in point of magnitude, with the house of Lord Egremont itself, though that is one of the largest mansions in the whole kingdom. The Bridewell has a wall round it that I should suppose to be twenty feet high. This place was not wanted, when the labourer got twice as much, instead of half as much as the common standing soldier. Here you see the true cause why the young labouring man is "*content,*" to exist upon 7*d.* a day, for six days in the week, and nothing for Sunday. Oh! we are a most free and enlightened people; our happy constitution in Church and state has supplanted Popery and slavery; but we go to a Bridewell unless we quietly exist and work upon 7*d.* a day!

Thursley,
Sunday, 13th Nov.

North Chapel is a little town in the Weald of Sussex, where there were formerly post-chaises kept; but where there are none kept now. And here is another complete revolution. In almost every country town the post-chaise houses have been lessened in number, and those that remain have become comparatively solitary and mean. The guests at inns are not now gentlemen, but *bumpers,* who, from being called (at the inns) "riders," became "travellers," and are now "commercial gentlemen," who go about in *gigs,* instead of on horseback, and who are in such numbers as to occupy a great part of the room in all the inns, in every part of the country. There are, probably, twenty thousand of them always out, who may perhaps have, on an average throughout the year, three or four thousand "ladies" travelling with them. The expense of this can be little short of fifteen millions a year, all to be paid by the country-people who consume the goods, and a large part of it to be drawn up to the Wen.

From North Chapel we came to Chiddingfold, which is in the Weald of Surrey; that is to say, the country of oak-timber.

This Chiddingfold is a very pretty place. There is a very pretty and extensive green opposite the church; and we were at the proper time of the day to perceive

---

[2] A characteristically romantic and absurd view of pre-Reformation society.
[3] George O'Brien Wyndham, 3rd Earl (1751–1837), patron of J. M. W. Turner.

130

that the modern system of education had by no means overlooked this little village. We saw *the schools* marching towards the church in military order. Two of them passed us on our road. The boys looked very hard at us, and I saluted them with "There's brave boys, you'll all be parsons or lawyers or doctors." Another school seemed to be in a less happy state. The scholars were too much in uniform, to have had their clothes purchased by their parents; and they looked, besides, as if a little more victuals, and a little less education, would have done as well. There were about twenty of them, without one single tinge of red in their whole twenty faces. In short, I never saw more deplorable-looking objects since I was born. And can it be of any use to expend money in this sort of way upon poor creatures that have not half a bellyful of food? We had not breakfasted when we passed them. We felt, at that moment, what hunger was. We had some bits of bread and meat in our pockets, however; and these, which were merely intended as stay-stomachs, amounted, I dare say, to the allowance of any half dozen of these poor boys for the day. I could, with all my heart, have pulled the victuals out of my pocket and given it to them; but I did not like to do that which would have interrupted the march, and might have been construed into a sort of insult. To quiet my conscience, however, I gave a poor man that I met soon afterwards sixpence, under pretence of rewarding him for telling me the way to Thursley, which I knew as well as he, and which I had determined, in my own mind, not to follow.

The weather being pretty cold we found ourselves most happily situated here by the side of an *American fireplace*, making extremely comfortable a room which was formerly amongst the most uncomfortable in the world. This is another of what the malignant parsons call Cobbett's Quackeries. But my real opinion is that the whole body of them, all put together, have never, since they were born, conferred so much benefit upon the country, as I have conferred upon it by introducing this fire-place. Mr. Judson of Kensington, who is the manufacturer of them, tells me that he has a great demand, which gives me much pleasure; but really, coming to conscience, no man ought to sit by one of these fire-places that does not go the full length with me both in politics and religion. It is not fair for them to enjoy the warmth without subscribing to the doctrines of the giver of the warmth. However, as I have nothing to do with Mr. Judson's affair, either as to the profit or the loss, he must sell the fire-places to whomsoever he pleases.

Kensington,
Sunday, 20th Nov.

Coming to Godalming on Friday, where business kept us that night, we had to experience at the inn the want of our American fire-place. A large and long room to sit in, with a miserable thing called a screen to keep the wind from our backs, with a smoke in the room half an hour after the fire was lighted, we, consuming a full bushel of coals in order to keep us warm, were not half so well off as we should have been in the same room, and without any screen, and with two gallons of coals, if we had our American fire-place. I gave the landlord my advice upon the

131

subject, and he said he would go and look at the fire-place at Mr. Knowles's. That was precisely one of these rooms which stand in absolute need of such a fire-place. It is, I should think, five-and-thirty, or forty feet long, and pretty nearly twenty feet wide. I could sooner dine with a labouring man upon his allowance of bread, such as I have mentioned above, than I would, in winter time, dine in that room upon turbot and sirloin of beef. An American fireplace, with a good fire in it, would make every part of that room pleasant to dine in, in the coldest day in winter. I saw a public-house drinking-room, where the owner has tortured his invention to get a little warmth for his guests, where he fetches his coals in a waggon from a distance of twenty miles or thereabouts, and where he consumes these coals by the bushel, to effect that, which he cannot effect at all, and which he might effect completely with about a fourth part of the coals.

It looked like rain on Saturday morning, we therefore sent our horses on from Godalming to Ripley, and took a post-chaise to convey us after them.

When we got to Ripley, we found the day very fine, and we got upon our horses and rode home to dinner, after an absence of just one month, agreeably to our original intention, having seen a great deal of the country, having had a great deal of sport, and having, I trust, laid in a stock of health for the winter, sufficient to enable us to withstand the suffocation of this smoking and stinking Wen.

But, Richard and I have done something else, besides ride, and hunt, and course, and stare about us, during this month. He was eleven years old last March, and it was now time for him to begin to know something about letters and figures. He has learned to work in the garden, and having been a good deal in the country, knows a great deal about farming affairs. He can ride any thing of a horse, and over any thing that a horse will go over. So expert at hunting, that his first teacher, Mr. Budd,[4] gave the hounds up to his management in the field; but now he begins to talk about nothing but *fox-hunting!* That is a dangerous thing. When he and I went from home, I had business at Reigate. It was a very wet morning, and we went off long before daylight in a post-chaise, intending to have our horses brought after us. He began to talk in anticipation of the sport he was going to have, and was very inquisitive as to the probability of our meeting with fox-hounds, which gave me occasion to address him thus: "Fox-hunting is a very fine thing, and very proper for people to be engaged in, and it is very desirable to be able to ride well and to be in at the death; but that is not ALL; that is not every thing. Any fool can ride a horse, and draw a cover; any groom or any stable-fellow, who is as ignorant as the horse, can do these things; but, all gentlemen that go a fox-hunting [I hope God will forgive me for the lie] are scholars, Richard. It is not the riding, nor the scarlet coats, that make them gentlemen; it is their scholarship." What he thought I do not know; for he sat as mute as a fish, and I could not see his countenance. "So," said I, "you must now begin to learn something; and you must begin with arithmetic."

---

[4] See note 6 on page 23.

Turner's powerful painting of an iron foundry. The effects of the Industrial Revolution on the rural poor were, in the short term, devastating.

One of Rowlandson's cartoons lampooning the over-indulgent clergy, who grow fat at the expense of 'half-starved labourers'.

He had learned from mere play, to read, being first set to work of his own accord, to find out what was said about Thurtell,[5] when all the world was talking and reading about Thurtell. That had induced us to give him Robinson Crusoe; and that had made him a passable reader. Then he had scrawled down letters and words upon paper, and had written letters to me, in the strangest way imaginable. His knowledge of figures he had acquired from the necessity of knowing the several numbers on the barrels of seeds brought from America, and the numbers upon the doors of houses. So that I had pretty nearly a blank sheet of paper to begin upon; and I have always held it to be stupidity in the last degree to attempt to put book-learning into children who are too young to reason with.

I began with a pretty long lecture on the utility of arithmetic; the absolute necessity of it, in order for us to make out our accounts of the trees and seeds that we should have to sell in the winter, and the utter impossibility of our getting paid for our pains unless we were able to make out our accounts, which accounts could not be made out unless we understood something about arithmetic. Having thus made him understand the utility of the thing, and given him a very strong instance in the case of our nursery affairs, I proceeded to explain to him the meaning of the word arithmetic, the power of figures, according to the place they occupied. I then, for it was still dark, taught him to add a few figures together, I naming the figures one after another, while he, at the mention of each new figure, said the amount, and if incorrectly, he was corrected by me. When we had got a sum of about 24, I said now there is another line of figures on the left of this, and therefore you are to put down the 4 and carry 2. "What is *carrying?*" said he. I then explained to him the *why* and the *wherefore* of this, and he perfectly understood me at once. We then did several other little sums; and, by the time we got to Sutton, it becoming daylight, I took a pencil and set him a little sum upon paper, which, after making a mistake or two, he did very well. By the time we got to Reigate he had done several more, and at last, a pretty long one, with very few errors. We had business all day, and thought no more of our scholarship until we went to bed, and then we did, in our post-chaise fashion, a great many lines in arithmetic before we went to sleep. Thus we went on mixing our riding and hunting with our arithmetic, until we quitted Godalming, when he did a sum very nicely in *multiplication of money*, falling a little short of what I had laid out, which was to make him learn the four rules in whole numbers first, and then in money, before I got home.

Now, when there is so much talk about education, let me ask how many pounds it generally costs parents to have a boy taught this much of arithmetic; how much time it costs also; and, which is a far more serious consideration, how much mortification, and very often how much loss of health, it costs the poor scolded broken-hearted child, who becomes dunder-headed and dull for all his life-time,

---

[5] Son of a mayor of Norwich, prize-fighter, hanged for murder of William Weare, to whom he owed gambling debts, 1824.

merely because that has been imposed upon him as a task which he ought to regard as an object of pleasant pursuit. I never even once desired him to stay a moment from any other thing that he had a mind to go at. I just wrote the sums down upon paper, laid them upon the table, and left him to tackle them when he pleased. In the case of the multiplication-table, the learning of which is something of a job, and which it is absolutely necessary to learn perfectly, I advised him to go up into his bed-room, and read it twenty times over out loud every morning, before he went a hunting, and ten times over every night, after he came back, till it all came as pat upon his lips as the names of persons that he knew. He did this, and at the end of about a week he was ready to set on upon multiplication. It is the irksomeness of the thing which is the great bar to learning of every sort. I took care not to suffer irksomeness to seize his mind for a moment, and the consequence was that which I have described. I wish clearly to be understood as ascribing nothing to extraordinary *natural* ability. There are, as I have often said, as many *sorts* of men as there are of dogs; but, I do not pretend to be of any peculiarly excellent sort, and I have never discovered any indications of it. There are, to be sure, sorts that are naturally stupid; but, the generality of men are not so; and I believe that every boy of the same age, equally healthy, and brought up in the same manner, would (unless of one of the stupid kinds) learn in just the same sort of way; but, not if begun to be thumped at five or six years old, when the poor little things have no idea of the utility of anything; who are hardly sensible beings, and have but just understanding enough to know that it will hurt them if they jump down a chalk pit. I am sure, from thousands of instances that have come under my own eyes, that to begin to teach children book-learning before they are capable of reasoning, is the sure and certain way to enfeeble their minds for life; and, if they have natural genius, to cramp, if not totally to destroy that genius.

I think I shall be tempted to mould into a little book these lessons of arithmetic given to Richard. I think that a boy of sense, and of age equal to that of my scholar, would derive great profit from such a little book.

Some people will say, here is a monstrous deal of vanity and egotism; and if they will tell me, how such a story is to be told without exposing a man to this imputation, I will adopt their mode another time. I get nothing by telling the story. I should get full as much by keeping it to myself; but it may be useful to others, and therefore I tell it. Nothing is so dangerous as supposing that you have eight wonders of the world. I have no pretensions to any such possession. I look upon my boy as being like other boys in general. Their fathers can teach arithmetic as well as I; and if they have not a mind to pursue my method, they must pursue their own. Let them apply to the outside of the head and to the back, if they like; let them bargain for thumps and the birch rod; it is their affair and not mine. I never yet saw in my house a child that was *afraid;* that was in any fear whatsoever; that was ever for a moment under any sort of apprehension, on account of the learning of anything; and I never in my life gave a command, an order, a request, or even advice, to look into any book; and I am quite satisfied that the way to make

136

children dunces, to make them detest books, and justify that detestation, is to tease them and bother them upon the subject.

As to the *age* at which children ought to begin to be taught, it is very curious, that, while I was at a friend's house during my ride, I looked into, by mere accident, a little child's abridgment of the History of England: a little thing about twice as big as a crown-piece. Even into this abridgment the historian had introduced the circumstance of Alfred's father, who, "through a *mistaken notion* of kindness to his son, had suffered him to live to the age of twelve years without any attempt being made to give him education." How came this writer to know that it was a *mistaken notion*? Ought he not rather, when he looked at the result, when he considered the astonishing knowledge and great deeds of Alfred—ought he not to have hesitated before he thus criticised the notions of the father? It appears from the result that the notions of the father were perfectly correct; and I am satisfied, that if they had begun to thump the head of Alfred when he was a child, we should not at this day have heard talk of Alfred the Great.

Great apologies are due to the OLD LADY[6] from me, on account of my apparent inattention towards her, during her recent, or rather, I may say, her present, fit of that tormenting disorder which, as I observed before, comes upon her by *spells*. Dr. M'CULLOCH may say what he pleases about her being "*wi' bairn*." I say it's the wet gripes; and I saw a poor old mare down in Hampshire in just the same way; but God forbid the catastrophe should be the same, for they shot poor old Ball for the hounds. This disorder comes by spells. It sometimes seems as if it were altogether going off; the pulse rises, and the appetite returns. By-and-by a fresh grumbling begins to take place in the bowels. These are followed by acute pains; the patient becomes tremulous; the pulse begins to fall, and the most gloomy apprehensions begin again to be entertained. At every spell the pulse does not cease falling till it becomes lower than it was brought to by the preceding spell; and thus, spell after spell, finally produces the natural result.

It is useless at present to say much about the equivocating and blundering of the newspapers, relative to the cause of the fall. They are very shy, extremely cautious; become wonderfully *wary*, with regard to this subject. They do not know what to make of it. They all remember, that I told them that their prosperity was delusive; that it would soon come to an end, while they were telling me of the falsification of all my predictions. I told them the Small-note Bill had only given a *respite*. I told them that the foreign loans, and the shares, and all the astonishing enterprises, arose purely out of the Small-note Bill; and that a short time would see the Small-note Bill driving the gold out of the country, and bring us back to another restriction, OR, to wheat at four shillings a bushel. They remember that I told them all this; and now, some of them begin to *regard me as the principal cause of the present embarrassments!* This is pretty work indeed! What! I! The poor deluded creature, whose predictions were all falsified, who knew nothing at all

---

[6] Cobbett's wife Ann, née Reid.

about such matters, who was a perfect pedlar in political economy, who was ''a conceited and obstinate old dotard,'' as the polite and enlightened paper, the *Morning Herald*, called me: is it possible that such a poor miserable creature can have had the power to produce effects so prodigious? Yet this really appears to be the opinion of one, at least, of these Mr. Brougham's best possible public instructors. The *Public Ledger*, of the 16th of November, has the following passage:—

''It is fully ascertained that the Country Banking Establishments in England have latterly been compelled to limit their paper circulation, for the writings of Mr. COBBETT are widely circulated in the Agricultural districts, and they have been so successful as to induce the *Boobies* to call for gold in place of country paper, a circumstance which has *produced a greater effect on the currency than any exportation of the precious metals* to the Continent, either of Europe or America, could have done, although it too must have contributed to render money for a season scarce.''

And, so, the ''*boobies*'' call for gold instead of country bank-notes! Bless the ''*boobies*''! I wish they would do it to a greater extent, which they would, if they were not so dependent as they are upon the ragmen. But, does the *Public Ledger* think that those unfortunate creatures who suffered the other day at Plymouth, would have been ''*boobies*,'' if they had gone and got sovereigns before the banks broke? This brother of the broad sheet should act justly and fairly as I do. He should ascribe these demands for gold to Mr. Jones of Bristol and not to me. Mr. Jones taught the ''boobies'' that they might have gold for asking for, or send the rag-men to jail. It is Mr. Jones, therefore, that they should blame, and not me. But, seriously speaking, what a mess, what a pickle, what a horrible mess, must the thing be in, if any man, or any thousand of men, or any hundred thousand of men, can change the value of money, unhinge all contracts and all engagements, and plunge the pecuniary affairs of a nation into confusion? I have been often accused of wishing to be thought the cleverest man in the country; but surely it is no vanity (for vanity means unjust pretension) for me to think myself the cleverest man in the country, if I can of my own head, and at my own pleasure, produce effects like these. Truth, however, and fair dealing with my readers, call upon me to disclaim so haughty a pretension. I have no such power as this public instructor ascribes to me. Greater causes are at work to produce such effects; causes wholly uncontrollable by me, and, what is more, wholly uncontrollable in the long run by the Government itself, though heartily co-operating with the bank directors. These united can do nothing to arrest the progress of events. Peel's bill produced the horrible distresses of 1822; the part repeal of that bill produced a respite, that respite is now about to expire; and neither Government nor bank, nor both joined together, can prevent the ultimate consequences. They may postpone them for a little; but mark, every postponement will render the catastrophe the more dreadful.

I see everlasting attempts by the ''Instructor'' to cast blame upon the bank. I can see no blame in the bank. The bank has issued no small notes, though it had liberty to do it. The bank pays in gold agreeably to the law. What more does any body want with the bank? The bank lends money I suppose when it chooses; and is not it to be the judge, when it shall lend and when it shall not? The bank is blamed for putting out paper and causing high prices; and blamed at the same time for not putting out paper to accommodate merchants and keep them from breaking. It cannot be to blame for both, and, indeed, it is blamable for neither. It is the fellows that put out the paper and then break, that do the mischief. However, a breaking merchant, whom the bank will no longer prop up, will naturally blame the bank, just as every insolvent blames a solvent, that will not lend him money.[7]

Uphusband (Hampshire),
Thursday, 24th Aug. 1826.

I saw, the other day, in the *Morning Herald*, London, "best public instructor," that all those had *deceived themselves*, who had expected to see the price of agricultural produce brought down by the lessening of the quantity of paper-money. Now, in the first place, corn is, on an average, a seventh lower in price than it was last year at this time; and, what would it have been, if the crop and the stock had now been equal to what they were last year? All in good time, therefore, good Mr. Thwaites.[8] Let us have a little time. The "best public instructors" have, as yet, only fallen, in number sold, about a third, since this time last year. Give them a little time, good Mr. Thwaites, and you will see them come down to your heart's content. Only let us fairly see an end to small notes, and there will soon be not two daily "best public instructors" left in all the "entire" great "British Empire."

But, as man is not to live on bread alone, so corn is not the *only* thing that the owners and occupiers of the land have to look to. There are timber, bark, underwood, wool, hides, pigs, sheep, and cattle. All these together make, in amount, four times the corn, at the very least. I know that *all* these have greatly fallen in price since last year; but, I am in a sheep and wool country, and can speak positively as to them, which are two articles of very great importance. As to sheep; I am speaking of South Downs, which are the great stock of these counties; as to sheep, they have fallen one-third in price since last August, lambs as well as ewes. And, as to the wool, it sold, in 1824, at 40s. a tod; it sold last year, at 35s. a tod; and it now sells at 19s. a tod! A tod is 28lb. avoirdupois weight; so that the price of South Down wool now is, 8d. a pound and a fraction over; and this is, I believe,

---

[7] In 1797 the Bank of England found itself likely to be obliged to suspend payments, and its notes were therefore declared (by law) a legal tender although no longer convertible into coin. There was thus no check upon the Bank as to the amount of its issues, and the currency became depreciated. Every man to whom £5 was due, was obliged to accept payment in a £5 note not worth £5. Peel's Act in 1819, however, declared that cash payments in the current coin of the realm should be made for notes if demanded. This led to a great commercial panic, and the Bank was more than once on the verge of a suspension of payments owing to foreign drains upon its gold. P.C.

[8] John Alexander Thwaites (1786–1844), owner of the *Morning Herald*.

cheaper than it has ever been known within the memory of the oldest man living! The "best public instructor" may, perhaps, think, that sheep and wool are a trifling affair. There are many thousands of farmers who keep each a flock of at least a thousand sheep. An ewe yields about 3lb. of wool, a wether 4lb., a ram 7lb. Calculate, good Mr. Thwaites, what a difference it is when this wool becomes 8d. a pound instead of 17d., and instead of 30d. as it was not many years ago! In short, every middling sheep farmer receives, this year, about £250 less, as the produce of sheep and wool, than he received last year; and, on an average, £250 is more than half his rent.

East Everley (Wiltshire),
Sunday, 27th August, Evening.

We set off from Uphusband on Friday, about ten o'clock, the morning having been wet. My sons came round, in the chaise, by Andover and Weyhill, while I came right across the country towards Ludgershall, which lies in the road from Andover to this place. I never knew the *flies* so troublesome, in England, as I found them in this ride. I was obliged to carry a great bough, and to keep it in constant motion, in order to make the horse peaceable enough to enable me to keep on his back. It is a country of fields, lanes, and high hedges; so that no *wind* could come to relieve my horse; and, in spite of all I could do, a great part of him was covered with foam from the sweat. In the midst of this, I got, at one time, a little out of my road, in, or near, a place called Tangley. I rode up to the garden-wicket of a cottage, and asked the woman, who had two children, and who seemed to be about thirty years old, which was the way to Ludgershall, which I knew could not be more than about *four miles* off. She did *not know!* A very neat, smart, and pretty woman; but, she did not know the way to this rotten borough, which was, I was sure, only about four miles off! "Well, my dear good woman," said I, "but you *have been* at LUDGERSHALL?"—"No."—"Nor at Andover?" (six miles another way)—"No."—"Nor at Marlborough?" (nine miles another way)—"No."—Pray, were you born in this house?"—"Yes."—"And, how far have you ever been from this house?"—"Oh! I have been *up in the parish* and over *to Chute.*" That is to say, the utmost extent of her voyages had been about two and a half miles! Let no one laugh at her, and, above all others, let not me, who am convinced, that the *facilities*, which now exist, of *moving human bodies from place to place*, are amongst the *curses* of the country, the destroyers of industry, of morals, and, of course, of happiness. It is a great error to suppose, that people are rendered stupid by remaining always in the same place. This was a very acute woman, and as well behaved as need to be.

Everley is but about three miles from Ludgershall, so that we got here in the afternoon of Friday: and, in the evening a very heavy storm came and drove away all flies, and made the air delightful. This is a real *Down*-country. Here you see miles and miles square without a tree, or hedge, or bush. It is country of green-sward. This is the most famous place in all England for *coursing*. I was here, at this very inn, with a party eighteen years ago; and the landlord, who is still the same, recognised me as soon as he saw me. There were forty brace of greyhounds taken out into the field on one of the days, and every brace had one course, and some of them two. The ground is the finest in the world; from two to three miles for the hare to run to cover, and not a stone nor a bush nor a hillock. It was here proved to me, that the hare is, by far, the swiftest of all English animals; for I saw three hares, in one day, *run away* from the dogs. To give dog and hare a fair trial, there should be but *one* dog. Then, if that dog got so close as to compel the hare *to turn*, that would be proof that the dog ran fastest. When the dog, or dogs, never get near enough to the hare to induce her to *turn*, she is said, and very justly, to *"run away"* from them; and, as I saw three hares do this in one day, I conclude, that the hare is the swifter animal of the two.

This inn is one of the nicest, and, in summer, one of the pleasantest, in England; for, I think, that my experience in this way will justify me in speaking thus positively. The house is large, the yard and the stables good, the landlord *a farmer* also, and, therefore, no cribbing your horses in hay or straw and yourself in eggs and cream. The garden, which adjoins the south side of the house, is large, of good shape, has a terrace on one side, lies on the slope, consists of well-disposed clumps of shrubs and flowers, and of short-grass very neatly kept. In the lower part of the garden there are high trees, and, amongst these, the tulip-tree and the live-oak. Beyond the garden is a large clump of lofty sycamores, and, in these a most populous rookery, in which, of all things in the world, I delight. The village, which contains 301 souls, lies to the north of the inn, but adjoining its premises. All the rest, in every direction, is bare down or open arable. I am now sitting at one of the southern windows of this inn, looking across the garden towards the rookery. It is nearly sun-setting; the rooks are skimming and curving over the tops of the trees; while, under the branches, I see a flock of several hundred sheep, coming nibbling their way in from the Down, and going to their fold.

My sons set off about three o'clock to-day, on their way to Herefordshire, where I intend to join them, when I have had a pretty good ride in this country. There is no pleasure in travelling, except on horse-back, or on foot. Carriages take your body from place to place; and, if you merely want to be *conveyed*, they are very good; but they enable you to see and to know nothing at all of the country.

East Everley, Monday Morning
5 o'clock, 28th Aug. 1826.

A very fine morning; a man, *eighty-two years of age*, just beginning to mow the short-grass, in the garden: I thought it, even when I was young, the *hardest work* that man had to do. To *look on*, this work seems nothing; but, it tries every sinew in your frame, if you go upright and do your work well. This old man never knew how to do it well, and he stoops, and he hangs his scythe wrong; but, with all this, it must be a surprising man to mow short-grass, as well as he does, at *eighty*. *I wish I* may be able to mow short-grass at eighty! That's all I have to say of the matter.

141

RIDE DOWN THE VALLEY OF THE AVON IN WILTSHIRE.

"Thou shalt not muzzle the ox when he treadeth out the corn; and, The labourer is worthy of his reward."—Deuteronomy, ch. xxv. ver. 4; 1 Cor. ix. 9; 1 Tim. v. 18.

Milston, Monday, 28th August.

I came off this morning on the Marlborough road, about two miles, or three, and then turned off, over the downs, in a north-westerly direction, in search of the source of the Avon River, which goes down to Salisbury. I had once been at Netheravon, a village in this valley; but I had often heard this valley described, as one of the finest pieces of land in all England; I knew that there were about thirty parish churches, standing in a length of about thirty miles, and in an average width, of hardly a mile; and I was resolved to see a little into the *reasons* that could have induced our fathers to build all these churches, especially if, as the Scotch would have us believe, there were but a mere handful of people in England *until of late years*.

At the end of about a mile, from the top of a very high part of the down, with a steep slope towards the valley, I first saw this *Valley of Avon*; and a most beautiful sight it was! Villages, hamlets, large farms, towers, steeples, fields, meadows, orchards, and very fine timber trees, scattered all over the valley. The shape of the thing is this: on each side *downs*, very lofty and steep, in some places, and sloping miles back, in other places; but the *out-sides* of the valley are downs. From the edge of the downs begin capital *arable fields*, generally of very great dimensions, and, in some places, running a mile or two back into little *cross-valleys*, formed by hills of downs. After the corn-fields come *meadows*, on each side, down to the *brook*, or *river*. The farm-houses, mansions, villages, and hamlets, are generally situated in that part of the arable land which comes nearest the meadows.

Great as my expectations had been, they were more than fulfilled. I delight in this sort of country; and I had frequently seen the vale of the Itchen, that of the Bourn, and also that of the Teste, in Hampshire; I had seen the vales amongst the South Downs; but I never before saw anything to please me like this valley of the Avon. I sat upon my horse and looked over Milston and Easton and Pewsey for half an hour, though I had not breakfasted. The hill was very steep. A road, going slanting down it, was still so steep, and washed so very deep, by the rains of ages, that I did not attempt to *ride* down it, and I did not like to lead my horse, the path was so narrow. So seeing a boy with a drove of pigs, going out to the stubbles, I beckoned him to come up to me; and he came and led my horse down for me. But now, before I begin to ride down this beautiful vale, let me give, as well as my means will enable me, a plan or map of it, which I have made in this way: a friend has lent me a very old map of Wiltshire, describing the spots where all the churches stand, and also all the spots where Manor-houses, or Mansion-houses, stood. I laid a piece of very thin paper upon the map, and thus traced the river upon my paper, putting *figures* to represent the spots where churches stand, and putting *stars* to represent the spots where Manor-houses or Mansion-houses

142

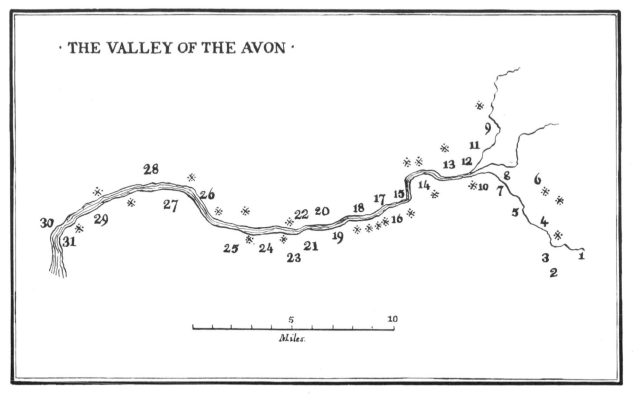

· THE VALLEY OF THE AVON ·

The sketch map of the Avon valley, here reproduced, is one traced by Cobbett from 'a very old map' lent him by a friend. The numbers represent 'spots where churches stand' and the stars 'spots where Manor-houses or Mansion-houses formerly stood.'

formerly stood. Endless is the variety in the shape of the high lands which form this valley. Sometimes the slope is very gentle, and the arable lands go back very far. At others, the downs come out into the valley almost like piers into the sea, being very steep in their sides, as well as their ends, towards the valley. They have no slope, at their other ends: indeed they have no *back ends*, but run into the main high land. There is also great variety in the width of the valley; great variety in the width of the meadows; but the land appears all to be of the very best; and it must be so, for the farmers confess it.

Having got to the bottom of the hill, I proceeded on to the village of Milston, the church of which is, in the map, represented by the figure 2. I left Easton (3) away at my right, and I did not go up to Wooton Rivers (1) where the river Avon rises, and which lies just close to the south-west corner of Marlborough Forest, and at about 5 or 6 miles from the town of Marlborough. Lower down the river, as I thought, there lived a friend, who was a great farmer, and whom I intended to call on. It being my way, however, always to begin making enquiries soon enough, I asked the pig-driver where this friend lived; and, to my surprise, I found that he lived in the parish of Milston (2). After riding up to the church, as being the centre of the village, I went on towards the house of my friend, which lay on my road down the

143

valley. I have many, many times witnessed agreeable surprise; but I do not know, that I ever in the whole course of my life, saw people so much surprised and pleased, as this farmer and his family were, at seeing me. People often *tell* you, that they are *glad to see* you; and in general they speak truth. I take pretty good care not to approach any house, with the smallest appearance of a design to eat or drink in it, unless I be *quite sure* of a cordial reception; but my friend at Fifield (it is in Milston parish) (2) and all his family, really seemed to be delighted beyond all expression.

When I set out this morning, I intended to go all the way down to the city of Salisbury (31) *to-day*; but, I soon found, that to refuse to sleep at Fifield, would cost me a great deal more trouble than a day was worth. So that I made my mind up, to stay in this farm-house, which has one of the nicest gardens, and it contains some of the finest flowers, that I ever saw, and all is disposed, with as much good taste, as I have ever witnessed. Here I am, then, just going to bed after having spent as pleasant a day, as I ever spent in my life.

Amesbury, Tuesday, 29th August.

I set off from Fifield, near Pawsey, this morning, and got here (25) about one o'clock, with my clothes wet. While they are drying, and while a mutton chop is getting ready, I sit down to make some notes of what I have seen since I left Enford (No. 15); but, here comes my dinner: and I must put off my notes till I have dined.

Salisbury, Wednesday, 30th August.

My ride yesterday, from Milston (No. 2) to this city of Salisbury, was, without any exception, the most pleasant; it brought before me the greatest number of, to me, interesting objects, and it gave rise to more interesting reflections, than I remember ever to have had brought before my eyes, or into my mind, in any one day of my life; and therefore, this ride was, without any exception, the most pleasant I ever had in my life, as far as recollection serves me. I got a little wet in the middle of the day; but I got dry again, and I arrived here in very good time.

Let us now, then, look back over this part of Wiltshire, and see whether the inhabitants ought to be "transported" by order of the "Emigration Committee," of which we shall see and say more by-and-by. I have before described this valley, generally; let me now speak of it a little more, in detail. The farms are all large, and, generally speaking, they were always large, I daresay; because *sheep* is one of the great things here; and sheep, in a country like this, must be kept in *flocks*, to be of any profit. The sheep principally manure the land. This is to be done only by *folding*; and, to fold, you must have *a flock*. Every farm has its portion of down, arable, and meadow; and, in many places, the latter are watered meadows, which is a great resource where sheep are kept in flocks; because these meadows furnish grass for the suckling ewes, early in the spring; and, indeed, because they have always food in them for sheep and cattle of all sorts. These meadows have had no part of the suffering from the drought, this year. They fed the ewes and lambs in

The Market Place in Salisbury, 1792.

the spring, and they are now yielding a heavy crop of hay; for I saw men mowing in them, in several places, particularly about Netheravon (18), though it was raining at the time.

The turnips look pretty well all the way down the valley; but, I see very few, except Swedish turnips. The early common turnips very nearly all failed, I believe. But, the stubbles, are beautifully bright; and the rick-yards tell us, that the crops are good, especially of wheat. This is not a country of peas and beans, nor of oats, except for home consumption. The crops are wheat, barley, wool and lambs, and these latter, not to be sold to butchers, but to be sold, at the great fairs, to those who are going to keep them for some time, whether to breed from, or, finally to fat for the butcher. It is the pulse and the oats, that appear to have failed most this year; and, therefore, this Valley has not suffered. I do not perceive that they have many *potatoes*; but what they have of this base root, seem to look well enough. It was one of the greatest villains upon earth (Sir Walter Raleigh), who (they say) first brought this root into England. He was beheaded at last! What a pity, since he was to be beheaded, the execution did not take place before he became such a mischievous devil as he was in the latter two-thirds of his life!

The stack-yards down this valley, are beautiful to behold. They contain from five to fifteen banging wheat-ricks, besides barley-ricks, and hay-ricks, and also besides the contents of the barns, many of which exceed a hundred, some two hundred, and I saw one at Pewsey (5), and another at Figheldean (19), each of which exceeded two hundred and fifty feet in length. At a farm, which, in the old maps, is called Chisenbury Priory (14) I think I counted twenty-seven ricks of one sort and another, and sixteen, or eighteen of them wheat-ricks. I could not conveniently get to the yard, without longer delay than I wished to make; but, I could not be much out in my counting. A very fine sight this was, and it could not meet the eye, without making one look round (and in vain) *to see the people who were to eat all this food*; and without making one reflect on the horrible, the unnatural, the base and infamous state, in which we must be, when projects are on foot, and are openly avowed, for *transporting*, those who raise this food, because they want to eat enough of it to keep them alive; and when no project is on foot for transporting the idlers, who live in luxury upon this same food; when no project is on foot for transporting pensioners, parsons, or dead-weight people!

A little while before I came to this farm-yard, I saw, in one piece, about four hundred acres of wheat-stubble, and I saw a sheep-fold, which, I thought, contained an acre of ground, and had in it, about four thousand sheep and lambs. The fold was divided into three separate flocks; but the piece of ground was one and the same; and I thought it contained about an acre. At one farm, between Pewsey and Upavon, I counted more than 300 hogs in one stubble. This is certainly the most delightful farming in the world. No ditches, no water-furrows, no drains, hardly any hedges, no dirt and mire even in the wettest seasons of the year: and though the downs, are naked and cold, the valleys are snugness itself. They are, as to the downs, what *ah-ahs!* are, in parks or lawns. When you are going over the downs, you look *over* the valleys, as in the case of the *ah-ah*; and, if you be not acquainted with the country, your surprise, when you come to the edge of the hill, is very great. The shelter, in these valleys, and particularly where the downs are steep and lofty on the sides, is very complete. Then the trees are every-where lofty. They are generally elms, with some ashes, which delight in the soil that they find here. There are, almost always, two or three large clumps of trees in every parish, and a rookery or two (not *rag*-rookery) to every parish. By the water's edge there are willows; and to almost every farm, there is a fine orchard, the trees being, in general, very fine, and, this year, they are, in general, well loaded with fruit. So that, all taken together, it seems impossible to find a more beautiful and pleasant country than this, or to imagine any life more easy and happy than men might here lead, if they were untormented by an accursed system, that takes the food from those that raise it, and gives it to those, that do nothing that is useful to man.

Here the farmer has always an abundance of straw. His farm-yard is never without it. Cattle and horses are bedded up to their eyes. The yards are put close under the shelter of a hill, or are protected by lofty and thick-set trees. Every animal seems comfortably situated; and, in the dreariest days of winter, these are, perhaps, the happiest scenes in the world; or, rather, they would be such, if those, whose labour makes it all, trees, corn, sheep and every thing, had but *their fair share* of the produce of that labour. What share they really have of it, one cannot exactly say; but, I should suppose, that every labouring *man* in this valley raises as much food, as would suffice for fifty, or a hundred persons, fed like himself!

The *stars*, in my map, mark the spots where manor-houses, or gentlemen's mansions, formerly stood, and stood, too, only about sixty years ago. Every parish had its manor-house in the first place; and then there were, down this Valley, twenty-one others; so that, in this distance of about thirty miles, there stood fifty mansion-houses. Where are they *now*? I believe there are but eight, that are at all worthy of the name of mansion houses; and even these are but poorly kept up, and, except in two or three instances, are of no benefit to the labouring people; they employ but few persons; and, in short, do not half supply the place of any eight of the old mansions. All these mansions, all these parsonages, aye, and their goods and furniture, together with the clocks, the brass kettles, the brewing-vessels, the good bedding, and good clothes, and good furniture, and the stock in pigs, or in money, of the inferior classes, in this series of once populous, and gay villages and hamlets; all these have been by the accursed system of taxing and funding and paper-money, by the well-known exactions of the state, and by the not less real, though less generally understood, extortions of the *monopolies* arising out of paper-money; all these have been, by these accursed means, conveyed away, out of this Valley, to the haunts of the tax-eaters, and the monopolizers. There are many of the *mansion houses*, the ruins of which you yet behold. At Milston (2) there are two mansion houses, the walls and the roofs of which yet remain, but which are falling gradually to pieces, and the garden walls are crumbling down. At Enford (15), Bennet the member for the county, had a large

Prize cattle at Birmingham, 1849. The developments in agriculture at this time were as far-reaching as those in industry, and had a profound effect on rural life in England.

mansion house, the stables of which are yet standing.[1] In several places, I saw, still remaining, indubitable traces of an ancient manor house, namely a dove-cote or pigeon-house. The poor pigeons have kept possession of their heritage, from generation to generation, and so have the rooks, in their several rookeries, while the paper-system has swept away, or, rather swallowed up, the owners of the dove-cotes and of the lofty trees, about forty families of which owners have been ousted in this one Valley, and have become dead-weight creatures, tax-gatherers, barrack-fellows, thief-takers, or, perhaps, paupers or thieves.

I have never been able to comprehend what the beastly Scotch *feelosofers* mean by their "national wealth;" but, as far as I can understand them, this is their meaning: that national wealth means, that which is *left* of the products of the country over and above what is *consumed*, or *used*, by those whose labour causes the products to be. This being the notion, it follows, of course, that the *fewer* poor devils, you can screw the products out of, the *richer* the nation is.

If the over-produce of this Valley of Avon were given, by the farmers, to the weavers in Lancashire, to the iron and steel chaps of Warwickshire, and to other makers or sellers of useful things, there would come an abundance of all these useful things into this valley from Lancashire and other parts; but if, as is the case, the over-produce goes to the fund-holders, the dead-weight, the soldiers, the lord and lady and master and miss pensioners and sinecure people; if the over-produce go to them, as a very great part of it does, nothing, not even the parings of one's nails, can come back to the valley in exchange. And, can this operation, then, add to the "national wealth"? It adds to the "wealth" of those who carry on the affairs of state; it fills their pockets, those of their relatives and dependents; it fattens all tax-eaters; but it can give no wealth to the "nation," which means the whole of the people.

What a *twist* a head must have before it can come to the conclusion, that the nation gains in wealth by the Government being able to cause the work to be done by those who have hardly any share in the fruit of the labour! What a *twist* such a head must have!

In taking my leave of this beautiful vale, I have to express my deep shame, as an Englishman, at beholding the general *extreme poverty* of those, who cause this vale to produce such quantities of food and raiment. This is, I verily believe it, the *worst used labouring people upon the face of the earth.* Dogs, and hogs, and horses, are treated with more civility; and as to food and lodging, how gladly would the labourers change with them! This state of things never can continue many years! *By some means or other* there must be an end to it, and my firm belief is, that that end will be dreadful. In the mean while I see, and I see it with pleasure, that the common people know that they are ill used; and that they cordially, most cordially, hate those who ill-treat them.

I got into Salisbury about half-past seven o'clock, less tired than I recollect ever

---

[1] See note 4 page 21.

to have been, after so long a ride; for, including my several crossings of the river, and my deviations to look at churches and farm-yards and rick-yards, I think I must have ridden nearly forty miles.

————

RIDE FROM SALISBURY TO WARMINSTER, FROM WARMINSTER TO FROME, FROM FROME TO DEVIZES, AND FROM DEVIZES TO HIGHWORTH.

"Hear this, O ye that swallow up the needy, even to make the poor of the land to fail: saying, When will the new moon be gone that we may sell corn? And the Sabbath, that we may set forth wheat, making the Ephah small, and the Shekel great, and falsifying the balances by deceit; that we may buy the poor for silver, and the needy for a pair of shoes; yea, and sell the refuse of the wheat? Shall not the land tremble for this; and every one mourn that dwelleth therein? I will turn your feasts into mourning, saith the Lord God, and all your songs into lamentations."—Amos, chap. viii, ver. 4 to 10.

Heytesbury (Wilts), Thursday,
31st August, 1826.

This place, which is one of the rotten boroughs of Wiltshire, and which was formerly a considerable town, is now but a very miserable affair. Yesterday morning I went into the Cathedral at Salisbury about 7 o'clock. When I got into the nave of the church, and was looking up and admiring the columns and the roof, I heard a sort of *humming*, in some place which appeared to be in the transept of the building. I wondered what it was, and made my way towards the place whence the noise appeared to issue. As I approached it, the noise seemed to grow louder. At last, I thought, I could distinguish the sounds of the human voice. This encouraged me to proceed; and, still following the sound, I at last turned in at a doorway to my left, where I found a priest and his congregation assembled. It was a parson of some sort, with a white covering on him, and five women, and four men: when I arrived, there were five couple of us. I joined the congregation, until they came to the *litany;* and then, being monstrously hungry, I did not think myself bound to stay any longer. I wonder what the founders would say, if they could rise from the grave, and see such a congregation as this, in this most magnificent and beautiful cathedral? I wonder what they would say, if they could know *to what purpose* the endowments of this Cathedral are now applied; and above all things, I wonder what they would say, if they could see the half-starved labourers, that now minister to the luxuries of those, who wallow in the wealth of those endowments. There is one thing, at any rate, that might be abstained from, by those, that revel in the riches of those endowments; namely, to abuse and blackguard those of our forefathers, from whom the endowments came, and who erected the edifice, and carried so far towards the skies, that beautiful and matchless spire, of which the

Cruickshank's view of 'clerical anticipation' in 1797. Cobbett was not alone in condemning the clergy for its greed and unchristian attitudes.

A watercolour by David Cox of Shakespeare's Cliff, Dover.

present possessors have the impudence to boast, while they represent as ignorant and benighted creatures, those who conceived the grand design, and who executed the scientific and costly work. These fellows, in big white wigs, of the size of half a bushel, have the audacity, even within the walls of the Cathedrals themselves, to rail against those who founded them; and Rennell and Sturges, while they were actually, literally, fattening on the spoils of the monastery of St. Swithin, at Winchester, were publishing abusive pamphlets against that Catholic religion which had given them their very bread.[1] For my part, I could not look up at the spire and the whole of the church at Salisbury, without *feeling* that I lived in degenerate times. Such a thing never could be made *now*. We *feel* that, as we look at the building. It really does appear that if our forefathers had not made these buildings, we should have forgotten, before now, what the Christian religion was!

Today has been exceedingly hot. Hotter, I think, for a short time, than I ever felt it in England before. In coming through a village called Wishford, and mounting a little hill, I thought the heat upon my back was as great as I had ever felt it in my life. There were thunder storms about, and it had rained at Wishford, a little before I came to it.

My next village was one that I had lived in, for a short time, when I was only about ten or eleven years of age. I had been sent down with a horse from Farnham, and I remember that I went by *Stone-henge*, and rode up and looked at the stones. From Stone-henge I went to the village of Steeple Langford, where I remained from the month of June till the fall of the year. I remember the beautiful villages, up and down this valley. I also remembered, very well, that the women at Steeple Langford used to card, and spin dyed wool. I was, therefore, somewhat filled with curiosity, to see this Steeple Langford again; and, indeed, it was the recollection of this village, that made me take a ride into Wiltshire this summer. I have, I dare say, a thousand times talked about this Steeple Langford, and about the beautiful farms and meadows along this valley. I have talked of these to my children, a great many times; and I formed the design of letting two of them see this valley this year, and to go through Warminster to Stroud, and so on to Gloucester and Hereford. But, when I got to Everley, I found that they would never get along fast enough to get into Herefordshire in time for what they intended; so that I parted from them in the manner, I have before described. I was resolved, however, to see Steeple Langford myself, and I was impatient to get to it, hoping to find a public-house, and a stable to put my horse in, to protect him, for a while against the flies, which tormented him to such a degree, that to ride him was work, as hard as threshing. When I got to Steeple Langford, I found no public-house, and I found it a much more miserable place than I had remembered it. The *Steeple*, to which it owed its distinctive appellation, was gone; and the place altogether seemed to me, to be very much altered for the worse.

---

[1] A reference to the controversy between John Sturges, Prebendary, and Thomas Rennell, Dean, of Winchester, and the Roman Catholic Bishop John Milner.

Warminster (Wilts), Friday, 1st Sept.

I set out from Heytesbury this morning about six o'clock. Last night, before I went to bed, I found that there were some men and boys in the house, who had come all the way from Bradford, about twelve miles, in order to get *nuts*. These people were men and boys, that had been employed in the *cloth factories* at Bradford and about Bradford. I had some talk with some of these nutters, and I am quite convinced, not that the cloth making is at *an end*; but that it *never will be again what it has been*. Before last Christmas these manufacturers had full work, at one shilling and threepence a yard at broad-cloth weaving. They have now a quarter work, at one shilling a yard! One and three-pence a yard for this weaving has been given at all times within the memory of man! Nothing can show more clearly than this, and in a stronger light, the great change which has taken place in the *remuneration for labour*. These poor nutters were extremely ragged. I saved my supper, and I fasted instead of breakfasting. That was three shillings, which I had saved, and I added five to them, with a resolution to save them afterwards, in order to give these chaps a breakfast for once in their lives. There were eight of them, six men, and two boys; and I gave them two quartern loaves, two pounds of cheese, and eight pints of strong beer. The fellows were very thankful, but the conduct of the landlord and landlady pleased me exceedingly. When I came to pay my bill, they had said nothing about my bed, which had been a very good one; and, when I asked, why they had not put the bed into the bill, they said they would not charge any thing for the bed, since I had been so good to the poor men. Yes, said I, but I must not throw the expense upon you. I had no supper, and I have had no breakfast; and, therefore, I am not called upon, to pay for them: but *I have had* the bed. It ended by my paying for the bed, and coming off, leaving the nutters at their breakfast, and very much delighted with the landlord and his wife; and I must here observe, that I have pretty generally found a good deal of compassion for the poor people to prevail amongst publicans and their wives.

The whole of the population of the twenty-four parishes down this vale, amounts to only 11,195 souls, according to the Official return to Parliament; and, mind, I include the parish of Fisherton Anger (a suburb of the city of Salisbury), which contains 893 of the number. I include the town of Heytesbury, with its 1,023 souls; and I further include this very good and large market town of Warminster, with its population of 5,000! So that I leave, in the other twenty-one parishes, only 4,170 souls, men, women, and children! That is to say, a hundred and ninety-eight souls to each parish; or, reckoning five to a family, thirty-nine families to each parish. Above one half of the population never could be expected to be in the church at one time; so that, here are one-and-twenty churches built for the purpose of holding two thousand and eighty people! There are several of these churches, any one of which would conveniently contain the whole of these people, the two thousand and eighty!

What a monstrous thing, to suppose that they were built without there being people to go to them; and built, too, without money and without hands! The

154

whole of the population in these twenty-one parishes could stand, and without much crowding too, in the bottoms of the towers of the several churches. Nay, in three or four of the parishes, the whole of the people could stand in the church porches. Then, the *church-yards* show you how numerous the population must have been. You see, in some cases, only here and there the mark of a grave, where the church-yard contains from half an acre to an acre of land, and sometimes more. In short, everything shows, that here was once a great and opulent population; that there was an abundance to eat, to wear, and to spare; that all the land that is now under cultivation, and a great deal that is not now under cultivation, was under cultivation in former times.[2]

As to the produce of this valley, it must be at least ten times as great as its consumption, even if we include the three towns that belong to it. I am sure I saw produce enough, in five or six of the farm-yards, or rick-yards, to feed the whole of the population of the twenty-one parishes. But the infernal system, causes it all to be carried away. Not a bit of good beef, or mutton, or veal, and scarcely a bit of bacon is left for those, who raise all this food and wool. The labourers here *look* as if they were half-starved.

For my own part, I really am ashamed to ride a fat horse, to have a full belly, and to have a clean shirt upon my back, while I look at these wretched countrymen of mine; while I actually see them reeling with weakness; when I see their poor faces present me nothing but skin and bone, while they are toiling to get the wheat and the meat, ready to be carried away to be devoured by the tax-eaters. I am ashamed to look at these poor souls, and to reflect that they are my countrymen; and particularly to reflect, that we are descended from those, amongst whom "beef, pork, mutton, and veal, were the food of the poorer sort of people."[3] We are reversing the maxim of the Scripture: our laws almost say, that those that work shall not eat, and that those who do not work, shall have the food. I repeat, that the baseness of the English land-owners surpasses that, of any other men that ever lived in the world. The cowards know well, that the labourers that give value to their land, are skin and bone. They are not such brutes, as not to know that this starvation, is produced by taxation. They know well, how unjust it is, to treat their labourers in this way.

Saturday, September 2nd.

After I got to Warminster yesterday, it began to rain, which stopped me in my way to Frome in Somersetshire, which lies about seven or eight miles from this place; but, as I meant to be quite in the northern part of the country, by to-morrow noon, or there-abouts, I took a post-chaise in the afternoon of yesterday, and went to Frome, where I saw, upon my entrance into the town, between two or three hundred weavers, men and boys, cracking stones, moving earth, and doing other

---

[2] Compare note 5 on page 97.
[3] Quoted from Sir John Fortescue's *De Laudibus Lequm Angliae* (1463).

The interior of a Dorset labourer's cottage, 1864.

sorts of work, towards making a fine road into the town. I drove into the town, and through the principal streets, and then I put my chaise up a little, at one of the inns.

This appears to be a sort of little Manchester. A very small Manchester, indeed; for it does not contain above ten or twelve thousand people, but, it has all the *flash* of a Manchester, and the innkeepers and their people look and behave like the Manchester fellows. I was, I must confess, glad to find proofs of the irretrievable decay of the place.

These poor creatures at Frome, have pawned all their things, or nearly all. All their best clothes, their blankets and sheets; their looms; any little piece of furniture that they had, and that was good for anything. Mothers have been compelled to pawn, all the tolerably good clothes, that their children had. In case of a man having two or three shirts, he is left with only one, and sometimes without any shirt; and, though this is a sort of manufacture, that cannot very well come to a complete end; still it has received a blow from which it cannot possibly recover. The population of this Frome, has been augmented to the degree of one-third, within the last six or seven years. There are here all the usual signs of

156

Frome, Somerset, in 1802, by George Walker.

accommodation bills, and all false paper stuff, called money: new houses, in abundance, half finished; new gingerbread "places of worship," as they are called; great swaggering inns; parcels of swaggering fellows going about, with vulgarity imprinted upon their countenances, but with good clothes upon their backs.

I found the working people at Frome very intelligent; very well informed as to the cause of their misery; not at all humbugged by the canters, whether about religion or loyalty. When I got to the inn, I sent my post-chaise boy back to the road, to tell one or two of the weavers to come to me at the inn. The landlord did not at first, like to let such ragged fellows, upstairs. I insisted, however, upon their coming up, and I had a long talk with them. They were very intelligent men; had much clearer views of what is likely to happen, than the pretty gentlemen of Whitehall seem to have; and, it is curious enough, that they, these common weavers, should tell me, that they thought that the trade, never would come back again, to what it was before; or, rather, to what it has been for some years past. This is the impression everywhere; that the *puffing is over*; that we must come back again to something like reality.

All salutary and humane law, really seems to be drawing towards an end, in this now miserable country, where the thousands are caused to wallow in luxury, to be surfeited with food and drink, while the millions are continually on the point of famishing. In order to form an idea of the degradation of the people of this country, and of the abandonment of every English principle, what need we of more than this one disgraceful and truly horrible fact, namely, that *the common soldiers, of the standing army in time of peace, subscribe, in order to furnish the meanest of diet, to keep from starving, the industrious people who are taxed to the amount of one-half of their wages, and out of which taxes, the very pay of these soldiers comes!* Is not this one fact; this disgraceful, this damning fact; is not this enough to convince us, *there must be a change;* that there must be a complete and radical change; or, that England must become a country of the basest slavery, that ever disgraced the earth?

Devizes, (Wilts),
Sunday Morning, 3rd Sept.

Before I speak of my ride from Warminster to this place, I must once more observe, that Warminster is a very nice town: every thing belonging to it is *solid* and *good*. There are no villanous gingerbread houses running up, and no nasty, shabby-genteel people; no women trapesing about with showy gowns and dirty necks; no jew-looking fellows with dandy coats, dirty shirts and half-heels to their shoes. A really nice and good town. It is a great corn-market: one of the greatest in this part of England; and here things are still conducted in the good, old, honest fashion. The corn is brought and pitched in the market before it is sold; and, when sold it is paid for on the nail; and all is over, and the farmers and millers gone home by day-light. Almost every where else the corn is sold by sample; it is sold by juggling in a corner; the parties meet and drink first; it is night work; there is no fair and open market; the mass of the people do not know what the prices are; and all this favours that *monopoly* which makes the corn change hands many times, perhaps, before it reaches the mouth, leaving a profit in each pair of hands, and which monopoly is, for the greater part, carried on by the villanous tribe of *Quakers, none of whom ever work,* and all of whom prey upon the rest of the community, as those infernal devils, the wasps, prey upon the bees. Monopolies compel those who labour to maintain those who do not labour; and hence the success of the crafty crew of Quakers, the very *existence* of which sect is a disgrace to the country.

Besides the corn market at Warminster, I was delighted, and greatly surprised, to see the *meat*. Not only the very finest veal and lamb that I had ever seen in my life, but so exceedingly beautiful, that I could hardly believe my eyes. I am a great connoisseur in joints of meat; a great judge, if five-and-thirty years of experience can give sound judgment. I verily believe that I have bought and have roasted more whole sirloins of beef than any man in England; I know all about the matter; a very great visitor of Newgate market; in short, though a little eater, I am a very great provider. It is a fancy, I like the subject, and therefore, I understand it; and

The Town Hall in Devizes, Wiltshire.

with all this knowledge of the matter, I say, I never saw veal and lamb half so fine as what I saw at Warminster. The town is famed for fine meat; and I knew it, and, therefore, I went out in the morning to look at the meat. It was, too, *2d.* a pound cheaper than I left it at Kensington.

Highworth (Wilts),
Monday, 4th Sept.

I got here yesterday, after a ride, including my deviations, of about thirty-four miles, and that, too, *without breaking my fast.* Before I got into the rotten-borough of Calne, I had two *tributes* to pay to the Aristocracy; namely, two *Sunday tolls;* and, I was resolved, that the country, in which these tolls were extorted, should have not a farthing of my money, that I could, by any means, keep from it. Therefore, I fasted, until I got into the free-quarters in which I am now. I would have made my horse fast too, if I could have done it without the risk of making him unable to carry me.

RIDE FROM HIGHWORTH TO CRICKLADE AND THENCE TO MALMSBURY.

Highworth (Wilts)
Monday, 4th Sept. 1826.

When I got to Devizes, on Saturday evening, and came to look out of the inn-window into the street, I perceived, that I had seen that place before, and, always having thought, that I should like to *see* Devizes, of which I had heard so much talk as a famous corn-market, I was very much surprised to find, that it was not new to me. Presently a stage-coach came up to the door, with "Bath and London" upon its panels; and then I recollected, that I had been at this place, on my way to Bristol, last year. Devizes is, as nearly as possible, in the centre of the county, and the *canal*, that passes close by it, is the great channel through which the produce of the country is carried away to be devoured by the idlers, the thieves, and the prostitutes, who are all tax-eaters, in the Wens of Bath and London. Pottern, which I passed through in my way from Warminster to Devizes, was once a place much larger than Devizes; and, it is now a mere ragged village, with a church large, very ancient, and of most costly structure. The whole of the people, here, might, as in most other cases, be placed in the *belfry*, or the church-porches.

All the way along, the mansion-houses are nearly all gone. There is now and then a great place, belonging to a borough-monger, or some one connected with borough mongers; but, all the *little gentlemen* are gone; and, hence it is, that parsons are now made justices of the peace! There are few other persons left, who are at all capable of filling the office in a way to suit the system! The monopolising brewers and rag-rooks are, in some places, the "magistrates;" and thus is the whole thing *changed*, and England, is no more what it was. Very near to the sides of my road from Warminster to Devizes, there were formerly (within a hundred years), 22 mansion-houses of sufficient note to be marked as such in the county-

Opposite above:
'Autumnal Sunset' by John Constable.

Opposite below:
A cartoon of 1819 attacking the spate of new taxes which were imposed on the English after the Napoleonic wars.

who the Devil woud have thought
of seeing you after I've paid you
so often well I see there is no Trusting any body

Fishing boats at Hastings making for
the shore in a breeze, by John Chalon.

Left:
An engraving of the Coronation procession of George IV in 1821, by G. Scharf.

Below:
'The Hop Garden' by W. F. Witherington. Hops were first grown in the Kentish weald in the sixteenth century, and by Cobbett's day were an important part of the rural economy.

map, then made. There are now only seven of them remaining. There were five parish-churches nearly close to my road; and, in one parish out of the five, the parsonage-house is, in the parliamentary return, said to be "too small" for the parson to live in, though the church would contain two or three thousand people, and though the living is a Rectory, and a rich one too! Thus has the church-property, or rather, that public property, which is called church property, been dilapidated! The parsons have swallowed the *tithes* and the rent of the glebes; and have, successively, suffered the parsonage-houses to fall into decay. But these parsonage-houses were, indeed, not intended for large families. They were intended for a priest, a main part of whose business it was to distribute the tithes amongst the poor and the strangers! The parson, in this case, at Corsley, says, "too small for an incumbent with a family." Ah! there is the mischief. It was never intended to give men tithes, as a premium for breeding! Malthus does not seem to see any harm in *this* sort of increase of population. It is the *working* population, those who raise the food and the clothing, that he and Scarlett want to put a stop to the breeding of![1]

I saw on my way through the down-countries, hundreds of acres of ploughed land in *shelves*. What I mean is, the side of a steep hill, made into the shape of *a stairs*, only the rising parts more sloping than those of a stairs, and deeper in proportion. The side of the hill, in its original form, was too steep to be ploughed, or, even to be worked with a spade. The earth, as soon as moved, would have rolled down the hill; and, besides, the rains would have soon washed down all the surface earth, and have left nothing for plants of any sort to grow in. Therefore the sides of hills, where the land was sufficiently good, and where it was wanted for the growing of corn, were thus made into a sort of steps or shelves, and the horizontal parts (representing the parts of the stairs that we put our feet upon,) were ploughed and sowed, as they generally are, indeed, to this day. Now, no man, not even the hireling Chalmers,[2] will have the impudence to say, that these shelves, amounting to thousands and thousands of acres in Wiltshire alone, were not made by the hand of man. It would be as impudent to contend, that the churches were formed by the flood, as to contend, that these shelves were formed by that cause. Yet, thus the Scotch scribes must contend; or, they must give up all their assertions about the ancient beggary and want of population in England; for, as in the case of the churches, what were these shelves made *for*? And could they be made at all, without a great abundance of hands? These shelves are everywhere to be seen throughout the down-countries of Sussex, Hampshire, Wiltshire,

---

[1] James Scarlett (1769–1844), Baron Abinger, Attorney General, regarded by Cobbett as a black reactionary.
[2] George Chalmers (1742–1825), author of *An Estimate of the Comparative Strength of Great Britain* (1782), much disliked by Cobbett.

Dorsetshire, Devonshire and Cornwall; and, besides this, large tracts of land, amounting to millions of acres, perhaps, which are now downs, heaths, or woodlands, still, if you examine closely, bear the marks of the plough. The fact is, I dare say, that the country has never varied very much in the gross amount of its population; but, formerly the people were pretty evenly spread over the country, instead of being, as the greater part of them now are, collected together in great masses, where, for the greater part, the idlers live on the labour of the industrious.

As I came on the road, for the first three or four miles, I saw great numbers of labourers either digging potatoes for their Sunday's dinner, or coming home with them, or going out to dig them. The land-owners, or occupiers, let small pieces of land to the labourers, and these they cultivate with the spade for their own use. They pay, in all cases, a high rent, and, in most cases, an enormous one. The practice prevails all the way from Warminster to Devizes, and from Devizes to nearly this place (Highworth). The rent is, in some places, a shilling a rod, which is, mind, 160s. or 8l. an acre! Still the poor creatures like to have the land: they work in it at their spare hours; and on Sunday mornings early: and the overseers, sharp as they may be, cannot ascertain precisely how much they get out of their plat of ground. But, good God! what a life to live; what a life to see people live; to see this sight in our own country, and to have the base vanity to *boast* of that country, and to talk of our "constitution" and our "liberties," and to affect to *pity* the Spaniards, whose working people, live like gentlemen, compared with our miserable creatures. Again I say, give me the Inquisition and well-healed cheeks and ribs, rather than "civil and religious liberty," and skin and bone. But, the fact is, that, where honest and laborious men can be compelled to starve quietly, whether all at once or by inches, with old wheat ricks and fat cattle under their eye, it is a mockery to talk of their "liberty," of any sort; for the sum total of their state is this, they have "liberty" to choose between death by starvation (quick or slow) and death by the halter!

Between Warminster and Westbury I saw thirty or more men *digging* a great field of I dare say, twelve acres. I thought, "surely, that 'humane,' half-mad fellow, Owen,[3] is not got at work here; that Owen, who, the *feelsofers* tell us, went to the Continent, to find out how to prevent the increase of the labourers' children." No: it was not Owen: it was the overseer of the parish, who had set these men to dig up this field, previously to its being sown with wheat. In short, it was a digging instead of a ploughing. The men, I found upon inquiry, got 9d. a day for their work. Plain digging, in the market gardens near London, is, I believe, 3d. or 4d. a rod. If these poor men, who were chiefly weavers or spinners from Westbury, or had come home to their parish from Bradford or Trowbridge; if they digged six rods each in a day, and *fairly* did it, they must work well. This would be 1½d. a rod, or 20s. an acre; and that is as cheap as ploughing and four times as good.

---

[3] Robert Owen (1771–1858), pioneer socialist and founder of the New Lanark Settlement, 1814.

But, how much better to give the men higher wages, and let them do more work? If married, how are their miserable families to live on 4s. 6d. a week? And, if single, they must and will have more, either by poaching, or by taking without leave. At any rate, this is better than the *road work:* I mean better for those who pay the rates; for here is something which they get for the money that they give to the poor; whereas, in the case of the roadwork, the money given in relief is generally wholly so much lost to the rate-payer. What a curious spectacle this is: the manufactories *throwing the people back again upon the land!* It is not above eighteen months ago, that the Scotch FEELOSOFERS, and especially Dr. Black,[4] were calling upon *the farm labourers to become manufacturers!* I remonstrated with the Doctor at the time; but, he still insisted, that such a transfer of hands, was the only remedy for the distress in the farming districts.

This is a *cheese country;* some corn, but, generally speaking, it is a country of dairies. The sheep here are of the large kind; a sort of Leicester sheep, and the cattle chiefly for milking. The ground is a stiff loam at top, and a yellowing stone under. The houses are almost all built of stone. It is a tolerably rich, but by no means, a gay and pretty country. Highworth has a situation corresponding with its name. On every side you go up-hill to it, and from it you see to a great distance all round, and into many counties.

Highworth, Wednesday, 6th Sept.

The great object of my visit to the Northern border of Wiltshire, will be mentioned when I get to Malmsbury, whither I intend to go to-morrow, or next day, and thence, through Gloucestershire, in my way to Herefordshire. But, an additional inducement, was to have a good long political *gossip*, with some excellent friends, who detest the borough-ruffians as cordially as I do, and who, I hope, wish as anxiously to see their fall effected, and no matter by what means. There was, however, arising incidentally, a third object, which had I known of its existence, would, of itself, have brought me from the South-West to the North-East corner of this county. One of the parishes adjoining to Highworth is that of Coleshill, which is in Berkshire, and which is the property of Lord Radnor, or Lord Folkestone,[5] and is the seat of the latter. I was at Coleshill twenty-two or three years ago, and twice at later periods. In 1824, Lord Folkestone bought some Locust trees[6] of me; and he has several times told me, that they were growing very finely; but, I did not know, that they had been planted at Coleshill; and, indeed, I always thought that they had been planted somewhere in the South of Wiltshire. I now found, however, that they were growing at Coleshill, and yesterday I went to see them,

---

[4] John Black (1783–1855), Scottish journalist and editor of the *Morning Chronicle*, a radical but too much of a Benthamite to suit Cobbett's taste.

[5] William Pleydell-Bouverie (1779–1869), Viscount Folkestone and Earl of Radnor, a Liberal peer on good terms with Cobbett.

[6] Carobs or false acacias, imported by Cobbett from America.

and was, for many reasons, more delighted with the sight, than with any that I have beheld for a long while. These trees stand in clumps of 200 trees in each, and the trees being four feet apart each way. These clumps make part of a plantation of 30 or 40 acres, perhaps 50 acres. The rest of the ground; that is to say, the ground where the clumps of Locusts do not stand, was, at the same time that the Locust clumps were, planted with chestnuts, elms, ashes, oaks, beeches, and other trees. These trees were stouter and taller than the Locust trees were, when the plantation was made. Yet, if you were now to place yourself at a mile's distance from the plantation, you would not think that there was any plantation at all, except the clumps. The fact is, that the other trees have, as they generally do, made, as yet, but very little progress; are not, I should think, upon an average, more than $4\frac{1}{2}$ feet, or 5 feet, high; while the clumps of Locusts are from 12 to 20 feet high; and, I think, that I may safely say, that the average height is sixteen feet. They are the most beautiful clumps of trees that I ever saw in my life.

The trees are, indeed, in good land, and have been taken good care of; but, the other trees are in the same land; and, while they have been taken the same care of, since they were planted, they had not, I am sure, worse treatment before planting, than these Locust trees had. At the time when I sold them to my Lord Folkestone, they were in a field at Worth, near Crawley, in Sussex. The history of their transport is this. A Wiltshire waggon came to Worth for the trees, on the 14th of March 1824. The waggon had been stopped on the way by the snow; and, though the snow was gone off before the trees were put upon the waggon, it was very cold, and there were sharp frosts and harsh winds. I had the trees taken up, and tied up in hundreds by withes, like so many fagots. They were then put in, and upon the waggon, we doing our best to keep the roots inwards in the loading, so as to prevent them from being exposed, but as little as possible, to the wind, sun and frost. We put some fern on the top, and, where we could on the sides; and we tied on the load with ropes, just as we should have done with a load of fagots. In this way, they were several days upon the road; and I do not know how long it was before they got safe into the ground again. All this shows how hardy these trees are, and it ought to admonish gentlemen to make pretty strict enquiries, when they have gardeners, or bailifs, or stewards, under whose hands Locust trees die, or do not thrive.

N.B. Dry as the late summer was, I never had my Locust trees so fine as they are this year. I have some, they write me, five feet high, from seed sown just before I went to Preston the first time, that is to say, on the 13th of May. I shall advertise my trees in the next Register. I never had them so fine, though the great drought has made the number comparatively small. Lord Folkestone bought of me 13,600 trees. They are, at this moment, worth the money they cost him, and, in addition the cost of planting, and in addition to that, they are worth the fee simple of the ground (very good ground) on which they stand; and this I am able to demonstrate to any man in his senses. What a difference in the value of Wiltshire, if all its Elms were Locusts! As fuel, a foot of Locust-wood is worth four or five of any English wood. It will burn better green, than almost any other wood will dry. If men want woods, beautiful woods, and *in a hurry*, let them go and see the clumps at Coleshill.

Malmsbury (Wilts),
Monday, 11th Sept.

I was detained at Highworth partly by the rain, and partly by company that I liked very much. I left it at six o'clock yesterday morning, and got to this town about three or four o'clock in the afternoon, after a ride, including my deviations, of 34 miles; and as pleasant a ride as man ever had. I got to a farm-house in the neighbourhood of Cricklade, to breakfast, at which house I was very near to the source of the river Isis, which is, they say, the first branch of the Thames. They call it the "Old Thames," and I rode through it here, it not being above four or five yards wide, and not deeper than the knees of my horse.

The land here, and all round Cricklade, is very fine. Here are some of the very finest pastures in all England, and some of the finest dairies of cows, from 40 to 60 in a dairy, grazing in them. Was not this *always* so? I saw in one single farmyard here, more food than enough for four times the inhabitants of the parish; and this yard did not contain a tenth, perhaps, of the produce of the parish; but, while the poor creatures that raise the wheat, and the barley, and cheese, and the mutton, and the beef, are living upon potatoes, an accursed *Canal* comes kindly through the parish to convey away the wheat, and all the good food to the tax-eaters and their attendants in the Wen! I could broom-stick the fellow who would look me in the face, and call this "an improvement."

I observed, some pages back, that, when I got to Malmsbury, I should have to explain my main object in coming to the North of Wiltshire. In the year 1818, the Parliament, by *an Act*, ordered the bishops to cause the beneficed clergy to give in an account of their livings, which account was to contain the following particulars, relating to each parish:

1. Whether a Rectory, Vicarage, or what.
2. In what rural Deanery.
3. Population.
4. Number of Churches and Chapels.
5. *Number of persons they* (the churches and chapels) *can contain*.

In looking into this account, as it was finally made up and printed by the parliamentary officers, I saw, that it was impossible for it to be true. I have always asserted, and indeed, I have clearly proved, that one of the two last population returns is false, barefacedly false; and, I was sure, that the account, of which I am now speaking, was equally false. The false-hood, consisted, I saw principally, in the account of the capacity of the church to contain people; that is, under the head No. 5, as above stated. I saw, that, in almost every instance, this account must of necessity be false, though coming from under the pen of a beneficed clergyman. I saw, that there was a constant desire to make it appear, that the church was now become too small! And thus to help along the opinion of a great recent increase of population, an opinion so sedulously inculcated by all the tax-eaters of every sort, and by the most brutal and best public instructor. In some cases the falsehood of this account was impudent almost beyond conception; and yet, it required going to the spot, to get unquestionable proof of the falsehood. Little Langford, or Landford, for instance, between Salisbury and Warminster, is returned as having a population under twenty, and a church that "can contain the population." This church, which I went and looked at, can contain, very conveniently, two hundred people! But, there was one instance, in which the parson had been singularly impudent; for, he had stated the population at eight persons, and had stated that the church could contain eight persons! This was the account of the parish of Sharncut, in this county of Wilts. It lies on the very northernmost edge of the county, and its boundary, on one side, divides Wiltshire from Gloucestershire. To this Sharncut, therefore, I was resolved to go, and to try the fact with my own eyes.

Sharncut, I found to consist of a church, two farm-houses, and a parsonage-house, one part of the buildings of which had become a labourer's house. The church has no tower, but a sort of crowning-piece (very ancient) on the transept. The church is sixty feet long, and, on an average, twenty-eight feet wide; so that the area of it contains one thousand six hundred and eighty square feet; or, one hundred and eighty-eight square yards! I found in the church eleven pews that would contain, that were made to contain, eighty-two people; and, these do not occupy a third part of the area of the church; and thus, more than two hundred persons, at least, might be accommodated, with perfect convenience, in this church, which the parson says "*can* contain *eight!*" Nay, the church porch, on its two benches, would hold twenty people, taking little and big promiscuously. I have been thus particular, in this instance, because I would leave no doubt as to the barefacedness of the lie. A strict inquiry would show, that the far greater part of the account is a most impudent lie, or, rather, string of lies. For, as to the subterfuge, that this account was true, because the church "*can* contain *eight*," it is an addition to the crime of lying. What the Parliament meant was, what "is the greatest number of persons that the church can contain at worship;" and, therefore to put the figure of 8 against the church of Sharncut was to tell the Parliament a wilful lie. This parish is a rectory; it has great and small tithes; it has a glebe, and a good solid house, though the parson says it is unfit for him to live in! In short, he is not here; a curate that serves, perhaps, three or four other churches, comes here at five o'clock in the afternoon.

The *motive* for making out the returns in this way is clear enough. The parsons see, that they are getting what they get in a declining, and a mouldering, country. The size of the church tells them, everything tells them, that the country is a mean and miserable thing, compared with what it was in former times. They feel the facts; but they wish to disguise them, because they know that they have been one great cause of the country being in its present impoverished and dilapidated state. They know, that the people look at them with an accusing eye: and they wish to put as fair a face as they can upon the state of things. If you talk to them, they will never acknowledge that there is any misery in the country; because they well know how large a share they have had in the cause of it. They were always haughty and insolent; but, the anti-jacobin times made them ten thousand times more so than ever. The cry of Atheism, as of the French, gave these fellows of ours a fine time of it: they became identified with loyalty, and what was more, with property; and, at one time, to say, or hint, a word against a parson, do what he would, was to be an enemy of God and of all property! Those were the glorious times for them. They urged on the war: they were the loudest of all the trumpeters. They saw their tithes in danger. If they did not get the Bourbons restored, there was no chance of re-establishing tithes in France; and then the example might be fatal. But, they forgot, that, to restore the Bourbons, a debt must be contracted; and that, when the nation could not pay the interest of that debt, it would, as it now does, begin to look hard at the tithes! In short, they over-reached themselves; and those of them who have common sense, now see it: each hopes that the thing will last out his time; but, they have, unless they be half-idiots, a constant dread upon their minds: this makes them a great deal less brazen than they used to be; and, I daresay, that, if the parliamentary return had to be made out again, the parson of Sharncut would not state that the church "*can* contain *eight persons*."

From Sharncut I came through a very long and straggling village, called Somerford, another called Ocksey, and another called Crudwell. Between Somerford and Ocksey, I saw, on the side of the road, more *goldfinches* than I had ever seen together; I think, fifty times as many as I had ever seen at one time in my life. The favourite food of the goldfinch is the seed of the *thistle*. This seed is just now dead ripe. The thistles are all cut and carried away from the fields by the harvest; but, they grow alongside the roads; and, in this place, in great quantities. So that the goldfinches were here in flocks, and, as they continued to fly along before me, for nearly half a mile, and still sticking to the road and the banks, I do believe I had, at last, a flock of ten thousand flying before me. *Birds* of every kind, including partridges and pheasants and all sorts of poultry, are most abundant this year. The fine, long summer has been singularly favourable to them; and you see the effect of it in the great broods of chickens and ducks and geese and turkeys in and about every farm-yard.

The churches of the last-mentioned villages are all large, particularly the latter, which is capable of containing, very conveniently, 3,000 or 4,000 people. It is a very large church; it has a triple roof, and is nearly 100 feet long; and master parson says, in his return, that it "*can* contain *three hundred* people!" At Ocksey the people were in church as I came by. I heard the singers singing; and, as the church-yard was close by the roadside, I got off my horse and went in, giving my horse to a boy to hold. The fellow says that his church "*can* contain *two hundred* people." I counted pews for about 450; the singing gallery would hold 40 or 50; two-thirds of the area of the church have no pews in them. On benches these two-thirds would hold 2,000 persons, taking one with another! But this is nothing rare;

the same sort of statement has been made, the same kind of falsehoods, relative to the whole of the parishes throughout the country, with here and there an exception.

When I got in here yesterday, I went, at first, to an inn; but I very soon changed my quarters for the house of a friend, who and whose family, though I had never seen them before, and had never heard of them until I was at Highworth, gave me a hearty reception, and precisely in *the style* that I like. This town, though it has nothing particularly engaging in itself, stands upon one of the prettiest spots that can be imagined. Besides the river Avon, which I went down in the South-East part of the country, here is another river Avon, which runs down to Bath, and two branches, or sources, of which meet here. There is a pretty ridge of ground, the base of which is a mile, or a mile and a half wide. On each side of this ridge a branch of the river runs down, through a flat of very fine meadows. The town and the beautiful remains of the famous old Abbey, stand on the rounded spot, which terminates this ridge; and, just below, nearly close to the town, the two branches of the river meet; and then they begin to be called *the Avon*. The land round about is excellent, and of a great variety of forms. The trees are lofty and fine: so that what with the water, the meadows, the fine cattle and sheep, and, as I hear, the absence of *hard*-pinching poverty, this is a very pleasant place. There remains more of the Abbey than, I believe, of any of our monastic buildings, except that of Westminster, and those that have become Cathedrals. The church-service is performed in the part of the Abbey that is left standing. The parish church has fallen down and is gone; but the tower remains, which is made use of for the bells; but the Abbey is used as the church, though the church-tower is at a considerable distance from it. It was once a most magnificent building; and there is now a *door-way*, which is the most beautiful thing I ever saw, and which was, nevertheless, built in Saxon times, in "the *dark* ages," and was built by men, who were not begotten by Pitt nor by Jubilee-George.[7]—What *fools*, as well as ungrateful creatures, we have been and are! There is a broken arch, standing off from the sound part of the building, at which one cannot look up without feeling shame at the thought of ever having abused the men who made it. No one need *tell* any man of sense; he *feels* our inferiority to our fathers, upon merely beholding the remains of their efforts to ornament their country and elevate the minds of the people. We talk of our skill and learning, indeed! How do we know how skilful, how learned *they* were? If, in all that they have left us, we see that they surpassed us, why are we to conclude, that they did not surpass us in all other things worthy of admiration?

---

[7] George III died in the sixtieth year of his reign. The reference is to George Chalmers's view that the population had increased enormously since 1760.

172

This famous Abbey was founded, in about the year 600, by Maidulf, a Scotch Monk,[8] who upon the suppression of a Nunnery here at that time selected the spot for this great establishment. For the great magnificence, however, to which it was soon after brought, it was indebted to Aldhelm, a Monk educated within its first walls, by the founder himself; and to St. Aldhelm, who by his great virtues became very famous, the Church was dedicated in the time of King Edgar. This Monastery continued flourishing during those *dark* ages, until it was sacked by the great enlightener, at which time it was found to be endowed to the amount of 16,077*l.* 11*s.* 8*d.*, of the money of the present day! Amongst other, many other, great men produced by this Abbey of Malmsbury, was that famous scholar and historian, William de Malmsbury.[9]

There is a *market-cross*, in this town, the sight of which is worth a journey of hundreds of miles. Time, with his scythe, and "enlightened Protestant piety,"[10] with its pick-axes and crow-bars; these united have done much to efface the beauties of this monument of ancient skill and taste, and proof of ancient wealth; but, in spite of all their destructive efforts, this Cross still remains a most beautiful thing, though possibly, and even probably, nearly, or quite, a thousand years old. There is a *market-cross* lately erected at Devizes, and intended to imitate the ancient ones. Compare that with this, and, then you have, pretty fairly, a view of the difference between us and our forefathers of the "dark ages."

To-morrow I start for Bollitree, near Ross, Herefordshire, my road being across the county, and through the city of Gloucester.

RIDE, FROM MALMSBURY, IN WILTSHIRE, THROUGH
GLOUCESTERSHIRE, HEREFORDSHIRE, AND WORCESTERSHIRE.

Stroud (Gloucestershire),
Tuesday Forenoon, 12th Sept., 1826.

I set off from Malmsbury this morning at 6 o'clock, in as sweet and bright a morning, as ever came out of the heavens, and leaving behind me as pleasant a house and as kind hosts as I ever met with in the whole course of my life, either in England or America; and that is saying a great deal indeed. This circumstance was the more pleasant, as I had never before either seen or heard of, these kind, unaffected, sensible, *sans-façons*, and most agreeable friends. From Malmsbury I first came, at the end of five miles, to Tutbury, which is in Gloucestershire, there

---

[8] A Scottish or Irish monk (died *c.* 675), founder of a school attended by St. Aldhem (640–709), Abbot of Malmesbury and Bishop of Sherborne.

[9] Early twelfth-century historian.

[10] Cobbett's term for alleged Protestant iconoclasm and vandalism.

being here, a sort of dell, or ravine, which, in this place, is the boundary line of the two counties, and over which you go on a bridge, one-half of which belongs to each county. And now, before I take my leave of Wiltshire, I must observe, that, in the whole course of my life (days of *courtship* excepted, of course), I never passed seventeen pleasanter days than those which I have just spent in Wiltshire. It is, especially in the Southern half, just the sort of country that I like; the weather has been pleasant; I have been in good houses and amongst good and beautiful gardens; and, in *every* case, I have not only been most kindly entertained, but my entertainers have been of just the stamp that I like.

I saw again, this morning, large flocks of *goldfinches*, feeding on the thistle-seed, on the roadside. The French call this bird by a name derived from the thistle, so notorious has it always been, that they live upon this seed. *Thistle* is, in French, *Chardon;* and the French call this beautiful little bird *Chardonaret*. I never could have supposed, that such flocks of these birds would ever be seen in England.

Just before I got into Tutbury, I was met by a good many people, in twos, threes, or fives, some running, and some walking fast, one of the first of whom asked me, if I had met an "old man" some distance back. I asked, what *sort* of a man: "A *poor* man." "I don't recollect, indeed; but, what are you all pursuing him for?" "He has been *stealing*." "What has he been stealing?" "Cabbages." "Where?" "Out of Mr. Glover, the hatter's, garden." "What! do you call that *stealing!* and would you punish a man, a poor man, and, therefore, in all likelihood, a hungry man too, and, moreover an old man; do you set up a hue-and-cry after, and would you punish, such a man for taking a few cabbages, when that Holy Bible, which, I dare say, you profess to believe in, and perhaps, assist to circulate, teaches you that the hungry man may, without committing any offence at all, go into his neighbour's vineyard and eat his fill of grapes, one bunch of which is worth a sack-full of cabbages?" "Yes; but he is a very bad character." "Why, my friend, very poor and almost starved people are apt to be 'bad characters;' but the Bible, in both Testaments, commands us to be merciful to the poor, to feed the hungry, to have compassion on the aged; and it makes no exception as to the 'character' of the parties." Another group or two of the pursuers had come up by this time; and I, bearing in mind the fate of Don Quixote, when he interfered in somewhat similar cases, gave my horse the hint, and soon got away; but, though, doubtless, I made no converts, I, upon looking back, perceived, that I had slackened the pursuit! The pursuers went more slowly; I could see that they got to talking; it was now the step of deliberation rather than that of decision; and, though, I did not like to call upon Mr. Glover, I hope he was merciful.

Tutbury is a very pretty town, and has a beautiful ancient church. The country is high along here for a mile or two toward Avening, which begins a long and deep and narrow valley, that comes all the way down to Stroud.

From Avening I came on through Nailsworth, Woodchester, and Rodborough, to this place. These villages lie on the sides of a narrow and deep valley, with a narrow stream of water running down the middle of it, and this stream turns the

174

wheels of a great many mills and sets of machinery for the making of *woollen-cloth*. The factories begin at Avening, and are scattered all the way down the valley. There are steam-engines as well as water powers. The work and the trade is so flat, that, in, I should think, much more than a hundred acres of ground, which I have seen to-day, covered with rails or racks, for the drying of cloth, I do not think that I have seen one single acre, where the racks had cloth upon them. The workmen do not get half wages; great numbers are thrown on the parish; but, overseers and magistrates, in this part of England do not presume that they are to leave anybody to starve to death; there is law here; this is in England, and not in "the North," where those who ought to see that the poor do not suffer, talk of their dying with hunger as Irish 'Squires do; aye, and applaud them for their patient resignation!

The Gloucestershire people have no notion of dying with hunger; and it is with

Pigs were an essential part of cottage economy, with almost every part of the animal being put to good use.

great pleasure that I remark, that I have seen no woe-worn creature this day. The sub-soil here is a yellowish ugly stone. The houses are all built with this; and, it being ugly, the stone is made *white* by a wash of some sort or other. The land on both sides of the valley, and all down the bottom of it, has plenty of trees on it; it is chiefly pasture land, so that the green and the white colours, and the form and great variety of the ground, and the water, and altogether make this a very pretty ride. Here are a series of spots, every one of which a lover of landscapes would like to have painted. Even the buildings of the factories are not ugly. The people seem to have been constantly well off. A pig in almost every cottage sty; and that is the infallible mark of a happy people. At present, indeed, this valley suffers; and, though cloth will always be wanted, there will yet be much suffering even here, while at Uly and other places, they say that the suffering is great indeed.

Huntley, between Gloucester and Ross.

I got to this village, about eight miles from Gloucester, by five o'clock: it is now half past seven, and I am going to bed with an intention of getting to Bollitree (six

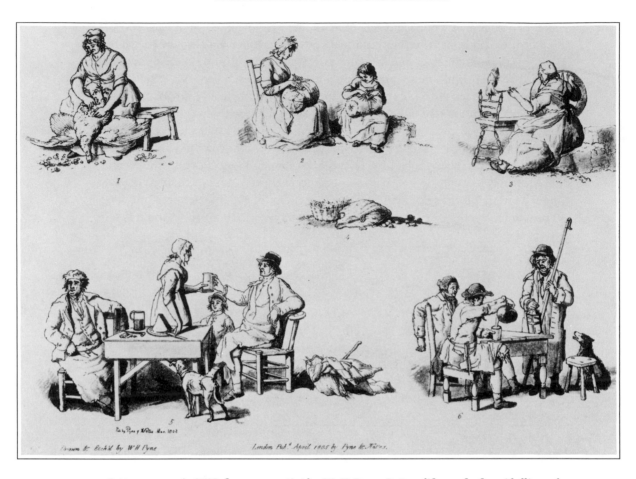

Cottage groups in 1805, from an aquatint by W. H. Pyne. Cottage life was far from idyllic, and Cobbett made great efforts to bring the plight of the rural poor to the notice of his fellow politicians.

miles only) early enough in the morning, to catch my sons in bed, if they play the sluggard.

Bollitree, Wednesday, 13th Sept.

This morning was most beautiful. There has been rain here now, and the grass begins (but only begins) to grow. When I got within two hundred yards of Mr. Palmer's[1] I had the happiness to meet my son Richard, who said that he had been up an hour. As I came along I saw one of the prettiest sights in the *flower* way that I ever saw in my life. It was a little orchard; the grass in it had just taken a start, and was beautifully fresh; and, very thickly growing amongst the grass, was the

[1] See note 1, page 23.

176

purple flowered *Colchicum*, in full bloom. They say, that the leaves of this plant which come out in the spring, and die away in the summer, are poisonous to cattle if they eat much of them in the spring. The flower, if standing by itself, would be no great beauty; but, contrasted thus, with the fresh grass, which was a little shorter than itself, it was very beautiful.[2]

Bollitree, Saturday, 23rd Sept.

What a thing it is to behold, poor people receiving rates, or alms, to prevent them from starving; and to behold one half, at least, of what they receive, taken from them in taxes! What a sight to behold soldiers, horse and foot, employed to prevent a distressed people from committing acts of violence, when the *cost* of the horse and foot would, probably, if applied in the way to relief to the sufferers, prevent the existence of the distress! *A cavalry horse has, I think, ten pounds of oats a day and twenty pounds of hay.* These at present prices, cost 16s. a week. Then there is stable room, barracks, straw, saddle, and all the trappings. Then there is the wear of the horse. Then the pay of them. So that one single horseman, with his horse, does not cost so little as 36s. a week; and that is more than the parish allowance to five labourers' or manufacturers' families, at five to a family; so that one horseman with his horse, costs what would feed twenty-five of the distressed creatures. If there be ten thousand of these horsemen, they cost as much as would keep, at the parish rate, two hundred and fifty thousand of the distressed persons.

Ryall, near Upton on Severn (Worcestershire),
Monday, 25th Sept.

Mr. Hanford, of this county, and Mr. Canning[3] of Gloucestershire, having dined at Mr. Price's yesterday, I went, to-day, with Mr. Price to see Mr. Hanford at his house and estate at Bredon Hill, which is, I believe, one of the highest in England. The ridge, or, rather, the edge of it, divides, in this part, Worcestershire from Gloucestershire. From Bredon Hill you see into nine or ten counties; and those curious bubblings-up, the Malvern Hills, are right before you, and only at about ten miles' distance, in a straight line. As this hill looks over the counties of Worcester, Gloucester, Hereford and part of Warwick, and the rich part of Stafford; and, as it looks over the vales of Esham,[4] Worcester, and Gloucester, having the Avon and the Severn, winding down them, you certainly see from this Bredon Hill one of the very richest spots of England.

The Avon (this is the *third* Avon that I have crossed in this Ride) falls into the Severn just below Tewkesbury, through which town we went in our way to Mr.

---

[2] Meadow saffron, sometimes called autumn crocus. P.C.

[3] Charles Edward Hanford of Wollas Hale, Worcs. and Robert Canning of Hartpury, Glos., both good friends of Cobbett.

[4] Evesham.

Hanford's. These rivers, particularly the Severn, go through, and sometimes overflow, the finest meadows of which it is possible to form an idea. Some of them contain more than a hundred acres each; and the number of cattle and sheep, feeding in them, is prodigious. Nine-tenths of the land, in these extensive vales, appears to me to be pasture, and it is pasture of the richest kind. The sheep are chiefly of the Leicestershire breed, and the cattle of the Hereford, white face and dark red body, certainly the finest and most beautiful of all horn cattle. The grass, after the fine rains that we have had, is in its finest possible dress; but, here, as in the parts of Gloucestershire and Herefordshire that I have seen, there are no turnips, except those which have been recently sown; and, though amidst all these thousands upon thousands of acres of the finest meadows and grass land in the world, hay is, I hear, seven pounds a ton at Worcester. However, unless we should have very early and even hard frosts, the grass will be so abundant, that the cattle and sheep will do better than people are apt to think. But, be this as it may, this summer has taught us, that our climate is the *best for produce*, after all; and that we cannot have Italian sun and English meat and cheese. We complain of the *drip;* but, it is the drip, that makes the beef and the mutton.

Mr. Hanford's house is on the side of Bredon Hill; about a third part up it, and is a very delightful place. The house is of ancient date, and it appears to have been always inhabited by and the property of Roman Catholics; for there is, in one corner of the very top of the building, up in the very roof of it, a Catholic chapel, as ancient as the roof itself. It is about twenty-five feet long and ten wide. It has arch-work, to imitate the roof of a church. At the back of the altar there is a little room, which you enter through a door going out of the chapel; and, adjoining this little room, there is a closet, in which is a trap-door made to let the priest down into one of those hiding places, which were contrived for the purpose of evading the grasp of those greedy Scotch minions, to whom that pious and tolerant Protestant, James I., delivered over those English gentlemen, who remained faithful to the religion of their fathers, and, to set his country free, from which greedy and cruel grasp, that honest Englishman, Guy Fawkes, wished, as he bravely told the King and his Scotch council, *"to blow the Scotch beggars back to their mountains again."* Even this King has, in his works (for James was an author), had the justice to call him "the English Scævola;"[5] and we Englishmen, fools set on by knaves, have the folly, or the baseness, to burn him in effigy on the 5th November, the anniversary of his intended exploit! In the hall of this house, there is the portrait of Sir Thomas Winter,[6] who was one of the accomplices of Fawkes, and who was killed in the fight with the sheriff and his party. There is also the portrait of his lady, who must have spent half of her life-time in the working of some very curious sacerdotal

---

[5] Caius Mucius Scaevola, Roman patriot, who attempted to assassinate the Etruscan invader Lars Porsenna, was caught but spared after demonstrating his courage by letting his right hand be burnt off. "Scaevola" means left-handed.

[6] Thomas Winter (1572–1606), fellow conspirator with Guy Fawkes, *not* "killed in the fight" but executed with the full barbarity reserved for traitors.

vestments, which are preserved here with great care, and are as fresh and as beautiful as they were the day they were finished.

Worcester, Tuesday, 26th Sept.

Mr. Price rode with us to this city, which is one of the cleanest, neatest, and handsomest towns I ever saw: indeed, I do not recollect to have seen any one equal to it. The *cathedral* is, indeed, a poor thing, compared with any of the others, except that of Hereford; and I have seen them all, but those of Carlisle, Durham, York, Lincoln, Chester, and Peterborough;[7] but the *town* is, I think, the very best I ever saw; and which is, indeed, the greatest of all recommendations, the *people* are, upon the whole, the most suitably dressed and most decent looking people. The town is precisely in character with the beautiful and rich country, in the midst of which it lies. Everything you see gives you the idea of real, solid wealth; aye! and thus it was, too, before, long before, Pitt, and even long before "good Queen Bess" and her military law, and her Protestant racks, were ever heard or dreamed of.

At Worcester, as everywhere else, I find a group of cordial and sensible friends, at the house of one of whom, Mr. George Brooke, I have just spent a most pleasant evening, in company with several gentlemen, whom he had had the goodness to invite to meet me. I here learned a fact, which I must put upon record before it escape my memory. Some few years ago (about seven, perhaps), at the public sale by auction of the goods of a then recently deceased Attorney of the name of Hyde, in this city, there were, amongst the goods to be sold, the portraits of *Pitt, Burdett,* and *Paine,* all framed and glazed. Pitt, with hard driving and very lofty praises, fetched fifteen shillings; Burdett fetched twenty-seven shillings. Paine was, in great haste, knocked down at five pounds; and my informant was convinced, that the lucky purchaser might have had fifteen pounds for it.

Stanford Park,
Wednesday, 27th Sept. (Morning).

In a letter which I received from Sir Thomas Winnington[8] (one of the Members for this county), last year, he was good enough to request that I would call upon him, if I ever came into Worcestershire, which I told him I would do; and accordingly here we are in his house, situated, certainly, in one of the finest spots in all England. We left Worcester yesterday about ten o'clock, crossed the Severn, which runs close by the town, and came on to this place, which lies in a north-western direction from Worcester, at 14 miles' distance from that city, and at about six from the borders of Shropshire. We crossed the Teme River just before we got here. Sir Thomas was out shooting; but he soon came home, and gave us a very polite reception. I had time, yesterday, to see the place, to look at trees, and the like, and I wished to get away early this morning; but, being prevailed on to

---

[7] It is notable how ignorant Cobbett still is of the Midlands and the North.
[8] Sir Thomas Winnington (1780–1839) M.P. for Worcestershire.

A view of the city of Worcester from the north-east.

stay to breakfast, here I am, at six o'clock in the morning, in one of the best and best-stocked private libraries that I ever saw; and, what is more, the owner, from what passed yesterday, when he brought me hither, convinced me that he was acquainted with the *insides* of the books. I asked, and shall ask, no questions about who got these books together; but the collection is such as, I am sure, I never saw before in a private house.

The house and stables and courts are such as they ought to be for the great estate that surrounds them; and the park is everything that is beautiful. On one side of the house, looking over a fine piece of water, you see a distant valley, opening between lofty hills: on another side the ground descends a little at first, then goes gently rising for a while, and then rapidly, to the distance of a mile perhaps, where it is crowned with trees in irregular patches, or groups, single and most magnificent trees being scattered all over the whole of the park; on another side, there rise up beautiful little hills, some in the form of barrows on the downs, only forty or a hundred times as large, one or two with no trees on them, and others topped with trees; but, on one of these little hills, and some yards higher than the lofty trees which are on this little hill, you see rising up the tower of the parish church, which hill is, I think, taken all together, amongst the most delightful objects that I ever beheld.

"Well then," says the devil of laziness, "and could you not be contented to live here all the rest of your life; and never again pester yourself with the cursed politics?" "Why, I think I have laboured enough. Let others work now. And such a pretty place for coursing and for hare-hunting and woodcock shooting, I dare say; and then those pretty wild-ducks in the water, and the flowers and the grass and the trees and all the birds in spring and the fresh air, and never, never again to be stifled with the smoke that from the infernal Wen ascendeth for ever more, and that every easterly wind brings to choke me at Kensington!" The *last word* of this soliloquy carried me back, slap, to my own study (very much unlike that which I am in), and bade me think of the GRIDIRON;[9] bade me think of the complete triumph, that I have yet to enjoy: promised me the pleasure of seeing a million of trees of my own, and sown by my own hands this very year. Ah! but the hares and the pheasants and the wild ducks! Yes, but the delight of seeing Prosperity Robinson[10] hang his head for shame: the delight of beholding the tormenting embarrassments of those who have so long retained crowds of base miscreants to revile me; the delight of ousting spitten-upon Stanley and bound-over Wood![11]

---

[9] A reference to Cobbett's offer to allow Castlereagh to broil him on a gridiron if Peel's economic measures succeeded.

[10] Cobbett's sarcastic name for Frederick John Robinson (1782–1859), Viscount Goderich and Earl of Ripon, ineffectual Prime Minister 1827–8.

[11] Edward George Stanley (1799–1869), Earl of Derby and, later, Prime Minister, and John Wood (1790–1838) were Cobbett's successful opponents in the Preston election of 1826. Stanley was "spat on" by the mob and Wood "bound over" for challenging a man to a duel.

Yes, but, then, the flowers and the birds and the sweet air! What, then, shall Canning never again hear of the "revered and ruptured Ogden!"[12] Shall he go into his grave, without being again reminded of "driving at the whole herd, in order to get at the *ignoble animal!*" Shall he never again be told of Six-Acts and of his wish "to extinguish that *accursed torch of discord for ever!*" Oh! God forbid! farewell hares and dogs and birds! what, shall Sidmouth,[13] then, never again hear of his *Power of Imprisonment Bill*, of his *Circular*, of his *Letter of Thanks to the Manchester Yeomanry!* I really jumped up when this thought came athwart my mind, and, without thinking of the breakfast, said to George[14] who was sitting by me, "Go, George, and tell them to saddle the horses;" for, it seemed to me, that I had been meditating some crime. Upon George asking me, whether I would not stop to breakfast? I bade him not order the horses out yet; and here we are, waiting for breakfast.

Ryall, Wednesday Night, 27th Sept.

After breakfast we took our leave of Sir Thomas Winnington, and of Stanford, very much pleased with our visit. We wished to reach Ryall as early as possible in the day, and we did not, therefore, stop at Worcester. We got here about three-o'clock, and we intend to set off, in another direction, early in the morning.

RIDE FROM RYALL, IN WORCESTERSHIRE, TO BURGHCLERE, IN HAMPSHIRE.

> "Alas, the country! How shall tongue or pen
> Bewail her now, *un*country gentlemen!
> The last to bid the cry of warfare cease,
> The first to make a malady of peace!
> For what were all these country patriots born?
> To hunt, and vote, and raise the price of corn,
> But corn, like ev'ry mortal thing, must fall:
> Kings, conquerors, and, *markets most of all*."
>
> LORD BYRON.

Ryall,
Friday Morning, 29th September, 1826.

I have observed, in this country, and especially near Worcester, that the working people seem to be better off than in many other parts, one cause of which is, I dare say, that *glove manufacturing*, which cannot be carried on by fire or by wind or by

---

[12] William Ogden (1753–1832), a printer who accompanied a workers' march on London in 1817, was arrested and ill-treated. Canning was said to have joked about the man's injuries.

[13] See note 4, page 33.

[14] Son of William Palmer of Bollitree.

water, and which is, therefore, carried on by the *hands* of human beings. It gives work to women and children, as well as to men; and that work is, by a great part of the women and children, done in their cottages, and amidst the fields and hop-gardens, where the husbands and sons must live, in order to raise the food, and the drink, and the wool. This is a great thing for the land. If this glove-making were to cease, many of these women and children, now, not upon the parish, must instantly be upon the parish. The glove-trade is, like all others, slack, from this last change in the value of money; but, there is no horrible misery here, as at Manchester, Leeds, Glasgow, Paisley, and other Holes of 84 degrees of heat. There misery walks abroad in skin, bone and nakedness. While there is an absolute destruction of life going on in the holes, there is no *visible* misery at, or near, Worcester; and I cannot take my leave of this county without observing, that I do not recollect to have seen, one miserable object in it. The working people, all seem to have good large gardens, and pigs in their styes; and this last, say the *feelosofers* what they will about her "antallectual enjoyments," is the *only* security for happiness, in a labourer's family.

Of all the mean, all the cowardly reptiles, that ever crawled on the face of the earth, the *English land-owners* are the most mean, and the most cowardly: for, while they support the churches, in their several parishes, while they see the population drawn away from their parishes, to the Wens, while they are taxed to keep the people in the Wens, and while they see their own Parsons pocket the tithes, and the glebe-rents, and suffer the parsonage-houses to fall down; while they see all this, they, without uttering a word in the way of complaint, suffer themselves and their neighbours to be taxed, to build new churches for the monopolizers and tax-eaters in those Wens! Never was there in this world, a set of reptiles so base as this. Of course, all they want is the income, and, the less the parsonage-house costs, the larger the spending income. But, in the meanwhile, here is a destruction of public property; and also, from a diversion of the income of the livings, a great injury, great injustice, to the middle and the working classes.

Is this, then, is this "church" a thing to remain untouched? Shall the widow and the orphan, whose money has been borrowed *by the land-owners* (including the Parsons) to purchase "victories" with; shall they be stripped of their interest, of their very bread, and shall the Parsons, who have let half the parsonage-houses fall down, or become unfit to live in, still keep all the tithes and the glebe-lands and the immense landed estates, called Church Lands? Oh, no! Sir James Graham "of Netherby,"[1] though you are a descendant of the Earls of Monteith, of John of the bright sword, and of the Seventh Earl of Galloway, K.T. (taking care, for God's sake, not to omit the K.T.); though you may be the *Magnus Apollo;* and, in short, be you what you may, you shall never execute your project of sponging the fund-holders and of leaving Messieurs the Parsons untouched! In many parishes, where the livings are good too, there is neither parsonage-house nor church! This is the

---

[1] Sir James Graham (1792–1861), a Cumberland squire, later Home Secretary, accused by Cobbett of plagiarising some of his ideas in a pamphlet of 1826.

case at Draycot Foliot, in Wiltshire. The living is a Rectory; the Parson has, of course, both great and small tithes; these tithes and the glebe-land are worth, I am told, more than three hundred pounds a year; and yet there is neither church nor parsonage-house; both have been suffered to fall down and disappear; and, when a new Parson comes to take possession of the living, there is, I am told, a temporary tent, or booth, erected, upon the spot where the church ought to be, for the performance of the *ceremony of induction!* What, then! Ought not this church to be repealed? An Act of Parliament made this church; an Act of Parliament can unmake it; and, is there any but a monster who would suffer this Parson to retain this income, while that of the widow and the orphan was taken away? Oh, no? Sir James Graham of Netherby, who, with the *gridiron before you*, say, that there was "no man, of any authority, who foresaw the effects of Peel's Bill;" oh, no! thou stupid, thou empty-headed, thou insolent aristocratic phamphleteer, the widow and the orphan *shall not* be robbed of their bread, while this Parson of Draycot Foliot keeps the income of his living!

On my return from Worcester to this place, yesterday, I noticed, at a village called Severn Stoke, a very curiously-constructed grape house; that is to say, a hot-house for the raising of grapes. Upon inquiry, I found, that it belonged to a Parson, of the name of St. John, whose parsonage-house is very near to it, and who, being *sure* of having the benefice, when the then Rector should die, bought a piece of land, and erected his grapery on it, just facing, and only about 50 yards from the windows, out of which the *old parson* had to look, until the day of his death, with a view, doubtless, of piously furnishing his aged brother with a *momento mori* (remember death), quite as significant as a death's head and crossbones, and yet done in a manner expressive, of that fellow-feeling, that delicacy, that abstinence from self-gratification, which are well known to be characteristics almost peculiar to "the cloth!" To those, if there be such, who may be disposed to suspect that the grapery arose, upon the spot where it stands, merely from the desire to have the vines in bearing state, against the time that the old parson should die, or, as I heard the Botley Parson once call it, "kick the bucket;"[2] to such persons, I would just put this one question; did they ever either from Scripture or tradition, learn that any of the Apostles or their disciples, erected graperies from motives such as this? They may, indeed, say, that they never heard of the Apostles, erecting any graperies at all, much less of their having erected them from such a motive. Nor, to say the truth, did I ever hear of any such erections on the part of those Apostles and those whom they commissioned to preach the word of God; and, Sir William Scott (now a *lord* of some sort)[3] never convinced me, by his parson-praising speech of 1802, that to give the church-clergy a due degree of influence over the minds of the people, to make the people

---

[2] The Revd Richard Baker, Cobbett's neighbour at Botley 1805–21, and his inveterate enemy and butt.

[3] Sir William Scott (1735–1846), elder brother of Lord Eldon and scarcely less of a Tory, created Lord Stowell in 1821.

revere them, it was necessary that the parsons and their wives should shine at *balls* and in *pump-rooms*. On the contrary, these and the like, have taken away almost the whole of their spiritual influence. They never had much; but, lately, and especially, since 1793, they have had hardly any at all; and, wherever I go, I find them much better known as *Justices of the Peace*, than as Clergymen. What they would come to, if this system could go on for only a few years longer, I know not; but go on, as it is now going, it cannot much longer; there must be *a settlement of some sort:* and that settlement never can leave that mass, that immense mass, of public property, called "church property," to be used as it now is.

I have seen, in this country, and in Herefordshire, several pieces of Mangel Wurzel; and, I hear, that it has nowhere failed, as the turnips have. Even the Lucerne has, in some places, failed to a certain extent; but, Mr. Walter Palmer, at Pencoyd, in Herefordshire, has cut a piece of Lucerne four times this last summer, and, when I saw it, on the 17th Sept. (12 days ago), it was got a foot high towards another cut. But, with one exception (too trifling to mention), Mr. Walter Palmer's Lucerne is on the Tullian plan, that is, it is in rows, at four feet distance from each other; so that you plough between, as often as you please, and thus, together with a little hand weeding between the plants, keep the ground, at all times, clear of weeds and grass. Mr. Palmer says, that his acre (he has no more) has kept two horses all the summer; and he seems to complain, that it has done no more. Indeed! A stout horse will eat much more than a fatting ox. This grass will fat any ox, or sheep; and would not Mr. Palmer like to have ten acres of land, that would fat a score of oxen? They would do this, if they were managed well. But, is it *nothing* to keep a team of four horses, for five months in the year, on the produce of two acres of land? If a man say that, he must, of course, be eagerly looking forward to another world; for nothing will satisfy him in this. A good crop of early cabbages, may be had between the rows of Lucerne.

Cabbages have, generally, wholly failed. Those that I see are almost all too backward to make much of heads; though it is surprising how fast they will grow and come to perfection, as soon as there is *twelve hours of night*. I am here, however, speaking of the large sorts of cabbage; for, the smaller sorts will loave in summer. Mr. Walter Palmer has now a piece of these, of which I think there are from 17 to 20 *tons* to the acre; and this, too, observe, after a season which, on the same farm, has not suffered a turnip of any sort to come. If he had had 20 acres of these, he might have almost laughed at the failure of his turnips, and at the short crop of hay. And, this is a crop of which a man may always be *sure*, if he take proper pains. These cabbages (Early Yorks, or some such sort) should, if you want them in June or July, be sown early in the previous August. If you want them in winter, sown in April, and treated as pointed out in my *Cottage Economy*. These small sorts stand the winter better than the large; they are more nutritious; and they occupy the ground little more than half the time. *Dwarf Savoys* are the finest and richest and most nutritious of cabbages. Sown early in April, and planted out early in July, they will, at 18 inches apart each way, yield a crop of 30 to 40 tons by Christmas.

But, all this supposes land very good, or, very well manured, and plants of a good sort, and well raised and planted, and the ground well tilled after planting; and a crop of 30 tons is worth all these, and all the care, and all the pains, that a man can possibly take.

I am here amongst the finest of cattle, and the finest sheep of the Leicester kind, that I ever saw. My host, Mr. Price, is famed as a breeder of cattle and sheep. The cattle are of the Hereford kind, and the sheep surpassing any animals of the kind that I ever saw. The animals seem to be made for the soil, and the soil for them.

In taking leave of this county, I repeat, with great satisfaction, what I before said about the apparent comparatively happy state of the labouring people; and I have been very much pleased, with the tone and manner in which they are spoken to, and spoken of, by their superiors. I hear of no *hard* treatment of them here, such as I have but too often heard of, in some counties, and too often witnessed in others; and I quit Worcestershire, and particularly the house in which I am, with all those feelings which are naturally produced, by the kindest of receptions, from frank and sensible people.

Hayden, Saturday Night,
30th Sept.

The Warwickshire Avon falls into the Severn here, and on the sides of both, for many miles back, there are the finest meadows that ever were seen. In looking over them, and beholding the endless flocks and herds, one wonders what can become of all the meat! By riding on about eight or nine miles farther, however, this wonder is a little diminished; for here we come to one of the devouring Wens; namely, Cheltenham, which is what they call a "watering place;" that is to say, a place, to which East India plunderers, West India floggers, English tax-gorgers, together with gluttons, drunkards, and debauchees of all descriptions, female as well as male, resort, at the suggestion of silently laughing quacks, in the hope of getting rid of the bodily consequences of their manifold sins and iniquities. When I enter a place like this, I always feel disposed to squeeze up my nose with my fingers. It is nonsense, to be sure; but I conceive that every two-legged creature, that I see coming near me, is about to cover me with the poisonous proceeds of its impurities.

After Cheltenham, we had to reach this pretty little town of Fairford, the regular turnpike road to which, lay through Cirencester; but I had from a fine map, at Sir Thomas Winnington's, traced out a line for us, along through a chain of villages, leaving Cirencester away to our right, and never coming nearer than seven or eight miles to it. We came through Dodeswell, Withington, Chedworth, Winston, and the two Colnes. At Dodeswell we came up a long and steep hill, which brought us out of the great vale of Gloucester, and up upon the Cotswold Hills, which name is tautological, I believe; for I think that *wold* meant *high lands of great extent*. Such is the Cotswold, at any rate, for it is a tract of country stretching across, in a south-eastern direction, from Dodeswell, to near Fairford, and in a north-easterly direction, from Pitchcomb Hill, in Gloucestershire (which, remember, I descended on the 12th September) to near Witney in Oxfordshire. Here we were, then, when we got fairly up upon the Wold, with the vale of Gloucester at our back, Oxford and its vale to our left, the vale of Wiltshire to our right, and the vale of Berkshire in our front: and from one particular point, I could see a part of each of them. This Wold is, in itself, an ugly country. The soil is what is called a *stone brash* below, with a reddish earth mixed with little bits of this brash at top, and, for the greater part of the Wold, even this soil is very shallow; and, as fields are divided by walls made of this brash, and, as there are, for a mile or two together, no trees to be seen, and, as the surface is not smooth and green like the downs, this is a sort of country, having less to please the eye than any other that I have ever seen, always save and except the *heaths* like those of Bagshot and Hindhead.

A *route*, when it lies through *villages*, is one thing on a *map*, and quite another thing on the ground. Our line of villages, from Cheltenham, to Fairford, was very nearly straight upon the map; but, upon the ground, it took us round about a great many miles, besides now and then a little going back, to get into the right road; and, which was a great inconvenience, not a public-house was there on our road, until we got within eight miles of Fairford. Resolved, that not one single farthing of my money should be spent in the Wen of Cheltenham, we came through that place, expecting to find a public-house in the first or second of the villages; but not one was there, over the whole of the Wold; and though I had, by pocketing some slices of meat and bread at Ryall, provided against this contingency, as far as related to ourselves, I could make no such provision for our horses, and they went a great deal too far, without baiting. Plenty of farm-houses, and, if they had been in America, we need have looked for no other. Very likely (I hope it at any rate) almost any farmer on the Cotswold, would have given us what we wanted, if we had asked for it; but the fashion, the good old fashion, was, by the hellish system of funding and taxing and monopolizing, driven across the Atlantic. And is England *never* to see it return? Is the hellish system to last *for ever*?

Burghclere (Hampshire), Monday, 2d October.

Yesterday was a really *unfortunate day*. The morning promised fair; but, its promises were like those of Burdett! There was a little snivelling, wet, treacherous frost. We had to come through Swindon, and Mr. Tucky had the kindness to come with us, until we got three or four miles on this side (the Hungerford side) of that very neat, and plain, and solid, and respectable market town. Swindon is in Wiltshire, and is in the real fat of the land, all being wheat, beans, cheese, or fat meat. In our way to Swindon, Mr. Tucky's farm[4] exhibited to me, what I never saw before, four score oxen, all grazing upon one farm, and all nearly fat! They were, some Devonshire and some Herefordshire. They were fatting on the grass only; and, I should suppose, that they are worth, or shortly will be, thirty pounds each.

---

[4] At "Haydon", possibly Haydon Wick just north-west of Swindon.

But, the great pleasure, with which the contemplation of this fine sight, was naturally calculated to inspire me, was more than counterbalanced by the thought, that these fine oxen, this primest of human food, was, aye, every mouthful of it, destined to be devoured in the Wen, and that, too, for the far greater part, by the Jews, loan-jobbers, tax-eaters, and their base and prostituted followers, dependents, purveyors, parasites and pimps, literary as well as other wretches, who, if suffered to live at all, ought to partake of nothing but the offal, and ought to come, but one cut, before the dogs and cats!

Mind you, there is, in my opinion, no land in England that surpasses this. There is, I suppose, as good in the three last counties, that I have come through; but, *better* than this is, I should think, impossible. There is a pasture-field, of about a hundred acres, close to Swindon, belonging to a Mr. Goddard, which, with its cattle and sheep, was a most beautiful sight. But, every thing is full of riches; and, as fast as skill, and care, and industry, can extract these riches from the land, the unseen grasp of taxation, loan-jobbing, and monopolizing takes them away, leaving the labourers not half a bellyfull, compelling the farmer to pinch them, or to be ruined himself, and making even the landowner, little better than a steward, or bailiff, of the tax-eaters, Jews and jobbers!

Just before we got to Swindon, we crossed a canal at a place where there is a wharf and a coal-yard, and close by these a gentleman's house, with coach-house, stables, walled-in garden, paddock *orné*, and the rest of those things, which, all together, make up *a villa*, surpassing the second, and approaching towards the first class. Seeing a man in the coal-yard, I asked him to what gentleman, the house belonged: "to the *head un* o' the canal," said he. And, when, upon further inquiry of him, I found that it was the villa of the chief manager, I could not help congratulating the proprietors of this aquatic concern; for, though I did not ask the name of the canal, I could readily suppose, that the profits must be prodigious, when the residence of the manager, would imply no disparagement of dignity, if occupied by a Secretary of State for the Home, or even for the Foreign, department. I mean an *English* Secretary of State; for as to an *American* one, his salary would be wholly inadequate, to a residence in a mansion like this.

From Swindon we came up into the *down-country;* and these downs, rise higher even than the Cotswold. We left Marlborough away to our right, and came along the turnpike road towards Hungerford, but with a view of leaving that town to our left, further on, and going away, through Ramsbury, towards the northernmost Hampshire hills, under which Burghclere (where we now are) lies. We passed some fine farms, upon these downs, the houses and homesteads of which were near the road. My companion, though he had been to London, and even to France, had never seen *downs* before; and it was amusing to me to witness his surprise, at seeing the immense flocks of sheep, which were now (ten o'clock) just going out from their several folds, to the downs for the day, each having its shepherd, and each shepherd his dog. We passed the homestead of a former Woodman, with *sixteen* banging wheat-ricks in the rick-yard, two of which were old ones; and

A cartoon of 1827 lampooning the Duke of Wellington, the 'greatest Captain of the Age' who, although the first politician to give way to the growing power of the people, as Prime Minister strenuously opposed the Reform Bill, and attracted the wrath of the London mobs.

Above:
Canterbury Cathedral in 1821, by J. Marten. Cobbett remarked on the city's 'cleanliness and niceness, notwithstanding it has a Cathedral in it.'

Left:
Joseph Farington's drawing of the Lady Oak near Cressage, Shropshire. Cobbett was particularly interested in the native trees of the English woods, and showed himself to be considerably knowledgeable in the subject.

rick-yard, farm-yard, waste-yard, horse-paddock, and all round about, seemed to be swarming with fowls, ducks, and turkeys, and on the whole of them, not one feather, but what was white! Turning our eyes from this sight, we saw, just going out from the folds of this same farm, three separate and numerous flocks of sheep, one of which (the *lamb*-flock) we passed close by the side of. The shepherd told us, that his flock consisted of thirteen score and five; but, apparently, he could not, if it had been to save his soul, tell us how many hundreds he had: and, if you reflect a little, you will find, that his way of counting is much the easiest and best. This was a most beautiful flock of lambs; short legged, and, in every respect, what they ought to be. George, though born and bred amongst sheep-farms, had never before seen sheep with dark-coloured faces and legs; but his surprise, at this sight, was not nearly so great as the surprise of both of us, at seeing numerous and very large pieces (sometimes 50 acres together) of very good early turnips, Swedish as well as White! All the three counties of Worcester, Hereford, and Gloucester (except on the Cotswold) do not, I am convinced, contain as great a weight of turnip bulbs, as we here saw in one single *piece;* for here there are, for miles and miles, no hedges, and no fences of any sort.

Doubtless they must have had *rain* here, in the months of June and July; but, as I once before observed (though I forget *when*) a chalk bottom does not suffer the surface to burn, however shallow the top soil may be. It seems to me to absorb and to *retain* the water, and to keep it ready to be drawn up by the heat of the sun. At any rate the fact is, that the surface above it does not burn; for, there never yet was a summer, not even this last, when the downs did not *retain their greenness to a certain degree*, while the rich pastures, and even the meadows (except actually *watered*) were burnt so as to be as brown as the bare earth.

This is a most pleasing circumstance, attending the down countries; and, there are no *downs* without a chalk bottom.

Along here, the country is rather *too bare:* here, until you come to Auborne, or Aldbourne, there are *no meadows* in the valleys, and no trees, even round the homesteads. This, therefore, is too naked to please me; but I love *the downs* so much, that, if I had to choose, I would live even here, and especially I would *farm* here rather than on the banks of the Wye in Herefordshire, in the vale of Gloucester, of Worcester, or of Evesham, or, even in what the Kentish men call their ''garden of Eden.'' I have now seen (for I have, years back, seen the vales of Taunton, Glastonbury, Honiton, Dorchester and Sherburne) what are deemed the richest and most beautiful parts of England; and, if called upon to name the spot, which I deem the brightest and most beautiful and, of its extent, *best* of all, I should say, the villages of *North Bovant and Bishopstrow*, between Heytesbury and Warminster in Wiltshire; for there is, as appertaining to rural objects, *every thing* that *I delight* in. Smooth and verdant downs in hills and valleys of endless variety as to height and depth and shape; rich corn-land, unencumbered by fences; meadows in due proportion, and those watered at pleasure; and, lastly, the homesteads, and villages, sheltered in winter, and shaded in summer, by lofty and beautiful trees; to which may be added, roads never dirty and a stream never dry.

Whoever tries it, will find, that the *less they eat and drink*, when travelling, the better they will be. I act accordingly. Many days I have no breakfast and no dinner. I went from Devizes to Highworth without breaking my fast, a distance, including my deviations, of more than *thirty miles*. I sometimes take, from a friend's house, a little bit of meat between two bits of bread, which I eat as I ride along; but, whatever I save from this fasting work, I think I have a clear right to give away; and, accordingly, I generally put the amount, in copper, into my waistcoat pocket, and dispose of it during the day. I know well, *that I am the better* for not stuffing and blowing myself out, and with the savings I make many and many a happy boy; and, now-and-then, I give a whole family a good meal with the cost of a breakfast, or a dinner, that would have done me mischief. I do not do this, because I grudge innkeepers, what they charge; for, my surprise is, how they can live, without charging *more* than they do in general.

It was dark by the time that we got to a village, called East Woodhay. Sunday evening is the time *for courting*, in the country. It is not convenient to carry this on before faces, and, at farm-houses and cottages, there are no spare apartments; so that the pairs turn out, and pitch up, to carry on their negociations, by the side of stile, or a gate. The evening was auspicious; it was *pretty dark*, the *weather mild*, and *Old Michaelmas* (when yearly services end) was fast approaching; and accordingly, I do not recollect ever having before seen, so many negociations going on, within so short a distance.

We got to Burghclere about eight o'clock, after a very disagreeable day; but we found ample compensation in the house, and all within it, that we were now arrived at.

RIDE FROM BURGHCLERE TO LYNDHURST, IN THE NEW FOREST.

"The reformers have yet many and powerful foes; we have to contend against a host, such as never existed before in the world. Nine-tenths of the press; all the channels of speedy communication of sentiment; all the pulpits; all the associations of rich people; all the taxing-people; all the military and naval establishments; all the yeomanry cavalry tribes. Your allies are endless in number, and mighty in influence. But, we have *one ally* worth the whole of them put together, namely, the DEBT! This is an ally, whom no honours or rewards can seduce from us. She is a steady, unrelaxing, persevering, incorruptible ally. An ally that is proof against all blandishments, all intrigues, all temptations, and all open attacks. She sets at definace all *'military,'* all *'yeomanry cavalry.'* They may as well fire at a ghost. She cares no more for the sabres of the yeomanry, or the Life Guards, than Milton's angels did for the swords of Satan's myrmidons. This ally cares not a straw about *spies*, and *informers*. She laughs at the employment of *secret-service money*. She is always erect, day and night, and is always firmly moving on in our cause, in spite of all the terrors of gaols, dungeons, halters and axes. Therefore, Mr. JABET, be not so pert. The combat is not so unequal as you seem to imagine; and, confident and insolent as you now are, the day of your humiliation may not be far distant."—LETTER TO Mr. JABET, of Birmingham, *Register*, v. 31, p. 477. (Nov. 1816.)

> *Hurstbourn Tarrant,*
> *(commonly called Uphusband,)*
> *Wednesday, 11th October, 1826.*

WHEN quarters are good, you are apt to *lurk* in them; but, really it was so wet, that we could not get away from Burghclere till Monday evening. Being here, there were many reasons for our going to the great fair at Weyhill, which began yesterday, and, indeed, the day before, at Appleshaw. These two days are allotted for the selling of sheep only, though the horse-fair begins on the 10th. The prices, take them on a fair average, were, at both fairs, just about one-half what they were last year. There were Dorsetshire ewes that sold last year, for 50s. a head. We could hear of none this year that exceeded 25s. And only think of 25s., for one of these fine, large ewes, nearly fit to kill, and having two lambs in her, ready to be brought forth in, on an average, six weeks' time! The average is *three lambs* to *two of these ewes*. In 1812 these ewes were from 55s. to 72s. each, at this same Appleshaw fair; and in that year, I bought South Down ewes at 45s. each, just such as were, yesterday, sold for 18s. Yet, the sheep and grass and all things are the same, in *real value*. What a false, what a deceptious, what an infamous thing, this paper-money system is!

Mr. Blount, at whose house (7 miles from Weyhill) I am, went with me to the fair; and we took particular pains to ascertain the prices. We saw, and spoke to, Mr. John Herbert, of Stoke (near Uphusband) who was *asking* 20s., and who did not expect to get it, for South Down ewes, just such as he *sold*, last year (at this fair), for 36s. Mr. Jolliff of Crux-Easton, was *asking* 16s. for just such ewes as he sold, last year (at this fair) for 32s. Farmer Holdway had sold "for less than half" his last year's price. A farmer that I did not know, told us, that he had sold to a great sheep-dealer of the name of Smallpiece, at the latter's own price! I asked him what that "own price" was: and he said that he was ashamed to say. The horse-fair appeared to have no business at all going on; for, indeed, how were people to purchase horses, who had got only half-price for their sheep?

What dreadful ruin will ensue! How many, many farmers' families are now just preparing the way for their entrance into the poor-house! How many? certainly many a score farmers did I see at Weyhill, yesterday, who came there as it were to *know their fate!* and who are gone home thoroughly convinced, that they shall, as farmers, never see Weyhill fair again!

When such a man, his mind impressed with such conviction, returns home and there beholds a family of children, half bred up, and in the notion that they were *not* to be mere working people, what must be his *feelings!* Why, if he have been a bawler against Jacobins and Radicals; if he have approved of the Power-of-Imprisonment Bill and of Six-Acts; aye, if he did not rejoice at Castlereagh's cutting his own throat; if he have been a cruel screwer down of the labourers, reducing them to skeletons; if he have been an officious detector of what are called "poachers," and have assisted in, or approved of, the hard punishments, inflicted on them; then, in either of these cases, I say, that his feelings, though they put the suicidal knife into his own hand, are short of what he deserves! I say this, and this I repeat with all the seriousness and solemnity with which a man can make a declaration; for, had it not been for these base and selfish and unfeeling wretches, the deeds of 1817 and 1819 and 1820 would never have been attempted. These hard and dastardly dogs, armed up to the teeth, were always ready to come forth to destroy, not only to revile, to decry, to belie, to calumniate in all sorts of ways, but, if necessary, absolutely to cut the throats of, those who had no object, and who could have no object, other than that of preventing a continuance in that course of measures, which have finally produced the ruin, and threaten to produce the absolute destruction, of these base, selfish, hard and dastardly dogs themselves. *Pity* them! Let them go for pity to those whom they have applauded and abetted.

The houses of the village are, in great part, scattered about, and are amongst very lofty and fine trees; and, from many, many points round about, from the hilly fields, now covered with the young wheat, or with scarcely less beautiful sainfoin, the village is a sight worth going many miles to see. The lands, too, are pretty beyond description. These chains of hills make, below them, an endless number of lower hills, of varying shapes and sizes and aspects and of relative state as to each other; while the surface presents, in the size and form of the fields, in the woods, the hedge-rows, the sainfoin, the young wheat, the turnips, the tares, the fallows, the sheep-folds and the flocks, and, at every turn of your head, a fresh and different set of these; this surface all together presents that, which I, at any rate, could look at with pleasure for ever. Not a sort of country that I like so well, as when there are *downs,* and a *broader valley,* and *more of meadow;* but, a sort of country that I like next to that; for, here, as there, there are no ditches, no water-furrows, no dirt, and never any drought to cause inconvenience. The chalk is at bottom, and it takes care of all. The crops of wheat have been very good here this year, and those of barley not very bad. The sainfoin has given a fine crop of the finest sort of hay in the world, and, this year, without a drop of wet.

I wish, that, in speaking of this pretty village (which I always return to with additional pleasure), I could give *a good account* of the state of *those, without whose labour, there would be neither corn, nor sainfoin, nor sheep.* I regret to say, that my account of this matter, if I gave it truly, must be a dismal account indeed! For, I have, in no part of England, seen the labouring people so badly off as they are here. This has made so much impression on me, that I shall enter fully into the matter, with names, dates, and all the particulars in the IVth Number of the "POOR MAN'S FRIEND." This is one of the great purposes for which I take these "Rides." I am

194

persuaded, that, before the day shall come when my labours must cease, *I shall have mended the meals of millions*. I may over-rate the effects of my endeavours; but, this being my persuasion, I should be guilty of a great neglect of duty, were I not to use those endeavours.

Andover, Sunday, 15th October.

I went to Weyhill, yesterday, to see the close of the hop and of the cheese fair; for, after the sheep, these are the principal articles. The crop of hops has been, in parts where they are grown, unusually large, and of super-excellent quality. The average price of the Farnham *hops* has been, as nearly as I can ascertain, seven pounds for a hundred weight; that of Kentish hops, five pounds, and that of the Hampshire and Surrey hops (other than those of Farnham), about five pounds also. The prices are, considering the great weight of the crop, very good; but, if it had not been for the effects of "*late* panic" (proceeding, as Baring said, from a "plethora of money,")[1] these prices would have been a full third, if not nearly one half, higher; for, though the crop has been so large and so good, there was hardly any stock on hand; the country was almost wholly without hops.

As to cheese, the price, considering the quantity, has been not one half so high, as it was last year. The fall in the positive price has been about 20 per cent., and the quantity made in 1826 has not been above two-thirds as great as that made in 1825. So that, here is a fall of *one-half* in real relative price; that is to say, the farmer, while he has the same rent to pay that he paid last year, has only half as much money to receive for cheese, as he received for cheese last year; and observe, on some farms, cheese is almost the only saleable produce.

Romsey (Hampshire),
Monday, Noon, 16th Oct.

Like a very great fool, I, out of senseless complaisance, waited, this morning, to breakfast with the friends, at whose house we slept last night, at Andover. We thus lost two hours of dry weather, and have been justly punished by about an hour's ride in the rain. I settled on Lyndhurst as the place to lodge at to-night; so we are here, feeding our horses, drying our clothes, and writing the account of our journey. We came, as much as possible, all the way through the villages, and, almost all the way, avoided the turnpike-roads. From Andover to Stockbridge (about seven or eight miles) is, for the greater part, an open corn and sheep country, a considerable portion of the lands being downs. The wheat and rye and vetch and sainfoin fields look beautiful here; and, during the whole of the way from Andover to Romsey, the early turnips of both kinds are not bad, and the stubble turnips very promising. The downs are green as meadows usually are in April. The grass is most abundant in all situations, where grass grows. From Stockbridge to Romsey we came nearly by the river side, and had to cross the river

---

[1] Sir Thomas Baring (1772–1848) of the great banking family, M.P. for Wycombe and Hampshire.

several times. This, the River Teste, which, as I described, in my Ride of last November, begins at Uphusband, by springs, bubbling up, in March, out of the bed of that deep valley. It is at first a bourn, that is to say, a stream that runs only a part of the year, and is the rest of the year as dry as a road. About 5 miles from this periodical source, it becomes a stream all the year round. After winding about between the chalk hills, for many miles, first in a general direction towards the south-east, and then in a similar direction towards the south-west and south, it is joined by the little stream that rises just above and that passes through, the town of Andover. It is, after this, joined by several other little streams, with names; and here, at Romsey, it is a large and very fine river, famous, all the way down, for trout and eels, and both of the finest quality.

Lyndhurst (New Forest),
Monday Evening, 16th October.

I have just time, before I go to bed, to observe that we arrived here, about 4 o'clock, over about 10 or 11 miles of the best road in the world, having a choice too, for the great part of the way, between these smooth roads, and green sward.

––––––––

RIDE: FROM LYNDHURST (NEW FOREST) TO BEAULIEU ABBEY;
THENCE TO SOUTHAMPTON AND WESTON.

> But where is now the goodly audit ale?
> The purse-proud tenant, never known to fail?
> The farm which never yet was left on hand?
> The marsh reclaim'd to most improving land?
> The impatient hope of the expiring lease?
> The doubling rental? What an evil's peace!
> In vain the prize excites the ploughman's skill,
> In vain the Commons pass their patriot Bill;
> The *Landed Interest*—(you may understand
> The phrase much better leaving out the *Land*)—
> The land self-interest groans from shore to shore,
> For fear that plenty should attain the poor.
> Up, up again, ye rents! exalt your notes,
> Or else the Ministry will lose their votes,
> And patriotism, so delicately nice,
> Her loaves will lower to the market price.
>
> LORD BYRON, *Age of Bronze.*

196

Weston Grove, Wednesday, 18 Oct., 1826.

Yesterday, from Lyndhurst to this place, was a ride, including our round-abouts, of more than forty miles; but the roads the best in the world, one half of the way green turf; and the day as fine an one as ever came out of the heavens. We took in a breakfast, calculated for a long day's work, and for no more eating till night. We had slept in a room, the access to which was only through another sleeping room, which was also occupied; and, as I had got up about *two o'clock* at Andover, we went to bed, at Lyndhurst, about *half-past seven* o'clock. I was, of course, awake by three or four; I had eaten little over night; so that here lay I, not liking (even after day-light began to glimmer) to go through a chamber, where, by possibility, there might be "a lady" actually *in bed;* here lay I, my bones aching with lying in bed, my stomach growling for victuals, imprisoned by my *modesty*. But, at last, I grew impatient; for, modesty here or modesty there, I was not to be penned up and starved: so, after having shaved and dressed and got ready to go down, I thrusted George out a little before me into the other room; and, through we pushed, previously resolving, of course, not to look towards *the bed* that was there. But, as the devil would have it, just as I was about the middle of the room, I, like Lot's wife, turned my head! All that I shall say is, first, that the consequences that befell her, did not befall me, and, second, that I advise those, who are likely to be hungry in the morning, not to sleep in *inner rooms;* or, if they do, to take some bread and cheese in their pockets. Having got safe down stairs, I lost no time in inquiry after the means of obtaining a breakfast to make up for the bad fare of the previous day; and finding my landlady rather tardy in the work, and not, seemingly, having a proper notion of the affair, I went myself, and, having found a butcher's shop, bought a loin of small, fat, wether mutton, which I saw cut out of the sheep and cut into chops. These were brought to the inn; George and I ate about 2 lb. out of the 5 lb., and, while I was writing a letter, and making up my packet, to be ready to send from Southampton, George went out and found a poor woman to come and take away the rest of the loin of mutton; for, our *fastings* of the day before enabled us to do this; and though we had about forty miles to go, to get to this place (through the route that we intended to take), I had resolved, that we would go without any more *purchase* of victuals and drink this day also. I beg leave to suggest to my *well-fed* readers; I mean, those who have at their command more victuals and drink than they can possibly swallow; I beg to suggest to such, whether this would not be a good way for them all to find the means of bestowing charity? Some poet has said, that that which is given in *charity* gives a blessing on both sides; to the giver as well as the receiver. But, I really think, that, if, *in general*, the food and drink given, came out of food and drink *deducted* from the usual quantity swallowed by the giver, the *blessing* would be still greater, and much more certain. I can speak for myself, at any rate. I hardly ever eat more than *twice* a day; when at home, never; and I never, if I can well avoid it, eat any meat later than about one or two o'clock in the day. I drink a little tea, or milk and water, at the usual tea-time (about 7 o'clock); I go to bed at eight, if I can; I write or read, from about four to about eight, and then, hungry as a hunter, I go to breakfast eating *as small a parcel* of cold meat and bread, as I can prevail upon my teeth to be satisfied with. I do just the same at dinner time. I very rarely taste *garden-stuff* of any sort. If any man can show me, that he has done, or can do *more work*, bodily and mentally united; I say nothing about good health, for of that, the public can know nothing; but, I refer to *the work:* the public know, they see, what I can do, and what I actually have done, and what I do; and, when any one has shown the public, that he has done, or can do more, then I will advise my readers attend to him, on the subject of diet, and not to me. As to *drink*, the less the better; and mine is milk and water, or, *not-sour* small beer, if I can get the latter; for the former I always can. I like the milk and water best; but I do not like much water; and, if I drink much milk, it loads, and stupifies, and makes me fat.

———————

RIDE: FROM WESTON, NEAR SOUTHAMPTON, TO KENSINGTON.

Hambledon, Sunday,
22nd Oct. 1826.

After quitting Soberton Down, we came up a hill leading to Hambledon, and turned off to our left to bring us down to Mr. Goldsmith's at West End, where we now are, at about a mile from the village of Hambledon. A village it *now* is; but it was formerly a considerable market-town, and it had three fairs in the year. There is now not even the name of market left, I believe; and the fairs amount to little more than a couple, or three gingerbread-stalls, with dolls and whistles for children. If you go through the place, you see that it has been a considerable town. The church tells the same story; it is now a tumble-down rubbishy place; it is partaking in the fate of all those places which were formerly a sort of rendezvous for persons who had things to buy and things to sell.[1] *Wens* have devoured market-towns and villages; and *shops* have devoured *markets and fairs;* and this, too, to the infinite injury of the most numerous classes of the people. Shop-keeping, merely as shop-keeping, is injurious to any community. What are the shop and the shop-keeper for? To receive and distribute the produce of the land. There are other articles, certainly; but the main part is the produce of the land. The shop must be paid for; the shop-keeper must be kept; and the one must be paid for and the other must be kept by the consumer of the produce; or, perhaps, partly by the consumer and partly by the producer.

When fairs were very frequent, shops were not needed. A manufacturer of shoes, of stockings, of hats; of almost any thing that man wants, could

---

[1] The great days of Hambledon as the best cricket side in England were also over. The club was wound up in 1796. It is odd that Cobbett, who approved of rural sports, does not mention this.

manufacture at home in an obscure hamlet, with cheap house-rent, good air, and plenty of room. He need pay no heavy rent for shop; and no disadvantages from confined situation; and, then, by attending three or four or five or six fairs in a year, he sold the work of his hands, unloaded with a heavy expense attending the keeping of a shop. He would get more for ten shillings in a booth at a fair or market, than he would get in a shop for ten or twenty pounds. Of course he could afford to sell the work of his hands for less; and thus a greater portion of their earnings, remained with those who raised the food, and the clothing from the land. I had an instance of this in what occurred to myself at Weyhill fair. When I was at Salisbury, in September, I wanted to buy a whip. It was a common hunting-whip, with a hook to it, to pull open gates with, and I could not get it for less than seven shillings and sixpence. This was more than I had made up my mind to give, and I went on with my switch. When we got to Weyhill fair, George had made shift to lose his whip some time before, and I had made him go without one, by way of punishment. But now, having come to the fair, and seeing plenty of whips, I bought him one, just such a one as had been offered me at Salisbury for seven and sixpence, for four and sixpence; and, seeing the man with his whips afterwards, I thought I would have one myself; and he let me have it for three shillings. So that, here were two whips, precisely of the same kind and quality as the whip at Salisbury, bought for the money which the man at Salisbury asked me for one whip. And yet, far be it from me to accuse the man at Salisbury of an attempt at extortion: he had an expensive shop, and a family in a town to support, while my Weyhill fellow had been making his whips in some house in the country, which he rented, probably for five or six pounds a year, with a good garden to it. Does not every one see, in a minute, how this exchanging of fairs, and markets for shops creates *idlers and traffickers;* creates those locusts, called middle-men, who create nothing, who add to the value of nothing, who improve nothing, but who live in idleness, and who live well, too, out of the labour of the producer and the consumer. The fair and the market, those wise institutions of our forefathers, and with regard to the management of which they were so scrupulously careful; the fair, and the market, bring the producer, and the consumer, in contact with each other. Whatever is gained is, at any rate, gained by one or the other of these. The fair and the market bring them together, and enable them to act for their mutual interest and convenience. The shop and the trafficker keep them apart; the shop hides from both producer and consumer, the real state of matters. The fair and the market lay every thing open: going to either, you see the state of things at once; and the transactions are fair and just, not disfigured, too, by falsehood, and by those attempts at deception, which disgrace traffickings in general.

Thursley, Monday Evening,
23rd October.

When I left Weston, my intention was, to go from Hambledon to Up Park,[2] thence to Arundel, thence to Brighton, thence to East-bourne, thence to Wittersham in Kent, and then by Cranbrook, Tunbridge, Godstone and Reigate to London; but, when I got to Botley, and particularly when I got to Hambledon, I found my horse's back so much hurt by the saddle, that I was afraid to take so long a stretch, and therefore resolved to come away straight to this place, to go hence to Reigate, and so to London.

I must here relate something that appears very interesting to me, and something, which, though it must have been seen by every man that has lived in the country, or, at least, in any hilly country, has never been particularly mentioned by anybody as far as I can recollect. We frequently talk of clouds coming from *dews;* and we actually see the heavy fogs become clouds. We see them go up to the tops of hills, and, taking a swim round, actually come, and drop down upon us, and wet us through. But, I am now going to speak of clouds, coming out of the sides of hills in exactly the same manner that you see smoke come out of a tobacco pipe, and, rising up, with a wider and wider head, like the smoke from a tobacco-pipe, go to the top of the hill or over the hill, or very much above it, and then come over the valleys in rain. At about a mile's distance from Mr. Palmer's house at Bollitree, in Herefordshire, there is a large, long beautiful wood, covering the side of a lofty hill, winding round in the form of a crescent, the bend of the crescent being towards Mr. Palmer's house. It was here, that I first observed this mode of forming clouds. The first time I noticed it, I pointed it out to Mr. Palmer. We stood and observed cloud after cloud, come out from different parts of the side of the hill, and tower up and go over the hill out of sight. He told me that that was a certain sign that it would rain that day, for that these clouds would come back again, and would fall in rain. It rained sure enough; and I found that the country people, all round about, had this mode of the forming of the clouds as a sign of rain. The hill is called Penyard, and this forming of the clouds, they call Old Penyard's *smoking his pipe;* and it is a rule that it is sure to rain during the day, if Old Penyard smokes his pipe in the morning. These appearances take place, especially in warm and sultry weather. It was very warm yesterday morning: it had thundered violently the evening before: we felt it hot even while the rain fell upon us at Butser-hill. Petersfield lies in a pretty broad and very beautiful valley. On three sides of it are very lofty hills, partly downs and partly covered with trees: and, as we proceeded on our way from the bottom of Butser-hill to Petersfield, we saw thousands upon thousands of clouds, continually coming puffing out from different parts of these hills and towering up to the top of them. I stopped George several times to make him look at them; to see them come puffing out of the chalk downs as well as out of

---

[2] Seat of Sir Harry Fetherstonhaugh (1754–1846) who had the future Lady Hamilton briefly as his mistress, and whose descendants employed as housekeeper the mother of H. G. Wells.

the woodland hills; and bade him remember to tell his father of it, when he should get home, to convince him that the hills of Hampshire, could smoke their pipes, as well as those of Herefordshire. This is a really curious matter. I have never read, in any book, anything to lead me to suppose that the observation has ever found its ways into print before. Sometimes you will see only one or two clouds during a whole morning, come out of the side of a hill; but we saw thousands upon thousands, bursting out, one after another, in all parts of these immense hills. The first time that I have leisure, when I am in the high countries again, I will have a conversation with some old shepherd about this matter: if he cannot enlighten me upon the subject, I am sure that no philosopher can.

Kensington,
Thursday, 26th Oct.

I have put an end to my Ride of August, September, and October, 1826, during which I have travelled five hundred and sixty-eight miles, and have slept in thirty different beds, having written three monthly pamphlets, called the "Poor Man's Friend," and have also written (including the present one) eleven Registers. I have been, in three cities, in about twenty market towns, in perhaps five hundred villages; and I have seen the people, no where so well off as in the neighbourhood of Weston Grove, and no where so badly off, as in the dominions of the Select Vestry of Hurstbourn Tarrant, commonly called Uphusband. During the whole of this ride, I have very rarely been a-bed after day-light; I have drunk, neither wine nor spirits. I have eaten no vegetables, and only a very moderate quantity of meat; and, it may be useful to my readers to know, that the riding of twenty miles, was not so fatiguing to me at the end of my tour, as the riding of ten miles was, at the beginning of it. Some ill-natured fools will call this *"egotism."* Why is it egotism? Getting upon a good strong horse, and riding about the country, has no merit in it; there is no conjuration in it; it requires neither talents nor virtues of any sort; but *health* is a very valuable thing; and when a man has had the experience which I have had, in this instance, it is the duty to state to the world, and to his own countrymen, and neighbours in particular, the happy effects of early rising, sobriety, abstinence, and a resolution to be active. It is his duty to do this; and it becomes imperatively his duty, when he has seen, in the course of his life, so many men; so many men of excellent hearts and of good talents, rendered prematurely old, cut off ten or twenty years before their time, by a want of that early rising, sobriety, abstinence and activity, from which he himself has derived so much benefit, and such inexpressible pleasure. During this ride, I have been several times wet to the skin. At some times of my life, after having indulged for a long while in coddling myself up in the house, these soakings would have frightened me half out of my senses; but I care very little about them: I avoid getting wet if I can; but, it is very seldom that rain, come when it would, has prevented me from performing the day's journey that I had laid out beforehand. And, this is a very good rule: stick to your intention, whether it be attended with inconveniences or

201

not; to look upon yourself as *bound* to do it. In the whole of this ride, I have met with no one untoward circumstance, properly so called, except the wounding of the back of my horse, which grieved me much more on his account, than on my own. I have a friend, who, when he is disappointed in accomplishing anything that he has laid out, says that he has been *beaten*, which is a very good expression for the thing. I was beaten in my intention to go through Sussex and Kent; but I will retrieve the affair in a very few months' time, or, perhaps few weeks'. THE COLLECTIVE[3] will be here now in a few days; and, as soon as I have got the Preston Petition fairly before them, and find (as I daresay I shall) that the petition will not be *tried* until February, I shall take my horse and with a resolution not to be beaten, next time, go along through the whole length of Sussex, and sweep round through Kent and Surrey till I come to Reigate again, and then home to Kensington; for I do not like to be beaten by a horse's sore back, or by any thing else; and besides that, there are several things in Sussex and Kent that I want to see and give an account of. For the present, however, farewell to the country, and now for the Wen and its villanous corruptions.

NORTHERN TOUR.

Sheffield, 31st January, 1830.

On the 26th instant I gave my third lecture at Leeds. I should in vain endeavour to give an adequate description of the pleasure which I felt at my reception, and at the effect which I produced in that fine and opulent capital of this great county of York; for the *capital* it is in fact, though not in name. On the first evening, the play-house, which is pretty spacious was not completely filled in all its parts; but on the second and third, it was filled brim full, boxes, pit and gallery; besides a dozen or two of gentlemen who were accommodated with seats on the stage. Owing to a cold which I took at Huddersfield, and which I spoke of before, I was, as the players call it, not in very good *voice;* but the audience made allowance for that, and very wisely preferred sense, to sound. I never was more delighted than with my audience at Leeds; and what I set the highest value on, is, that I find I produced a prodigious effect in that important town.

From Leeds, I proceeded on to this place, not being able to stop at either Wakefield or Barnsley, except merely to change horses. The people in those towns were apprised of the time that I should pass through them; and, at each place, great numbers assembled to see me, to shake me by the hand, and to request me to stop. I

---

[3] Meaning that Parliament is about to meet. Cobbett intended to send in a petition against the malpractices which lost him the Preston election.

was so hoarse as not to be able to make the post-boy hear me, when I called to him; and, therefore, it would have been useless to stop; yet I promised to go back if my time and my voice would allow me. They do not; and I have written to the gentlemen of those places to inform them, that when I go to Scotland in the spring, I will not fail to stop in those towns, in order to express my gratitude to them. All the way along, from Leeds to Sheffield, it is coal and iron, and iron and coal. It was dark before we reached Sheffield; so that we saw the iron furnaces, in all the horrible splendour of their everlasting blaze. Nothing can be conceived more grand or more terrific than the yellow waves of fire, that incessantly issue from the top of these furnaces, some of which are close by the way-side. Nature has placed the beds of iron and the beds of coal alongside of each other, and art has taught man to make one, to operate upon the other so as to turn the iron-stone into liquid matter, which is drained off from the bottom of the furnace, and afterwards moulded into blocks and bars, and all sorts of things. The combustibles are put into the top of the furnace, which stands thirty, forty, or fifty feet up in the air, and the ever-blazing mouth of which is kept supplied with coal and coke and iron-stone, from little iron waggons forced up by steam, and brought down again to be re-filled. It is a surprising thing to behold; and it is impossible to behold it without being convinced that, whatever other nations may do with cotton and with wool, they will never equal England, with regard to things made of iron and steel. This Sheffield, and the land all about it, is one bed of iron and coal. They call it Black Sheffield, and black enough it is; but from this one town and its environs go nine-tenths of the knives that are used in the whole world; there being, I understand, no knives made at Birmingham; the manufacture of which place consists of the larger sorts of implements, of locks of all sorts, and guns and swords, and of all the endless articles of hardware which go to the furnishing of a house. As to the land, viewed in the way of agriculture, it really does appear to be very little worth. I have not seen, except at Harewood and Ripley, a stack of wheat since I came into Yorkshire; and even there, the whole I saw, and all that I saw during a ride of six miles that I took into Derbyshire the day before yesterday, all put together would not make the one-half of what I have many times seen in one single rick-yard of the vales of Wiltshire. But this is all very proper: these coal-diggers, and iron-smelters, and knife-makers, compel us to send the food to them, which, indeed, we do very cheerfully, in exchange for the produce of their rocks, and the wondrous works of their hands.

The trade of Sheffield has fallen off, less in proportion than that of the other manufacturing districts. North America, and particularly the United States, where the people have so much victuals to cut, form a great branch of the custom of this town. If the people of Sheffield could only receive a tenth part of what their knives sell for by retail in America, Sheffield might pave its streets with silver. A *gross* of knives and forks is sold to the Americans, for less than three knives and forks, can be bought at retail in a country store in America. No fear of rivalship in this trade. The Americans may lay on their tariff, and double it, and triple it; but as long as they continue to *cut* their victuals, from Sheffield, they must have the things to cut it with.[1]

The ragged hills all round about this town, are bespangled with groups of houses inhabited by the working cutlers. They have not suffered like the working weavers; for, to make knives, there must be the hand of man. Therefore, machinery cannot come to destroy the wages of the labourer. The home demand, has been very much diminished; but still the depression has here, not been what it has been, and what it is, where the machinery can be brought into play.

Upon my arriving here on Wednesday night, the 27th instant, I by no means intended to lecture, until I should have a little recovered from my cold; but to my great mortification, I found that the lecture had been advertised, and that great numbers of persons had actually assembled. To send them out again, and give back the money, was a thing not to be attempted. I, therefore, went to the Music Hall, the place which had been taken for the purpose, gave them a specimen of the state of my voice, asked them whether I should proceed, and they answering in the affirmative, on I went. I then rested until yesterday, and shall conclude my labours here tomorrow, and then proceed to *"fair Nottingham,"* as we used to sing when I was a boy, in celebrating the glorious exploits of "Robin Hood and Little John." By the by, as we went from Huddersfield to Dewsbury, we passed by a hill which is celebrated as being the burial-place of the famed Robin Hood, of whom the people in this country talk to this day.

It is very curious that I have always had a very great desire to see Nottingham. This desire certainly originated in the great interest that I used to take, and that all country boys took, in the history of Robin Hood, in the record of whose achievements, which were so well calculated to excite admiration in the country boys, this Nottingham, with the word *"fair"* always before it, was so often mentioned. The word *fair*, as used by our forefathers, meant fine; for we frequently read in old descriptions of parts of the country of such a district or such a parish, containing a *fair* mansion, and the like; so that this town appears to have been celebrated as a very fine place, even in ancient times; but within the last thirty years. Nottingham has stood high in my estimation, from the conduct of its people; from their public spirit; from their excellent sense as to public matters; from the noble struggle, which they have made from the beginning of the French war, to the present hour; if only forty towns in England equal in size to Nottingham, had followed its bright example, there would have been no French war against liberty;[2] the Debt would have been now nearly paid off, and we should have known nothing of those manifold miseries, which now afflict, and those greater miseries, which now menace, the country. The French would not have been in Cadiz; the Russians would not have been at Constantinople; the

---

[1] Cobbett's late conversion to qualified approval of the American way of life did not lead him to approve of American tariffs.

[2] Cobbett means the war against the French Revolution.

Americans would not have been in the Floridas; we should not have had to dread the combined fleets of America, France and Russia; and, which is the worst of all, we should not have seen the jails four times as big as they were; and should not have seen Englishmen reduced to such a state of misery, as for the honest labouring man to be fed, worse than the felons in the jails.

EASTERN TOUR.

"You permit the Jews openly to preach in their synagogues, and call Jesus Christ an impostor; and you send women to jail (to be brought to bed there, too), for declaring their unbelief in Christianity." — *King of Bohemia's Letter to Canning, published in the Register, 4th of January,* 1823.

Hargham, 22nd March, 1830.

I set off from London on the 8th of March, got to Bury St. Edmund's that evening; and, to my great mortification, saw the county-election, and the assizes both going on, at Chelmsford, where, of course, a great part of the people of Essex were met. At Bury St. Edmund's I gave a lecture on the ninth, and another on the tenth of March, in the playhouse, to very crowded audiences. I went to Norwich on the 12th, and gave a lecture there on that evening, and on the evening of the 13th. The audience here was more numerous than at Bury St. Edmund's, but not so numerous in proportion to the size of the place; and, contrary to what has happened in most other places, it consisted more of town's people than of country people.

During the 14th and 15th, I was at a friend's house at Yelverton, half way between Norwich and Bungay, which last is in Suffolk, and at which place I lectured on the 16th to an audience consisting chiefly of farmers, and was entertained there in a most hospitable and kind manner, at the house of a friend.

The next day, being the 17th, I went to Eye, and there lectured in the evening in the neat little playhouse of the place, which was crowded in every part, stage and all. I staid at Eye all the day of the 18th, having appointed to be at Ipswich on the 19th. Eye is a beautiful little place, though an exceedingly rotten borough.[1]

All was harmony and good humour: everybody appeared to be of one mind; and as these friends observed to me, so I thought, that more effect had been produced by this one lecture in that neighbourhood, than could have been produced in a whole year, if the Register had been put into the hands of every one of the hearers, during that space of time; for though I never attempt to put forth that sort of stuff which the "intense" people on the other side of St. George's Channel call "*eloquence*," I bring out strings of very interesting facts; I use pretty powerful arguments; and I hammer them down so closely upon the mind, that they seldom fail to produce a lasting impression.

---

[1] A borough returning more members to Parliament than its population now warranted.

On the 19th I proceeded to Ipswich, not imagining it to be the fine, populous and beautiful place that I found it to be. On that night, and on the night of the 20th, I lectured to boxes and pit, crowded principally with opulent farmers, and to a gallery filled, apparently, with journeymen tradesmen and their wives. On the Sunday before I came away, I heard, from all quarters, that my audiences had retired deeply impressed with the truths which I had endeavoured to inculcate.

About twelve o'clock, my son and I set off for this place (Hargham), coming through Needham Market, Stow-market, Bury St. Edmund's, and Thetford, at which latter place I intended to have lectured to-day and to-morrow, where the theatre was to have been the scene, but the mayor of the town thought it best not to give his permission until the assizes (which commence to-day the 22nd) should be over, lest the judge should take offence, seeing that it is the custom, while his Lordship is in the town, to give up the civil jurisdiction to him. Bless his worship! what in all the world should he think would take me to Thetford, *except it being a time for holding the assizes!* At no *other* time should I have dreamed of finding an audience in so small a place, and in a country so thinly inhabited. I was attracted, too, by the desire of meeting some of my *"learned friends"* from the Wen; for I deal in arguments, founded on the *law of the land*, and on *Acts of Parliament*. The deuce take this Mayor for disappointing me; and, now, I am afraid that I shall not fall in with this learned body during the whole of my spring tour.

I know of no town to be compared with Ipswich, except it be Nottingham; and there is this difference in the two; that Nottingham stands high, and, on one side, looks over a very fine country; whereas Ipswich is in a dell, meadows running up above it, and a beautiful arm of the sea below it. The town itself is substantially built, well paved, every thing good and solid, and no wretched dwellings to be seen on its outskirts. From the town itself, you can see nothing; but you can, in no direction, go from it a quarter of a mile without finding views, that a painter might crave, and then, the country round about it, so well cultivated; the land in such a beautiful state, the farm-houses all white, and all so much alike; the barns, and every thing about the homesteads so snug; the stocks of turnips so abundant every where; the sheep and cattle in such fine order; the wheat all drilled; the ploughman so expert; the furrows, if a quarter of a mile long, as straight as a line, and laid as truly as if with a level: in short, here is every thing to delight the eye, and to make the people proud of their country; and this is the case throughout the whole of this county. I have always found Suffolk farmers great boasters of their superiority over others; and I must say that is is not without reason.

To conclude an account of Suffolk, and not to sing the praises of Bury St. Edmund's, would offend every creature of Suffolk birth; even at Ipswich, when I was praising *that place*, the very people of that town asked me if I did not think Bury St. Edmund's the nicest town in the world. Meet them wherever you will, they have all the same boast; and indeed, as a town *in itself*, it is the neatest place that ever was seen. It is airy, it has several fine open places in it, and it has the remains of the famous abbey walls and the abbey gate entire; and it is so clean and

Right:
An engraving by James Pollard,
depicting cottagers giving hospitality
to benighted travellers.

Below:
Buckingham House (later Palace) from
Green Park in 1825.

The Valley of the Stour by John Constable.

so neat that nothing can equal it in that respect. It was a favourite spot in ancient times; greatly endowed with monasteries and hospitals. Besides the famous Benedictine Abbey, there was once a college and a friary; and as to the abbey itself, it was one of the greatest in the kingdom; and was so ancient as to have been founded only about forty years after the landing of Saint Austin in Kent. The land all round about it is good; and the soil is of that nature as not to produce much dirt at any time of the year; but the country about it is *flat*, and not of that beautiful variety that we find at Ipswich.

That which we *admire* most, is not always that, which would be *our choice*. One might imagine, that after all that I have said about this fine country, I should certainly prefer it as a place of residence. I should not, however: my choice has been always very much divided between the woods of Sussex, and the downs of Wiltshire. I should not like to be compelled to decide: but if I were compelled I do believe that I should fix on some vale in Wiltshire. Water meadows at the bottom, corn-land going up towards the hills, those hills being *down land*, and a farm-house, in a clump of trees, in some little cross vale between the hills, sheltered on every side but the south. In short, if Mr. Bennet[2] would give me a farm, the house of which lies on the right-hand side of the road going from Salisbury to Warminster, in the parish of Norton Bovant, just before you enter that village; if he would be so good as to do that, I would freely give up all the rest of the world to the possession of whoever may get hold of it. I have hinted this to him once or twice before, but I am sorry to say that he turns a deaf ear to my hinting.

Horncastle, 13th April, morning.

I made a speech last evening to from 130 to 150, almost all farmers, and most men of apparent wealth, to a certain extent. I have seldom been better pleased with my audience. It is not the clapping and huzzaing that I value so much as the *silent attention*, the *earnest look* at me from *all eyes* at once, and then when the point is concluded, the *look and nod at each other*, as if the parties were saying, *"Think of that"*! And of these, I had a great deal at Horncastle. They say that there are *a hundred parish churches within six miles of this town*. I dare say that there was one farmer, from almost every one of these parishes. This is sowing the seeds of truth, in a very sure manner: it is not scattering broad-cast; it is really *drilling the country*.

Spittal, near Lincoln, 19th April, 1830.

It is time for me now, withdrawing myself from these objects visible to the eye, to speak of the state of *the people*, and of the manner in which their affairs are affected by the workings of the system. With regard to the labourers, they are, every where, miserable. The wages for those who are employed on the land are, through all the counties that I have come, twelve shillings a week for married men, and less for single ones; but a large part of them are not even at this season employed on the

---

[2] See note 4 on page 21.

THE LIFE OF A LABOURER

CONTENT HAVING FOOD & RAIMENT

The labourer is poor but content, having food and raiment for himself and his family.

land. The farmers, for want of means of profitable employment, suffer the men to fall upon the parish; and they are employed in digging and breaking stone for the roads; so that the roads are nice, and smooth, for the sheep and cattle to walk on, in their way to the all-devouring jaws of the Jews and other tax-eaters in London and its vicinity. None of the best meat, except by mere accident, is consumed here. To-day (the 20th of April), we have seen hundreds upon hundreds of sheep, as fat as hogs, go by this inn door, their toes, like those of the foot-marks at the entrance of the lion's den, all pointing towards the Wen; and the landlord gave us for dinner a little skinny, hard leg of old ewe mutton! Where the man got it, I cannot imagine. Thus it is: every good thing is literally driven or carried away out of the country.

One of the great signs of the poverty of people in the middle rank of life, is the falling off of the audiences at the playhouses. There is a playhouse in almost every country town, where the players used to act occasionally; and in large towns almost always. In some places they have of late abandoned acting altogether. In others they have acted, very frequently, to not more than *ten or twelve persons*. At

Now a pauper, beggared by tithes and taxes, he is forced to receive alms from the parish.

Norwich, the playhouse had been shut for a long time. I heard of one manager who has become a porter to a warehouse, and his company dispersed. In most places, the insides of the buildings seem to be tumbling to pieces; and the curtains and scenes that they let down, seem to be abandoned to the damp and the cobwebs. *My* appearance on the boards seemed to give new life to the drama.

Another respect in which our situation so exactly resembles that of France on the eve of the Revolution, is, the *fleeing from the country* in every direction. When I was in Norfolk, there were four hundred persons, generally young men, labourers, carpenters, wheelwrights, millwrights, smiths, and bricklayers; most of them with some money, and some farmers and others with good round sums. These people were going to Quebec, in timber-ships, and from Quebec, by land, into the United States. They had been told that they would not be suffered to land in the United States from board ship. The roguish villains had deceived them: but no matter; they will get into the United States; and going through Canada will do them good, for it will teach them to detest every thing belonging to it. Those that

PETITIONS.

He petitions for help, and is rebuffed.

The end of this series of the 1830s sees the unfortunate labourer hanged.

have most money, go direct to the United States. From the Thames, and from the several ports down the Channel, about two thousand have gone this spring. All the flower of the labourers of the east of Sussex, and west of Kent, will be culled out and sent off in a short time. From Glasgow, the sensible Scotch are pouring out amain. The Unites States form another England without its unbearable taxes, its insolent game-laws, its intolerable dead-weight, and its tread-mills.

———

EASTERN TOUR ENDED, MIDLAND TOUR BEGUN.

Leicester, 26th April, 1830.

At the famous ancient city of Lincoln I had crowded audiences, principally consisting of farmers, on the 21st and 22nd; exceedingly well-behaved audiences; and great impression produced.

The country from Lincoln to Newark (sixteen miles), is by no means so fine as that which we have been in for so many weeks. The land is clayey in many parts. A pleasant country; a variety of hill and valley; but not that richness which we had so long had, under our eye: fields smaller; fewer sheep, and those not so large, and so manifestly loaded with flesh. The roads always good. Newark is a town very

In his helplessness and frustration he wrecks the machinery which he sees as the instrument of his suffering. (The original 'Luddites', from their leader, Ned Lud, tried to wreck machinery and stocking-frames around Nottingham between 1812 and 1816, when several of them were tried and hanged.)

much like Nottingham, having a very fine and spacious market-place; the buildings every where good; but it is in the villages that you find the depth of misery.

We got to Leicester on the 24th, at about half-past five o'clock; and the time appointed for the lecture was six. Leicester is a very fine town; spacious streets, fine inns, fine shops, and containing, they say, thirty or forty thousand people. It is well stocked with jails, of which a new one, in addition to the rest, has just been built, covering three acres of ground! And, as if *proud* of it, the grand portal has little turrets, in the castle style, with *embrasures* in miniature on the caps of the turrets. Nothing speaks the want of reflection in the people so much, as the self-gratulation which they appear to feel in these edifices in their several towns. Instead of expressing shame at these indubitable proofs of the horrible increase of misery and of crime, they really boast of these "improvements," as they call them.

Hull, *c.* 1840.

Yesterday morning (Sunday the 25th), I walked out to the village of Knighton, two miles on the Bosworth road, where I breakfasted, and then walked back. This morning I walked out to Hailstone, nearly three miles on the Lutterworth road, and got breakfast there. You have nothing to do but to walk through these villages, to see the cause of the increase of the jails. View the large, and once the most beautiful, churches; see the parson's house, large, and in the midst of pleasure-gardens; and then look at the miserable sheds in which the labourers reside! Look at these hovels, made of mud and of straw; bits of glass, or of old off-cast windows, without frames or hinges, frequently, but merely stuck in the mud wall. Enter them, and look at the bits of chairs or stools; the wretched boards tacked together, to serve for a table; the floor of pebble, broken brick, or of the bare ground; look at the thing called a bed; and survey the rags on the backs of the wretched inhabitants; and then wonder if you can, that the jails and dungeons and tread-mills increase, and that a standing army and barracks are become the favourite establishments of England!

Worcester, 18th May, 1830.

I set off from Lutterworth early on the 29th of April, stopped to breakfast at Birmingham, got to Wolverhampton by two o'clock (a distance altogether of about 50 miles), and lectured at six in the evening. I repeated, or rather continued, the lecturing, on the 30th, and on the 3rd of May. On the 6th of May went to Dudley, and lectured there: on the 10th of May, at Birmingham; on the 12th and 13th, at Shrewsbury; and on the 14th, came here.

TOUR IN THE WEST.

3rd July, 1830.

Just as I was closing my third Lecture (on Saturday night), at Bristol, to a numerous and most respectable audience, the news of the death of George IV. arrived. I had advertised and made all the preparations for lecturing at Bath on Monday, Tuesday, and Wednesday; but, under the circumstances, I thought it would not be proper to proceed thither, for that purpose, until after the burial of the King. When that has taken place, I shall, as soon as may be, return to Bath, taking Hertfordshire and Buckinghamshire in my way; from Bath, through Somerset, Devon, and into Cornwall; and back through Dorset, South Wilts, Hants, Sussex, Kent, and then go into Essex, and, last of all, into my native county of Surrey. But never shall I see another place to interest me, and so pleasing to me, as Bristol and its environs, taking the whole together. A good and solid and wealthy city: a people of plain and good manners; private virtue and public spirit united; no empty noise, no insolence, no flattery. And, as to the seat of the city and its environs, it surpasses all that I ever saw. A great commercial city in the midst of

215

The city of Bristol from Rownham Ferry, in 1841.

corn-fields, meadows and woods, and the ships coming into the centre of it, miles from any thing like sea, up a narrow river, and passing between two clefts of a rock probably a hundred feet high; so that from the top of these clefts you *look down* upon the main-top gallant masts of lofty ships, that are gliding along!

———

PROGRESS IN THE NORTH.

Newcastle-upon-Tyne, 24 September, 1832.

Every demonstration of respect and kindness met me at the door of the coach in which I came from Leeds, on Friday, the 21st September. In the early part of Saturday, the 22d, a deputation waited upon me with *an address*. Let the readers, in my native county and parish, remember, that I am now at the end of thirty years of calumnies, poured out incessantly upon me from the poisonous mouths and pens, of three hundred mercenary villains, called newspaper editors and reporters; that I have written and published more than three hundred volumes in those thirty years; and that more than a thousand volumes (chiefly paid for out of the taxes) have been written and published for the sole purpose of impeding the progress of these truths that dropped from my pen; that my whole life has been a life of sobriety and labour; that I have invariably shown that I loved and honoured my country, and that I preferred its greatness and happiness far beyond my own; that, at four distinct periods, I might have rolled in wealth derived from the public money, which I always refused in any way to touch; that, for having thwarted this Government in its wastefulness of the public resources, and particularly for my endeavours to produce that Reform of the Parliament which the Government itself has at last been compelled to resort to; that, for having acted this zealous and virtuous part, I have been twice stripped of all my earnings by the acts of this Government; once lodged in a felon's jail for two years,[1] and once driven into exile for two years and a half; and that, after all, here I am on a spot within a hundred miles of which I never was before in my life; and here I am receiving the unsolicited applause of men amongst the most intelligent in the whole kingdom.

Sunderland, 4th Oct. 1832.

You see nothing here that is pretty; but everything seems to be abundant in value; and one great thing is, the working people live well. Theirs is not a life of ease to be sure, but it is not a life of hunger. The pitmen have twenty-four shillings a week; they live rent-free, their fuel costs them nothing, and their doctor costs them

---

[1] Though sentenced to two years in Newgate (1810–11), Cobbett in fact only served eight months and was enabled to have comfortable quarters and free use of his pen. But he did die a poor man, having sold most of his copyrights to his publisher. He left everything (reckoned as worth £1500), including the bones of Tom Pain, to his eldest son William, who in turn went bankrupt in 1836.

nothing. Their work is terrible, to be sure; and, perhaps, they do not have what they ought to have; but, at any rate, they live well, their houses are good and their furniture good; and though they live not in a beautiful scene, they are in the scene where they were born, and their lives seem to be as good as that of the working part of mankind can reasonably expect.

Alnwick, 7th Oct., 1832.

They tell me that Lord Howick,[2] who is just married by-the-by, made a speech here the other day, during which he said, "that the Reform was only the means to an end; and that the end was cheap government." Good! stand to that, my Lord, and, as you are now married, pray let the country fellows and girls marry too: let us have *cheap government*, and I warrant you, that there will be room for us all, and plenty for us to eat and drink. It is the drones, and not the bees, that are too numerous; it is the vermin who live upon the taxes, and not those who work to raise them, that we want to get rid of. We are keeping fifty thousand tax-eaters to breed gentlemen and ladies for the industrious and laborious to keep. These are the opinions which I promulgate; and whatever your flatterers may say to the contrary, and whatever *feelosofical* stuff Brougham and his rabble of writers may put forth, these opinions of mine will finally prevail. I repeat my anxious wish (I would call it a *hope* if I could), that your father's resolution may be equal to his sense, and that he will do that, which is demanded by the right which the people have, to insist upon measures necessary, to restore the greatness and happiness of the country; and, if he show a disposition to do this, I should deem myself the most criminal of all mankind, if I were to make use of any influence that I possess, to render his undertaking more difficult than it naturally must be; but, if he show not that disposition, it will be my bounden duty to endeavour to drive him from the possession of power; for, be the consequences to individuals what they may, the greatness, the freedom, and the happiness of England must be restored.

---

[2] Better known as Charles Earl Grey of the Reform Bill (1764–1845), Prime Minister 1831–4.

INDEX

Page numbers in italics refer to illustrations; page numbers followed by n refer to footnotes.

ACKNOWLEDGEMENTS

The publishers would like to thank the following for supplying illustrations:

Colour

Bodleian Library, Oxford 77 below, 106 above, 161 below; E.T. Archive 25, 26, 27 below, 28, 37, 38, 55, 56, 66, 67 above, 68, 77 above, 78, 95 below, 96 above, 105, 106 below, 108, 133, 152, 161 above, 162–3, 164, 189, 190, 207, 208; Mansell Collection 27 above, 65, 67 below, 107, 134, 151; National Trust 95 above, 96 below.

Black and white

British Museum (E. T. Archive) 93, (Eileen Tweedy) 64, 71, 157; City Art Gallery, Manchester 30; Malcolm Couch 143; E. T. Archive 34, 58, 80; Gloucestershire County Library 22; Guildhall Library (Godfrey New Photographics) 16; Mansell Collection 53, 59, 60, 63, 69, 83, 85, 90, 100, 121, 156, 175, 176, 180, 210, 211, 212, 213, 214, 216; Museum of English Rural Life, Reading 148; National Portrait Gallery 32, 113, 115; Parker Gallery 62; Victoria and Albert Museum frontispiece, 50, 120, 145; Wiltshire Archaeological and Natural History Society 159.